Vilain and Courtois

Kathryn Gravdal

University
of Nebraska
Press
Lincoln and
London

Vilain

and

Courtois

Transgressive
Parody in French
Literature of the
Twelfth and Thirteenth
Centuries

Acknowledgment for the use of previously
published material appears on page xii.
Library of Congress Cataloging-in-Publication Data
Gravdal, Kathryn, 1954–
    Vilain and courtois: transgressive parody
in French literature of the twelfth and
thirteenth centuries / Kathryn Gravdal.
        p.   cm. — (Regents studies in medieval culture)
    Bibliography: p.
    Includes index.
    ISBN 0-8032-2126-6 (alk. paper)
    1. French literature—To 1500—History and
criticism. 2. Social classes in literature.
3. Peasantry in literature. 4. Nobility
in literature. 5. Parody. I. Title. II. Series.
PQ155.S7G73   1989
840'.9'001—dc19   88–27730
                                                    CIP

For Stephen

CONTENTS

ILLUSTRATIONS

ACKNOWLEDGMENTS

This book is in part the development of a project initially under-taken in Paris, under the direction of Jean Dufournet, to whom I am indebted for years of support and training. Many friends in Paris were also mentors and teachers at that time, and I am partic-ularly grateful to Jean-Marc Dilettato and Geneviève Pichon for their unstinting help.

The generosity of friends and colleagues never ceases to amaze me. Above all, I thank Katharine Jensen, Terese Lyons, Mary Shaw, and Margeret Waller; without their hard work and encouragement this book would not have been possible. My thanks to Elizabeth Houlding, Cheryl Morgan, and Karen Sullivan, whose energy saw me through the final stages of this project. I cannot say how much strength and hope I drew from friends like Mary Kimble.

I am eager to acknowledge the support, encouragement and ex-ample of Eugene Vance, who made this book possible, and R. Howard Bloch, who offered invaluable guidance. Ross Cham-bers, Nancy K. Miller, and Domna Stanton were always willing not only to read my work but also to be supportive mentors.

Several people took the time to read my drafts at various stages of progress, and I especially thank Gérard Genette and Paul Zumthor. Michelle Freeman was good enough to read an early version of Chapter I.

For his attentive support at every point of my work, his exam-ple as a scholar, and his interest in a project so distant from the field of his own undertakings, I am in debt to my teacher Michael Riffaterre.

To no one does this book owe more than to Nancy Freeman Re-galado, and each page should carry a footnote of acknowledg-ment to her. I cannot imagine greater intellectual generosity than that which she has shown at every step in my work. She gave of herself freely and warmly in shaping the direction of this book.

Vilain and Courtois

This book is affectionately dedicated to my husband, who made countless sacrifices, both comic and epic, while it was being written.

Portions of Chapter 3 have previously been published in "Kingship and Kingdoms in the *Roman de Renart*," ACTA II (1986): 113–20, and are used by permission of the Center for Medieval and Early Renaissance Studies.

All of the illustrations are reprinted courtesy of the Bibliothèque Nationale, Paris.

Signs and Paradigms

INTRODUCTION

The tendency to perceive signs and paradigms in all things, and the need to impose models on experience, are distinguishing marks of medieval thought. It has become widely acknowledged in recent years that the Middle Ages possessed and practiced a theory of signs long before the semioticians of the twentieth century.[1] Modern readers are often struck by the medieval imposition of paradigms and codes on all facets of experience. In twelfth-century theology, for instance, the dominant model of biblical hermeneutics was a four-tiered typology, a system which interpreted all of human history at four levels: anagogical, moral, allegorical, and literal.[2] In social theory, a triadic model was created as a way of seeing and organizing social experience: the human community was seen as built of three groups, those who pray, those who fight, those who work the soil.[3] In literary theory, commentators put forth a circular model which was to describe and prescribe the rules of literary composition and genre: the wheel of Vergil.[4]

The wheel of Vergil is a fraud in two senses at least: it was not the creation of Vergil at all and its prescriptions were never actually obeyed by medieval poets. But the wheel is genuine, and worthy of study, in other respects. The Vergilian wheel expresses and illustrates the fundamental medieval habit of coding and of reading signs as parts of codes. Literature both codes and is made up of codes, tightly bound up in the whole of life, the visible world of signs. Literary texts of the Middle Ages are governed by rules prescribing a strict adequation of genre and setting, genre and character, genre and stylistic level, genre and moral ethos. This observation holds true even in the presence of "mixed" texts; their very evident transgression of the rules of genre expressed by the concentric rings in the Vergilian wheel and their rupture of codes testify to the strength and authority of literary models.

In twelfth- and thirteenth-century French literature, one of the

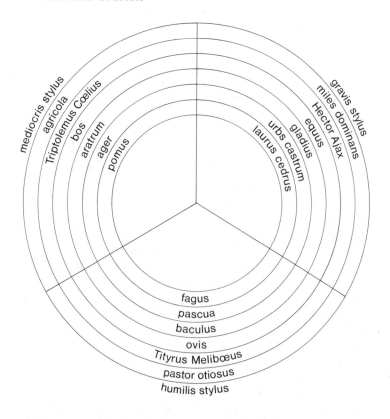

chief preoccupations of written texts is the coding and interpreting of the social order. The preoccupation with social class apparent in Vergil's wheel has not lessened in the France of Louis VII, Philippe II, or Louis VIII. The writers of literature continue to be fascinated by the recording and the shaping of social structures. The opposition of the social and the nonsocial, of the "high" social and the "low" social, finds infinite, delighted, and delightful expression in the literary texts of this period of expansion and development. Writers and their audiences, extremely conscious of social hierarchies, look to literature as a space in which to contemplate social constructs.

Since much of the literature of these two centuries shows a marked preoccupation with the idea of the social, and of the signs that order society, it is not surprising that the parodic literature of this same period seizes upon this use of the social to express moral oppositions of "good" and "bad." Just as "serious" literature becomes a place of social visions and thought, so too does parody become the space in which the literary preoccupation with social hierarchy can be used as comic material. Parody exaggerates the tendency to social codification already present in twelfth- and thirteenth-century literary texts. An author has only to focus on the highly coded rules of genre, each with its corresponding social milieu, characters, and language, to set upon the path to parody. In medieval parody, the poet's accomplishment is complex, his target multiple; in transgressing and distorting the literary rules of social representation, the parodist makes light of the literary model, but also of the medieval mental habit of conceptualizing in terms of models, of encoding all signs with heavily determined meanings, social, linguistic, and moral.

In the European Middle Ages, it was believed that in creating the world, God was creating signs. "And God said, Let there be lights in the firmament of the heaven to divide the day from the night; and let them be for signs" (Gen. 1:14). It was the responsibility of the human community to interpret those signs. Nothing could be a truer description of a medieval "way of seeing" than to speak of it as reading and interpreting the signs of the universe.[5] The whole of life was perceived in terms of models, or arrangements of signs. Theologians, philosophers, scientists, political theorists and poets looked for the signal patterns ruling and expressing human experience. Indeed, men and women saw themselves as the visible earthly signs of the invisible, the celestial.

Only when we have grasped the pervasive presence of codes and paradigms in medieval French literature can we begin to understand the significance of comic parody in the Middle Ages. Perhaps because of the silence and distance that separate us from the Middle Ages, transgressive representations of social class and social structure have been interpreted as direct revelations of societal change or attitude. Too often medievalists have approached literary texts as mirrors of the poet's or audience's heartfelt wishes for change, or need for permanence, in the social order. But socially marked characters are not simple historical referents; they are complex signs. They are specifically medieval signs in the sense that Saint Augustine gave to Genesis 1:14: "I am convinced that this is what was meant, O Lord, when you commanded man and the creatures of the sea to increase and multiply. I believe that by this blessing you granted us the faculty and the power both to give expression in many different ways to things which we understand in one way only and to understand in many different ways what we find written obscurely in one way."[6]

In medieval parody, socially stereotyped characters are complex signs that can be understood in many different ways: as markers of literary genre; as references to social practices, such as the practice of regulating social hierarchy; and as references to discursive practices, such as rhetoric. They reflect the primacy and fixity of the cultural practice of making signs into paradigms. In medieval France, parody "gives expression in many different ways" to the codes and hierarchies of space, social class, language, and ethos that govern the literary text. Parody is therefore a useful and pertinent approach to the study of the juncture of medieval literature and the medieval conceptualization of social class.

Parody in medieval literature warrants volumes of studies in its own right. Paul Lehmann's seminal work on Latin medieval literature, *Die Parodie im Mittelalter,* remains the single comprehensive study on the subject.[7] But countless types of parody existed (indeed, flourished) in the Middle Ages. Religious parody enjoyed great success. The liturgical parodies studied by Lehmann are in many ways akin to the carnivalesque parodies discussed by Bakhtin. Mixed parodies, of which the anonymous *Aucassin et Nicolette* offers an example, are common in thirteenth-century literature, and their composite nature has thrown the critics into some confusion as to whether they ought to be considered parody.[8] Not all medieval parody is comic. The "summa," or anthologized sum of a body of texts, a popular form in medieval writing, constitutes serious parody. Local parody—the imitation of one text or one corpus—can be comic (as are some of the texts studied in this book) or serious (as in Guillaume de Lorris's *Roman de la Rose*). The *Queste del Saint Graal* constitutes an example of serious religious parody, in its duplication of the Christian eucharist.

This book studies the literary manifestations of one social paradigm in medieval parody, the hierarchical opposition of *vilain,* the "vile" peasant, to *courtois,* the "courtly" nobleman. We will ask whether Old French parodies reflect, affirm, or deny the cultural values a social historian could describe. Do medieval texts constitute a mimesis of social class structures, or simply create their own aesthetic constructs?

Recent scholarship on the medieval coding of the social and the nonsocial, or the "high" social and the "low" social, has broached the question of the relation between history and literature in the phenomenon known as carnival. Medieval carnival has been much discussed since the appearance of Mikhail Bakhtin's splendid book *Rabelais and His World,* which examines the relation between the Rabelaisian text in the sixteenth century and popular culture in the Middle Ages.[9] Bakhtin's Marxist analysis presents an image of the extreme stability of social classes in the Middle Ages, in life as in literature. Even in carnival, according to Bakhtin, reversal reinforces the stability of medieval culture, and ultimately confirms it. The literary texts studied in the following chapters disclose representations of vilains and courtois that are not as stable as Bakhtin and other scholars have assumed. The opposing signs of peasant and nobleman often appear in contradictory, not fixed or stable, manifestations. The cultural significance of many medieval texts lies not so much in their support of existing social structures as in their "play" on social models and with serious cultural issues.

The present study focuses on varieties of comic, rather than serious, parody, for the simple reason that anomalous vilains and courtois consistently appear in humorous texts. It presents examples both of local parody, in which the target imitated is a single, well-known text, and also of generic parody, in which it is a corpus of texts, or an entire canon, that is being mocked.

Thus far I have used the term *parody* as if it were self-explanatory. The truth of the matter is that the term as well as the textual phenomenon it attempts to classify admit of no easy definition and are the object of some debate. Those medievalists who have worked on parodic texts have struggled with traditional and general definitions of parody as "the world upside down." But if we hope to account for the variety of *vilains courtois* and *courtois vilains* in Old French parodies of the twelfth and thirteenth centuries, we must go beyond the simple notion of semantic overturning.

Traditional definitions of parody, from Aristotle to Abrams, confuse the issue of parody's literariness by equating literary genre with social class, and by labelling the parodic text an inferior or parasitic variation of the model parodied. But the presence of parody cannot lead to any conclusions concerning the social status or moral standards of a putative audience.[10] Nor can Freud's definition, which holds that parody is tendentious and destructive, be useful to the study of medieval literature.[11] Anglo-American scholars tend to categorize parody as a subgenre of satire.[12] Nothing could be more misleading: parody and satire are quite distinct systems of text production. Parody is a textual play on literary traditions and conventions, while satire is a literary commentary on the real world, usually meliorative in its pragmatism. As Vladimir Nabokov wrote, "Satire is a lesson, parody is a game."[13]

If parody cannot be explained in aesthetic or political terms of lowness as opposed to highness, vulgarity as opposed to nobility, how then are we to speak of it? Perhaps it can be best understood in terms of the conspicuousness of its repetition of paradigms. The specificity of parody lies in the way it exhibits its relation to other texts: overt, systematic, and partial reproduction and transformation of literary models.

Just as parody cannot be defined in terms of highbrow as opposed to lowbrow art, it cannot be defined by the notion of upside-downness. It means nothing, for example, to speak of turning Chrétien de Troyes's Arthurian corpus topsy-turvy, for a parody of Chrétien's texts could take any number of directions, and distortion could occur in varying degrees. The parodic hero could be ugly or fat, short or stupid, cowardly or bloodthirsty, concupiscent or slothful. The language used to parody Chrétien's style could be epic or obscene, religious or scatological, precious or nonsensical. The parodic hero's feats could be outlandishly diminished or exaggerated, or wholly unrelated to chivalry. The possibilities are legion, yet the choices made by any given parody are directed and focussed, not random or inadvertent.

Contemporary literary theory has done much to help us understand and define parody. The structuralism of the 1960s and 1970s, despite its sometimes simplistic insistence on formalism, made an important point: the text is not a window on social history; the puzzles it presents are often literary, and answers can be found within the text itself.[14] This insight made a valuable contribution to the study of parody, and especially with regard to the age-old critical confusion of parody and satire. Parody could now be viewed as a literary play on literature, rather than a mockery of society or a condemnation of certain historical authors. In 1982, Gérard Genette published an important work on literary parody entitled *Palimpsestes*. This monumental study of "second-degree literature" (its subtitle) brought together a vast amount of critical history and research on parody, opening many new doors. Briefly, the subject of *Palimpsestes* is "hypertextuality": "toute relation unissant un texte B (hypertexte) à un texte antérieur A (hypotexte) sur lequel il se greffe d'une manière qui n'est pas celle du commentaire." "Hypertextuality" is Genette's reworking of "intertextuality," "relation de coprésence entre deux ou plusieurs textes," a term he finds both too imprecise and too local. Genette's study is an encyclopedic compendium of parodic texts, ranging from classical Greek literature to the cinema of Woody Allen, and also an examination of numerous parodic phenomena, including allusion, quotation, pastiche, travesty, burlesque, plagiarism, mock epic, caricature, and satire. The student of the theory of parody will find an invaluable *summa* of material in this work. Interestingly, Genette argues for a restriction of the much-abused term *parody* (usually taken to refer to satirical pastiche), and gives the category "parody" itself a very small part in his systematic breakdown of second-degree genres, defining it as a "détournement de texte à *transformation minimale.*"[15]

Medieval parody does not play a large role in the pages of *Palimpsestes* for the simple reason that Genette is not a medievalist. Two comments can be made on Genette's study of parody, for they are directly pertinent to the discussion of our medieval texts. First, Genette's work is a purely formal classification of texts that analyzes parody as text relations. It offers a transhistorical and formalist definition of parody and second-degree literature, and foregoes questions concerning historical context, hermeneutics, the reader, or ideology. Such restrictions (deliberately placed by Genette himself) limit the usefulness of *Palimpsestes* for the study of medieval parody, which the modern reader cannot understand or examine without knowledge of the specificity of medieval literary traditions and medieval ideology. Secondly, Genette's schematic classifications, while they account for every type and degree of distortion, do not study the direction of the "détournement" in any given parody.[16] In other words, Genette's system cannot account for the specificity of the individual parodic actualization, nor can it account for the fact of difference within each category of second-degree literature. This question of specific orientation is key, however, to my theory of medieval parody, as is the question of historical context.

In 1985 Linda Hutcheon published *A Theory of Parody: The Teachings of Twentieth-Century Art Forms,* an interdisciplinary study of contemporary parody that both draws on and extends Genette's work in *Palimpsestes.* Despite the modesty of Hutcheon's claims that her study of twentieth-century art forms is necessarily limited and local, her work is extremely pertinent to our discussion of medieval parody. Hutcheon insists on the need to go beyond the formal considerations of structuralism and semiotics in order to take on questions of context and ideology. "In parody, art reveals its awareness of the context-dependent nature of meaning, of the importance of the circumstances surrounding any utterance." Any definition of parody, Hutcheon argues, must be historical. Indeed, parody is by its very nature historical and historicizing; as it looks back on past texts and traditions, it posits its own relationship to literary history. Taking up questions ranging from semiotics to reader response and deconstruction, each of Hutcheon's chapters is rich in material for the student of medieval parody. Three points in particular bear mention in their relevance to the Middle Ages. Hutcheon describes parody structurally as a bitextual synthesis that is a stylistic confrontation endowed with its own internal function as literary critique. This notion of a literary criticism existing within literary texts themselves describes medieval literature quite aptly: medieval theory as a discursive practice is located within medieval texts, rather than in some external metabody of criticism. Further, Hutcheon understands parody not as negative in ethos but rather as an inscription of continuity and change; parody preserves continuity within discontinuity and is the intersection of tradition and renewal. Therein lies one of the distinguishing features of medieval parody; its relation to literary tradition is commonly conservative, rarely destructive.

The third point to be retained from Hutcheon's study is that in taking up Mikhail Bakhtin's discussion of medieval carnival and its relation to parody, Hutcheon examines the ambivalence of transgression in parody, what she names "the paradox of parody."[17] Parody has a double virtual tendency: conservative or revolutionary. It presupposes both a law and the transgression of that law. This notion of parody as authorized transgression, or legalized subversion, aptly depicts the ideological status of medieval parody. Neither revolutionary nor reforming, parody in the Middle Ages is temporary and limited play; it neither ridicules nor defends ideological norms or deviations.

Hutcheon's call for historical definitions of parody brings us once again to the description of the medieval specificity of parody. Hutcheon does not, any more than Genette, attempt to account for the unique difference of every parodic manifestation. Simply to speak of a "bitextual synthesis" does not explain how or why there can exist more than one parody of a given author or more than one parody of a given text. This difference or variance among parodies will be the object of my study and theory of medieval parody.

This book explores a model of parody that is tripartite rather than bipartite, and therefore able to account for the specific difference of every parody. A tripartite model of the linguistic sign first appeared in the work of the American semiotician Charles S. Peirce in the 1930s. According to Peirce, language is composed not only of mimetic signs, referring us to objects in the world around us, but also of signs that are interpretive, bearing on our understanding of the relation between a sign and an object. Peirce gave the name of "interpretant" to this third type of sign.[18] Another American semiotician, Michael Riffaterre, demonstrated that Peirce's triadic sign structure obtains in literature as well as in linguistics.[19] In the Riffaterrean model, the sign-text refers to a second text (the object of the first), and the relation between the two gives rise to the textual interpretant, a third text, which enables us to read the initial text.[20] The notion of the literary interpretant is particularly useful in the study of parody, for it enables the critic to go beyond the limited concept of semantic overturning, and to recognize parody as a form of textual production that can go in any "direction," take on any cast. It was not enough to say that, in parody, "high" shifts to "low," or "low" replaces "high," for the question remained, Which "high"? which "low"? The tripartite model, with its inclusion of a third presence, a third textual direction or literary model, enables the reader to identify the precise nature of the parodic distortion, and thus to understand more fully the parodic text.

The triadic model of parody, in its imposition of paradigmatic order on complex signs, is not unlike medieval models. The tripartite theory illuminates twelfth- and thirteenth-century literature, a literature built on fixed conventions and well-defined codes, and in which texts commonly refer both to an intertext and to an interpretant. Such a model also permits us to go beyond the boundaries of genre to the extent that it allows us to place side by side medieval genres not frequently studied together and to discover the density of the signals, exchanges, and communications that exist between and among them. The discovery that medieval texts are commonly related in unsuspected ways, intergenerically as well as intertextually, opens the door to the possibility of redefining medieval literature: not from without, but from within.

The four comic texts studied in this book, though heterogeneous in many ways, have a unity of their own in that they practice forms of comic transgression. They disobey the rules, so important to this period, concerning the adequation of social class and diction, social class and literary characters, social class and literary genre.[21] While the features of their rule-breaking may vary, all four texts, in choosing to focus on the vilain and the courtois, attest to an acute cultural awareness of the theoretical relation between language, social class, and literary codes.

The term *transgression* carries distinctly religious and moral overtones and should be defined further. By *transgression,* and *transgressive,* we will understand parodic (which is to say literary, not ethico-religious) rule-breaking. In parody, transgression is twofold. First, it is oppositional, in that it introduces an opposing diction, character, stylistic tendency, or social space in a literary genre to which they do not belong. Second, it is combinational, in that it juxtaposes registers, characters, or scenes from different genres, placing them side by side. Thus, parodic transgression means, quite simply, the formal transgression of literary norms and conventions. So strong was the literary coding of the Middle

Ages that the transgressive oppositions and the juxtaposed combinations were quickly understood by the medieval public.

The parodies we will examine cover a time span of approximately one century, from the period of genre canonization occurring in the second half of the twelfth century, to the creation and institution of literary automatisms at the turn of the century and the development of vernacular narrative in the first half of the thirteenth century.[22] These four comic texts teach us that play, and the freedom it represents, was an unshakeable cultural value in the Middle Ages. *Fergus, Audigier, Le Roman de Renart,* and *Trubert* toy with literary oppositions and stylistic combinations, just as they toy with cultural oppositions and societal combinations. In playing with the rules of literary practice, they are also, always, and already, playing with social practice.

Fergus, by Guillaume le Clerc, is an Arthurian romance from the first third of the thirteenth century, parodying the elegant register of the romance corpus of Chrétien de Troyes. The anonymous *Audigier* is an epic parody from the second half of the twelfth century, in which nonsense poetry and scatological language mock the genealogical epic. The *Roman de Renart* is a collection of beast fables, dated from 1174 to 1250, that parody epic paradigms. *Trubert,* by Douin de Lavesne, belongs to the mid-thirteenth century, and rewrites a universal folktale type known as "The Youth Cheated Selling Oxen." Each makes transgressive use of the vilain and courtois opposition, whether at the level of social class, space, rhetoric, stylistics, or literary genre. In other words, in all four the parody is generated by anomalous combinations of vilain elements and courtois elements. Yet each parody is wholly unlike the others; each develops its own strategies and exploits certain transgressive elements more than others. To speak of the "world upside down" cannot possibly account for the humor and beauty of these four texts.

In reading and rereading medieval parodies, the critic comes to admire the inventiveness of such expressions of difference in a world that often looks to us to be rudimentary, unaware, and unmoving. Contrary to what we might have been taught about the Middle Ages, we learn from these parodies that the force and weight of literary tradition account for the ever nascent laughter in medieval literature.[23]

Vilain and Courtois

Having affirmed the complexity and variety of vilains, courtois, vilains courtois and courtois vilains in these parodies, it is time we place these categories in their historical context. Although the function and values of parody are chiefly aesthetic, they cannot be divorced from the time and place of their production. While avoiding the common taxonomic confusion of satire and parody, we can still point out the fact that *vilain* and *courtois* do not simply designate literary characters. First, they are Old French words, and we must study their linguistic content as such. Secondly, they refer to literary characters whose history reaches back before the twelfth century, characters whose status as *dramatis personae* in Old French literature we must examine. Finally, *vilain* and *courtois* designate historical categories, and we can acquaint ourselves with the literary characters only if we look at those characters in the context of their historical counterparts, peasants and noblemen in twelfth- and thirteenth-century France.

The terms *vilain* and *courtois* are central semes in the discourse of medieval ideology. They express the cultural opposition of the social and the nonsocial, or rather the high and the low social, on which feudal society is built. It is not surprising, then, that the mere word *vilain* constitutes a dramatic chapter in Old French philology. The vulgar Latin *villanus* designated a villa or country home. In Gallo-Roman *villanus* referred to the man who worked the land outside an urban agglomeration or in the village surrounding the urban cluster. But unlike the term *rusticus, villanus* was not initially pejorative. In the French of the Middle Ages a social connotation joined the professional denotation: the *vilain* both lived outside the city and belonged to the lowest social class. Other words existed to designate a peasant or farmer, such as *laboureur* or *brassier*. The distinct fate (and notoriety) of the term *vilain* results from its homonymic confusion with *vil* (from the Latin *vilem*, "of little worth," "of low price"). The Old French *vil*, with its moral connotation of abjection, contaminates the term *vilain*. A negative expansion occurs: the meaning "low-born" comes to include the meaning "ugly," then "unrefined," then "stingy." The next development left its mark on the English language as well as French: the vilain is morally ugly, of ignoble ideas and base instincts. The peasant has become the villain.

At each step of the negative expansion, *vilain* metamorphoses in contradistinction to the Old French *courtois*. Thus, early in the eleventh century, the *courtois* is he who comes from the court, the *vilain* from the "villa," or farm. Gradually, where *courtois* means "generous," *vilain* means "stingy"; where *courtois* means "handsome," *vilain* signifies "repulsive." In a final stage, a religious acceptation joins the others: the *courtois* is pious, the *vilain* a heathen.[24] These simple words come to constitute self-authenticating justifications for the structures of medieval feudalism.

This linguistic opposition functions in Old French literature, in which the two terms are transformed into key literary characters. The *vilain* and the *courtois* have traditionally been presented and regarded as unchanging features in both the language of medieval society and the languages of medieval literature. In Stanley Galpin's 1905 study of this social nexus, *Cortois and Vilain: A Study of the Distinctions Made between Them by the French and Provençal Poets of the Twelfth, Thirteenth, and Fourteenth Centuries,* the author presents the two literary characters as fixed and diametrically opposed markers, suffering almost no exceptions.[25] Galpin relegates anomalous representations of vilain and courtois to the footnotes of his book, in an effort to push them to the margins, for they contradict the very premise on which his book was written. Anomalous vilain and courtois characters are exceptions indeed, but deserve more—rather than less—attention for that very reason. The present study will bring the transgressive uses of vilain and courtois from the margins to the center of our field of investigation. The permutations of opposition and oxymoron are complex and shifting in medieval representations of social class. While the figures of courtois and vilain are highly stylized, they are neither unmoving signs of a monolithic age, nor even the markers of a rigidly hierarchic and conservative society. Medieval literature presents infinite combinations of those variables. Jean de Condé expresses the attitude of literary texts of the twelfth and thirteenth centuries when he writes:

> Vilain et courtois sont contraire;
> De l'un ne puet on bien retraire,
> Et en l'autre n'a fors que bien.[26]

> *Vilain* and *courtois* are opposites; from one no good can come, and in the other is all good things.

The *pastourelle* genre also presents the vilain-courtois opposition in a way that is regarded as universal. Its opposition of a male

courtois and a female vilain is typical of medieval French literature:

> . . . segon dreitura
> Cerca fols sa follatura,
> Cortes cortez' aventura,
> E il vilans ab la vilana;
> En tal loc fai sens fraitura
> On hom non garda mezura.[27]
>
> . . . in accordance with what is fitting, a fool seeks folly, *cortes* seeks courtly
> adventure, and the *vilans* man belongs with a *vilana* woman; but in many
> places the right thing isn't done because men do not respect limits.

But the reader of medieval texts also encounters vilains courtois
and courtois vilains; in point of fact, medieval texts constantly re-
define the connotations of these terms, as we see when we go beyond abusive generalization and study individual cases. In the
thirteenth-century epic *Gaydon,* for example, a courtois chooses
to become a vilain and exalts the advantages of that life. Gaydon
makes a clear distinction between the social and moral meanings
of the term: "Cil est vilains qui fait la vilennie."[28]

By the time these words, and the literary characters they en-
gender, appear in twelfth- and thirteenth-century texts, they are
no longer simple linguistic elements, substantives or adjectives.
These opposing semes, originally social designations, come to
constitute stylistic categories, and those stylistic registers are inextricably linked to literary genres. *Vilain* becomes a sign capable of
signifying (1) a space, that of the rural countryside; (2) a social
class, that of the medieval peasantry; (3) a moral sphere, that of
the base and vile; (4) a stylistic register, that of vilains mots, gross
words and crude self-expression; (5) a literary sphere, or constellation of genres, that of the fabliaux, the beast fable, the pastourelle. In other words, the term *vilain* has become highly coded,
and has taken on its own power to code, in medieval discourse.

Literature and history, as areas of research, are not as discrete
as structuralists, semioticians, and deconstructionists have
claimed.[29] Our knowledge of medieval culture, and in this case of
medieval social class, is discursive: it comes to us through the discourse of individuals, through fictional texts and nonfictional
texts, through songs, poems, and prayers. We can never discover

the "reality" of medieval life; we can only study the discourse of medieval culture about itself. And since much of what we know about the Middle Ages comes to us through literary texts, it becomes bootless to ask whether social changes caused literary texts to be written, in a kind of mechanical causality, or whether, as Michel Foucault claimed, discourse preexists social reality.[30] History comes to us through texts: therefore, history comes to us already and always textualized. History *is* discourse: thousands of disparate voices speaking to us through torn manuscripts, rent tapestries, and ruined cathedrals.

The view that literature and history are interdependent may appear to contradict the intertextual approach that informs this book. But in point of fact, while intertextuality may be one of the universals of literature, the critic must acknowledge that its actualization is always historical. The copresence of one text in another occurs in time. My working notion of intertextuality views the intertext and interpretant as historical in the sense that they play on and with historically informed categories: "vilain," "courtois," "dame," "seigneur." The act of turning to social history does not imply that the meaning of the literary vilain can be explained by the historical context of the medieval peasant. The study of historical context neither posits a relation of cause and effect between history and literature nor assigns a purely mimetic function to the literary character. It does recognize the fact that no literary text is produced by invisible forces. The historical question of this book becomes, How can we situate the transgressive vilain and courtois characters in a time, a place, a society?

Georges Duby contextualizes the literary characters of vilain and courtois in the following way: "One of the themes to become increasingly popular in the late twelfth century in a literature composed for knightly audiences is that of the upstart villein, the man of rustic origins who has climbed up the rungs of the social ladder, taken the place of well-born men in the exercise of seignorial authority by paying cash for it, and endeavored to ape their manners while succeeding only in making himself ridiculous and hated."[31] Vilain and courtois come into existence, as textual configurations, in a society made up of peasants and noblemen, of real people who think of themselves and others as vilain or courtois. The unwonted representations of social class, social space, language level, professional hierarchy, and so on, do not arise *in vacuo*. These parodies are the dynamic production of a particular group in a particular historical moment—indeed, a historical moment in which social structures were undergoing noticeable changes, and in which "peasant" and "nobleman" were not stable categories.

Some readers will wonder whether the key interpretant of parody is literary or historical. Are these parodies really "about" literary forms and genres, or are they about social class structures in medieval France? If the vilain becomes the hero of a twelfth- or thirteenth-century romance parody, but never of an eleventh- or fourteenth-century romance, these parodies must be understood as part of a preoccupation with shifting social classes in the one hundred years during which the parodies were composed and first performed.

The opposition of vilain and courtois is one expression of the familiar, age-old opposition of court and country.[32] But wherever the medieval vilain figures, whether in literary, economic, religious or political texts, he is a figure of specific medieval tensions. During the preceding centuries, the social and political status and condition of the peasant (whether slave, serf, or freeman) had remained relatively stable. With the economic explosion of the twelfth century, a boom originating in rural agriculture, the (historical) peasant of northern France is no longer a static figure in feudal economy and society.[33] The linguistic marker *vilain* takes on key cultural significance in a society witnessing changes in feudalism. The peasant classes, though their members do not reap the benefits of the economic expansion for which they are partially responsible, represent a new phenomenon, a sign of social change that was sensed as threatening. When the authors of our parodies take up the stock literary cliché known today as the *paysan parvenu,* they both allude to and dissipate social tensions created by shifts in class structure and economic wealth. If the play in these parodies is literary, it is not innocent literary play; it refers to historical conflicts and to deeply felt social problems.

The history of relations between peasants, knights, and lords in twelfth- and thirteenth-century France is not a tidy account of a smooth evolution, either from bad to worse or good to better. It is a history of change in agricultural organization and of technological revolution, but above all it is a story of shifting power, in which each side of the struggle presents multiple threats to the other. Moreover, the changes in relations between peasant and chivalric classes are both material and ideological.

While avoiding notions of mechanical causality, in which the billiard ball of history knocks into the eight ball of literature, causing a certain type of text to appear, we can look at the institutions of chivalry and serfdom in this time period. Four historical issues constitute a contextual backdrop for this book: that of a peasant's right to own land, that of a peasant's right to hold municipal office, that of a peasant's right to marry a woman of a higher class, and that of a peasant's right to bear arms.

The great clearing of land, felling of forests, and draining of marshes in the twelfth century affected feudal structures in various ways. Petty lords experienced greater difficulty in managing the increasing size of their arable properties and were frequently obliged to parcel up the far reaches of their land and sell plots to their free peasants, who then became property-holders in their own right, creating an uneasy parity between peasant and nobleman.[34] Such land-ownership was deceptive, however, for it did not mean that peasants accrued power, wealth, or security. They were generally forced to "surrender" their property to the protection of the nobleman from which it was purchased, for they themselves could not defend it, or even farm it, alone.[35] The freedom gained therefore in the right to own property, in the twelfth century, was essentially chimerical. The peasant remained a slave to the feudal system. Indeed, in many ways the situation of the peasantry in the twelfth century became more intolerable, despite the new prosperity, because of several practices. Lords discovered that the payments they could exact in exploiting their bannal rights (rights to their "ban," or feudal dominion) were incomparably greater than the revenues from their landholdings.[36] Peasants still had to make gifts of their own production, render seasonal services, pay for the use of the lord's mills or winepress, and pay countless taxes in goods, services, and money. What appeared to be economic and social emancipation disguised increased burdens. The issue of a peasant's right to own land appears, indirectly, in several of the literary parodies studied in this book, and especially in the story of Grimberge, a peasant property-holder, in the anonymous *Audigier* (Chapter 2).

Vilain and Courtois

A more real emancipation of peasants occurred in the course of the thirteenth century. By the early thirteenth century, two out of every ten peasants had grown wealthy, with only one in ten living in destitute poverty.[37] More important still, with the growth of towns and cities, and the subsequent commercial freedom available to peasants who could trade or work in the urban sphere, peasants and former peasants began entering the municipal and political life of the community, began acquiring power, could buy political office and intermarry with the daughters of the lesser nobility.

The questions of interclass marriage and the subsequent political powers derived by peasants are raised quite directly by the story of Soumilloit, the hero's father, in *Fergus* (Chapter 1), and indirectly through the vilains of the *Roman de Renart* (Chapter 3). Historical records show that as far as the institution of marriage was concerned, social class lines were flexible and changing at this time. Theodore Evergates's study of feudal society in Troyes from the late twelfth through the thirteenth century—which is to say the period during which Champagne was a center of literary production—reveals that the classifications of peasant, knight, and aristocrat were in a constant state of flux, a mobility that can be charted through marriage contracts.[38]

Georges Duby, in the passage cited above, wrote of the popularity of the comic bumpkin knight in Old French literature. How can we situate the literary cliché of the vilain courtois, or vilain chevalier in the context of late-twelfth- and early-thirteenth-century France? Why do these laughable horsemen suddenly flourish in Old French parody? Medievalists have commonly interpreted these comic scenes as allusions to the increasing wealth of peasants at the turn of the century and to the inferred fear, on the part of the upper class, that these "arrivistes" would aspire to knighthood. The literary joke is read as an attempt to mock (and chastise) ambitious peasants in an effort to maintain a certain purity of caste. The interpretation is certainly plausible.[39] On the other hand, we must not assume that peasants were growing wealthy, and showing upwardly mobile tendencies, for the first time. Affluent peasants attempting to join the upper classes had been witnessed as early as the tenth century. Nor were peasants bearing arms and armor for the first time in the thirteenth century. Formerly, lords raised their archers, pikers, and foot soldiers among their villeins. The change lay in new laws and ordinances, appearing in the late twelfth and early thirteenth century, that increasingly curtailed the lower classes' right to bear arms. The official explanation given was that peasants were needed in the fields more than on the battlegrounds. Another powerful explanation lay in a new social practice. In thirteenth-century France, serfdom and knighthood, between which the line had traditionally remained shifting, were now judged incompatible. By the end of the thirteenth century, it had become illegal to knight a villein. The real crisis of feudalism, of course, took place in the fourteenth century.[40]

For a poet of this period to depict a vilain inept at riding or at bearing arms was to do more than rework a stock gag. All the antinomical heroes tumbling from their steeds are so many signs in the medieval semiotics of social coding.[41] They are a comic examination of social regulation and constitute an attempt to deal with social tensions of the time. While the pratfalls of these characters may seem simple burlesque to a modern reader, they signalled an ongoing preoccupation with the lines of social class, a preoccupation to which the thirteenth-century audience would have been keenly alive. Indeed, in using the comic vilain courtois and its various manifestations—vilain chevalier, riche vilain—medieval parodists deliberately draw on the contradictions in twelfth- and thirteenth-century feudalism to rehearse certain cultural preoccupations about the changing world in which the audience lived. The texts draw on the overdetermined nature of the vilain and courtois categories, in literary tradition, in the ideological values it reflects and creates, and in the feudal structure itself, where peasants and noblemen are tangled in a shifting system of uneasy exchanges. Just as the distinction between satire (the literary critique of extraliterary institutions) and parody (literary mockery of literary texts and paradigms) is crucial to a proper evaluation of comic medieval literature, so too is the distinction between real and symbolic empowerment of social classes essential to the analysis of these parodies and to an understanding of their historical meaning. In these comic figures, poets and audiences seek one form of resolution, albeit artistic, to the social conflicts and anxieties of their historical world.

Fergus:
The Courtois Vilain

CHAPTER ONE

Aristotle uses the term *spoudaios,* "weighty," for noble characters in literature and the term *phaulos,* "light," for vulgar characters. Northrop Frye, elaborating on Aristotle's distinction, defines the hero of romance as *spoudaios,* a weighty character in a weighty genre.[1] Neither Aristotle nor Frye contemplates the possibility of a light hero in a weighty romance. Yet such is the case of the thirteenth-century *Fergus.*[2]

Fergus is an Arthurian romance that narrates fantastic quests, creates an image of ideal society and ideal government, examines the nature of honor, and debates the value of a life without love. Concomitantly, the hero of the romance busies himself with eating and drinking, fights enemies with an ignoble wooden spit, seeks adventure in rusted armor, and flees the love of the heroine.

Literary historians have disparaged *Fergus* on two counts. One faction has condemned the text as a mediocre imitation because of its adherence to the romance model and its overt borrowings from the work of Chrétien de Troyes.[3] Another party deems the romance to be second-rate because it does *not* conform to romance tradition, and in particular because its hero does not behave like the heroes of Chrétien. Rather than judge *Fergus,* we could with greater profit discover why this text makes such obvious allusions to the work of Chrétien, and ask why it presents the reader with such blatant and comical "mistakes," or transgressions of the strict medieval adequation of genre, character, style, and setting.

In this chapter we will discover that the comic anomalies in the character of the hero signal a deliberate poetic project; the humor of *Fergus* reveals a coherent pattern, which modern readers have overlooked. Mikhail Bakhtin has written that the literature of certain periods, such as that of the Middle Ages, may contain more humor and irony than we today expect, or grasp. "We often lose the sense of parody and would doubtless have to reread many a text of world literature to hear its tone in another key."[4]

Any discussion of Guillaume's *Fergus* must begin with a concomitant discussion of Chrétien's work, quite simply because the *Fergus* romance deliberately defines itself with respect to that work. The study of French Arthurian romance is today dominated by a corpus of five texts, composed by Chrétien de Troyes.[5] The labor of such a comparison has been spared us by the careful research of W. L. Frescoln, whose 1961 study of *Fergus* provides a detailed catalogue of its relation to medieval romance, and to Chrétien's production in particular.[6] Frescoln outlines the Arthurian paradigm and charts the progress of Guillaume le Clerc along the path established by Chrétien. If, in his effort to defend the literary value of the later romance, Frescoln has downplayed the anomalies in the text, he nonetheless documents its deliberate reproduction of Chrétien's best-known scenes.

In the Arthurian pattern, a young and untried or unknown knight accepts a challenge at King Arthur's court. Love, ambition, or both motivate the hero to set off on a dangerous quest, of which the object is to restore social order and justice.[7] The Arthurian hero simultaneously proves his valor as a knight and his devotion as a lover or husband, and then returns to receive the adulation of Arthur's court. Recent critical studies underline the ways in which Arthurian romance constantly reworks an established stock of narrative phrases in each actualization of this relatively fixed pattern.[8] Every romance text selects conventional variations in its invention of the hero's origins, the erotic plot, the chivalric combats, and the transitions which lead from quest to quest.

The following narrative summary shows that Guillaume's *Fergus* faithfully actualizes the conventional pattern: A young peasant boy, Fergus, leaves the farm of his vilain father in Scotland to seek Arthur's court at Carduel. When Fergus tells the court he wishes to become a knight, Keu mocks the naive rustic by sending him to the Black Mountain in quest of the Horn and Wimple. Fergus sets off, and on his way meets the heroine when he stays at her uncle's castle. Fergus rejects Galiene's offers of love and rides on to win the Horn and Wimple. When Fergus later returns to visit Galiene, he learns she has disappeared. The hero must undertake the Quest of the Beautiful Shield in order to regain her love.

After adventuresome wanderings, Fergus successfully defeats the hideous old hag who guards the shield. Fergus then learns that an enemy king is besieging Galiene, now queen of Lodien. Disguised as the Knight of the Beautiful Shield, Fergus rescues the queen. King Arthur announces a tournament to entice Fergus back to the court. Still dressed as the Knight of the Beautiful Shield, Fergus triumphs and is given Galiene's hand in marriage, as well as the kingdom of Lodien. The romance concludes with their wedding and coronation.

The transgressions in *Fergus* are comic reworkings of romance patterns. Those rewritings break literary rules that exist not in any ethical sense but in the expectations of the audience. These expectations exist at multiple levels: stylistic, spatial, social, and moral. The audience assumes that the rhetorical level of a romance's language, the setting of its action, the social class of its characters, and the moral message of the story will all correspond to the genre being performed. The hero of a romance must be handsome and brave, never misshapen or peevish. The stylistic level of the poetry will be elevated, not rustic or grotesque. The romance will be set in the kingdom of Arthur, not in the stables of a local peasant. Good, not evil, will triumph at the close of the narrative.

The strength of these literary rules is confirmed whenever a text transgresses them, as does Guillaume's *Fergus*. We have only to turn to key narrative moments in the Arthurian pattern in order to study the infractions of *Fergus*.

The prologue or opening verses of any medieval text constitute a paradigmatic key to the entire work. When we begin Guillaume's *Fergus* we find no prologue per se. Instead, there is a sort of operatic overture, a comprehensive review of themes and variations frequently found at the opening of Arthurian romance. Such is the effect created by the first passages of *Fergus*. The audience hears familiar strains: the feast of Pentecost at King Arthur's court; the friendship of Gauvain and Yvain; the beauty of the queen, and a description of her robes; the hunt of the white stag. Then, like the curtain rising after an overture, the words of *Fergus* lead us to expect a magnificent event, or the appearance of an important character: Arthur's hunting party sees a castle rising on the horizon. But such expectations are raised only to be thwarted by transgression:

Ens en l'issue d'Ingeval
En un castiel desus un val
Manoit uns vilains de Pelande.
(*Fergus* 303–5)
There at the edge of Galloway, in a castle atop a valley, lived a vilain from
Pelande.

"Vilain" immediately strikes a jarring note: a peasant in a castle, when the audience expected the hero. The verses following are overdetermined by the insistent repetition of that one incongruous word:

Li vilains ert molt aaisies.
(314)
The vilain was very well-off.

Del vilain mentir ne vos quier.
(321)
I have no desire to lie to you about this vilain.

Li vilains ot non Soumilloit.
(326)
The vilain's name was Soumilloit.

Mais li vilains rustes campestre. . .
(334)
But the country bumpkin vilain. . .

. . . Al riche vilain Soumeillet.
(353)
. . . of the rich vilain Soumeillet.

The vilain Soumilloit does indeed turn out to be our introduction to the unprepossessing hero: Soumilloit is the hero's father. Fergus appears, but he is dressed in rough peasant garb sweating at his father's plow, and when he sees Arthur's company pass by, he hides in comic fright. *Fergus* thus sets a precedent, establishing a tactic that is to dominate most of the romance: a heavily marked allusion to Chrétien's corpus that generates audience expectations is followed by a comic transgression of romance rules.

The first comic "error" in the story is a transgression of social class among its characters. *Fergus* opened with mentions of Yvain and his lion, of Perceval and his vermillion armor, creating the expectation of a noble hero, perhaps the son of a king. Furthermore, the usage of social class in romance dictates that a weighty role such as that of the hero cannot be played by a local peasant. *Fergus* defies that rule throughout; its hero frequently insists on calling attention to himself as "le fils de vilain."

The hero's father is unlike most literary vilains, for he has a proper name, Soumilloit. Scholars, recognizing that the literary use of a proper name frequently signals an important reference, or hermeneutic clue, have attempted to establish the historical identity of the patron who commissioned this romance in the person of an Anglo-Saxon named Somerlord, or Somarled, a Scottish chieftain who warred regularly against the king of Scotland and died in 1164.[9] It has been surmised that Guillaume le Clerc must therefore have travelled to Scotland in the expedition of Prince Louis (later Louis VIII) of France, or that Guillaume was among the many French-speaking monks who lived in Scotland long before that expedition (led in 1216 and 1217).[10] But the text itself offers a more likely explanation of the proper name. Guillaume frequently uses the verb soumillier, "to sleep," or "to doze":

Si commenche Fergus a soumiller.
(913)
Then Fergus began to doze.

Aval garde par la fenestre
Et vit soumilier le dansiel.
(916–17)
[The girl] looked down from her window and saw the young man drowsing.

The adjective *someillos* describes someone who needs sleep, who likes to sleep, or who is indolent. Its connotations are those of unenlightenment. The peasant's proper name is overdetermined further by a homonymic contamination with the Old French *somelier* or *someillier,* someone who leads or shepherds beasts of burden (*bêtes de somme*).[11] And that is precisely what Soumilloit and his sons do. Soumilloit's name simply serves to impress us with the fact that he is a true vilain, benighted and heavy like sleep itself, no better than a cowherd.

The hero's peasant father breaks the rules of romance because of his social class. The vilain father is linked to another transgression in *Fergus*: it is an Arthurian romance set in Scotland. At once wild and laughable, Scotland constitutes an element of antiexoticism in a genre usually set in England. The old school of philological criticism studied maps of medieval Scotland to show that Guillaume le Clerc, even if he had travelled to Scotland, possessed a poor sense of geography and a weak memory for spelling.[12] The misspellings in fact suggest an oral transmission of unfamiliar terms. Scholarly articles have pointed out the improbability of the characters' itinerary.[13] Yet the text's aim here is not to excel in nineteenth-century realism *avant la lettre*, but to establish the comic strangeness of Scotland, thus preparing for the appearance of the unusual hero. Guillaume will perpetuate this spatial transgression throughout, in a series of slurs on things Scottish:

> Et Percevals lance levee
> Le siut adies amont aval,
> Tant qu'est venus en Ingeval,
> Une terre d'avoir molt riche.
> Mais cil del pais sont molt niche:
> Que ja n'enterront en mostier.
> Pas ne leur calt de Diu proier:
> Tant sont niches et bestiaus.
> (192–99)

So Perceval, lance held high, followed [the stag] over hill and dale, until he reached Galloway, a land of great wealth. But the people of the country are quite foolish, for they will never set foot in church. Little do they care for praying to God, so foolish and brutish are they.

Like Brittany, which is represented in medieval romance as a fictional frontier between this world and the marvelous Other World, Scotland functions as a fictional frontier between serious Arthurian romance and the realm of parody. The laughable aspects of Scotland and the Scots are underlined, and their threatening wildness is "tamed" through humor. Scotland becomes a a literary joke and a generic marker for transgressive romance.

To the social transgression of the vilain father and the spatial transgression of the Scottish setting, *Fergus* adds another comic "mistake" in the introduction of its hero. The knighting of the Arthurian hero is a key moment in any romance. The description of armor constitutes one of the stylistic showcases of Arthurian romance (as do the descriptions of castles, combats, and women). The medieval audience was listening closely to the following passage in *Fergus,* expecting to hear of shining knightly array, the guarantee of the hero's heroic status:

> Si a un cofre deffreme,
> Si en traist unes armes tels
> Que je vos sai bien dire quels.
> Li haubers estoit si vermaus
> Tout autresi con li solaus,
> Quant li lieve vers Ethipe.
> Mais ce n'iert mie de sinople
> Ne de bresil, bien le sachies:
> Ains estoit un poi ruillies.
> (534–42)

Then he opened a chest and drew from it a suit of armor that I can describe for you exactly. The hauberk was as vermillion as the sun, when it rises over Ethiopia. But it was not made of sinople, nor of brazil, make no mistake: on the contrary, it was a bit rusted.

The parodic crescendo mocks the stylistic convention of the description of beautiful objects and in so doing undercuts the standard rhetorical description of a knight's armor.

The vilain father, foolish in his eagerness to display this family treasure, orders the armor to be thrown to the floor, where a black cloth serves to accentuate the blood-red rust in a parody of the aestheticism we find in the descriptions typical of romance:

> Li vilains ne vaut plus atendre:
> Ains fist enmi la sale estendre
> Un grant drap plus noir conme meure.
> Puis jete les armes deseure
> Qui erent rouges comme sanc.
> (555–59)

The vilain could no longer bear to wait. In the middle of the room he had a great cloth, blacker than blackberries, spread across the floor. Then he threw the armor, red as blood, upon it.

The great poetic clichés of medieval description—"noir conme meure," "rouges comme sanc"—are mocked by their juxtaposition to the rusty possessions of a Scots easant.

It will be obvious to the student of medieval romance that in this introduction of his hero, Guillaume le Clerc alludes openly to Chrétien's young Welsh hero, Perceval, in the *Conte du Graal*. In other words, Guillaume has not invented transgressive combination and juxtaposition; he is rendering homage to an ironic tendency already present in the work of Chrétien. Guillaume is not attacking Chrétien, but rather acknowledging him as a model. This form of parodic playfulness is not aberrant, in medieval literature; it is an integral feature, a common discursive practice.[14] We see this absence of malice when Fergus insists on riding forth with the accoutrements of a country boy rather than with the arms of a knight, much like the rustic young Perceval:

> Si demande sis gavellos.
> Savoir poes qu'il estoit sos.
> Car s'il fust sages, sans doutance
> Il ne demandast que sa lance.
> (601–4)
>
> He asked for his six darts. You can tell that he was an ignorant child, for if he were wise, without a doubt, he would have asked only for a lance.

The reader must not imagine that the *Graal* and *Fergus* are alone in exploiting the traditionally weighty scene of the hero's knighting to establish and confirm the text's transgressive project. Literary history informs us that this comic version of a key Arthurian scene comes to constitute a narrative cliché in a number of thirteenth-century romances. In Hue de Rotelande's *Ipomédon* and in the anonymous *Aiol,* the heroes' undignified processions through a town mark important transitions.[15] And in two of the texts to be studied in later chapters, *Audigier* and *Trubert,* the traditional heroic apogee becomes a comic perigee in the same way: the hero's accession to chivalry is a bathetic debacle.

The midpoint of the hero's quest is a key moment in any Arthurian romance. In the case of *Fergus*, this central point occurs when Fergus, in his effort to obtain the Beautiful Shield which will enable him to find Galiene, reaches Dunostre Castle, where the shield is jealously guarded. Here Guillaume transgresses chivalric motifs in a most comic manner. Fergus quests after the "bel ecu" at Dunostre Castle, where it is guarded by an old hag, "la vielle moussue" (3738). The adjective *moussue* signals the introduction of a comic turn. Of uncertain origin, *mossu*, "hairy," is supposed to derive from the Francian *mossa*, "moss." The old woman is mossy with hair. *Mossu* frequently appears with the adjective *vieil*, referring to the undignified hair that appears in the noses and ears and on the faces of the elderly. Where the audience expected a dragon or a black knight, it meets with a hairy old woman brandishing a steel scythe.

> Le vielle laide et hirechie
> Et a son col le fauc drecie.
> S'ot les grenons lons et trecies,
> Entre deux eols ot bien deus pies,
> Les dens agus et sors et les.
> Bien sanble aversiers u maufes.
> (4076−81)
> The ugly and bristling old woman stood with her scythe ready, about her neck. Her moustache was long and braided; there were a good two feet between her two eyes; her teeth were sharp and yellow and wide. She looked quite like a demon or a devil.

The expectation of fear is attenuated by the comic elements of the description: hirsute ugliness; the moustache, braided in a touch of coquetterie; the absurd precision of the space between her two eyes; the yellowness of her teeth.

As Fergus approaches, the old woman begins to whistle: "Si commence fort a sifler" (4083):

> La vielle avoit leve sa hure,
> Si commencha sorcillier.
> (4089−90)
> The old woman raised her mangey head and began to frown.

Rather than *teste* or *chief*, the text chooses the term *hure*, which connotes the hair or head of a beast. All potentially frightening marks in the description of this foe are rendered laughable by the references to femaleness and to old age. To this comic description the text simultaneously contrasts a genuinely frightened hero. Thus, transgressive juxtaposition and combination continue to undercut the hero's heroicness; Fergus is represented as fearful even as the cause of that fear is undermined.

It is a commonplace to point out that medieval romance has

two plots, or two economies: one, chivalric, the other erotic. Guillaume's strategies in portraying Fergus as lover are not unlike those he uses in subverting the hero as knight. Like the representation of the hero's dubbing, the portrayal of the main characters as they fall in love constitutes a prominent point in medieval romance. In *Fergus*, the initial development of this crucial moment conforms to the conventions of the genre: the beautiful and noble heroine falls in love at first sight of the hero, then spends long hours suffering from her secret feelings. Galiene, the heroine of *Fergus*, repeats fragments of a love discourse the audience has heard before: the amorous ratiocinatio closely resembles the language of Fenice and Soredamor in Chrétien's *Cligès*, as well as that of the lovers in the earlier twelfth-century *Roman d'Eneas* and *Roman de Thebes*.[16] In the thirteenth century, Hue de Rotelande's *Ipomédon* will offer a comic version of such speeches, as we will see in Chapter 4. But in *Fergus*, the laments of Galiene are not comic; as poignant as those of Chrétien's heroines, they create strong expectations in the audience. Those expectations are heightened when Guillaume virtually quotes the *Conte du Graal* in describing the heroine as she arises in the night to waken the sleeping hero. In Chrétien's *Conte du Graal*, Blancheflor's declaration of love is received, quite literally, with open arms; Perceval swears to defend her against all foes, and they remain side by side through the night. In Guillaume's *Fergus*, the scene begins properly enough, but abruptly goes awry. Galiene, in tears, has lost her heart:

"Mon cuer ai perdu, se ne truis
Qui me die qu'est devenus.
Car il est cha a vos venus.
Rendes le moi, vostre merchi."
(1930–33)
"I have lost my heart, and cannot find anyone who will tell me what has become of it. In truth, it has gone out to you. Give it back to me, I beg you."

Fergus replies, densely, that he has not seen it:

Fergus respont "Onques ne vi,
Ma demoisele, vostre cuer.
Je nel retenroie a nul fuer,

Se je l'avoie en ma baillie.
Mais sacies que je ne l'ai mie."
(1934–38)

Fergus answered, "I never saw your heart, young lady. I would not keep it
from you at any price, if I had it in my possession. But know that I do not
have it."

Galiene insists that Fergus possesses her heart, her life, and her
death. Fergus, in poor form, laughs:

Fergus li respont en riant
"Pucele, je vois el querrant
Que amors ne que druerie.
J'ai une bataille aatie,
Que jou vaurai avant parfaire."
(1951–55)

Laughing, Fergus answers her: "Maiden, I am seeking for something other
than love or romance. I must engage in a fierce battle, which I want to win
before anything else."

Hearing this, Galiene faints outright:

Ariere sor le pavement
Est recheue, si se pasme.
(1974–75)

Backwards onto the stone floor [Galiene] fell, and fainted.

To conclude, at two crucial moments in the love-interest story,
Fergus takes care to build the audience's expectations of the conventional Arthurian scene, only to dash them, like poor Galiene,
on the castle pavement. *Fergus* here practices a transgressive juxtaposition. The author illustrates his knowledge of the rules of
love scenes, for Galiene's role and speeches conform perfectly to
the model. The text thus prepares the audience to recognize
Fergus's language and behavior as incorrect or out-of-place, belonging to another space and to another stylistic register.

Weaving these two quests, the knightly and the erotic, medieval
romance must find a way of leading its audience from displays of
chivalry to scenes of love and back again. The memory of having
been loved, the intuition of danger, the knowledge of an un-
avenged wrong—such are the clichés that commonly function as

narrative transitions in Arthurian romance, leading the hero from adventure to adventure. They are conventions of a stylistic, a social, and a moral order. The framework of the unending Arthurian quest must be clothed in upper-class manners and noble motivations, expressed in elegant language. Guillaume le Clerc makes a point of breaking with the usages governing narrative transitions, just as he transgresses the decorum of combat and that of love. Though Guillaume effects narrative transitions with skill and speed, the anecdotal justification for the transitions, far from conforming to the expectations of the audience, jolts them because of its transgressive nature. The text utilizes two types of events to spur the hero on in his quest: when one episode ends and the hero must leave in search of another adventure, either he can find none or he grows too hungry to look.

When Fergus first sallies forth from King Arthur's court, eager to test his own mettle, the reader expects him to meet with a signal danger or hear a prophecy that will foretell his future. Guillaume undercuts his hero, however, creating a comic disappointment for the reader. Fergus can find nothing to do:

> Fergus s'en part, tos sols chemine
> Ne tenoit pas la chiere encline,
> De fierte resanble lion.
> En tot le mont ne trovast on
> Chevalier de lui plus hardi.
> Trestote jor dusqu'a midi
> Son cemin chevauche a droiture.
> Onques ne trova aventure:
> Se li anuie durement.
> (1487–95)

Fergus departed, wending his way alone. He did not hold his head low; in his pride he resembled a lion. In all the world one could not find a braver knight than he. All the day long, in fact until noon, he rode straight on his way. But he did not find a single adventure, and was sorely grieved.[17]

Not only is this hero plagued by boredom; he is also tormented by a less than heroic preoccupation—hunger. It is hunger that leads Fergus to his greatest feats, and eating that brings them to a conclusion. Now, in the Arthurian scheme of things, tables, linens, golden washbasins, and menus may be described, for they function as markers of the social class of the characters and of the stylistic level of the genre. But twelfth- and thirteenth-century romance practice forbids talk of eating, as Guillaume's *Fergus* firmly states:

> Des mes ne vos quer faire fable.
> Ases orent a lor voloir
> S'õr voloie dire le voir
> De lor mes, con faire saroie,
> Ma matere en alongeroie
> Et l'ovre en poroie enpirier.
> Por ce ne m'en vel travillier.
> Car au mius dire vel pener,
> Si je m'en puis aporpenser,
> Ne n'estudie a pior metre.
> Tot d'el me vauroie entremetre.
> (1028–38)

As for the dishes served, I don't want to lie to you. They all had as much as they desired. If I were to tell the whole truth concerning their fare, as I know very well how to do, I would lengthen my material and could worsen my work; for that reason I do not care to give myself such trouble. For I want to strive at expressing things in the best possible way, and I want to be able to reflect on how to do so, not to work at making a thing worse. Now let me go on to take up an entirely different matter.

After this lengthy narratorial digression, Guillaume reiterates the rules, implying that they are not empty formulae but points of contemporary literary theory and of artistic pride:

> De mes orent dusques a dis.
> Mes borderes resanbleroit
> Qui cascun mes deviseroit.
> Por ce ne m'en vel entremettre:
> Car aillors veul mon penser metre,
> Se mon sens i puis apoier.
> (1712–17)

They had as many as ten different dishes, but it would seem like a poor joke to describe each one of them. That is why I do not want to set about such a task, for I want to turn my thoughts to other matters, if I can apply my intelligence in another way.

Gregoire Lozinski, in his critical edition of the carnival text *La Bataille de Caresme et de Charnage*, documents the transgressive nature of food and eating in the social and moral codes of "high" culture, whence their significance as key rituals in medieval carnival. Commenting on medieval literature, Lozinski formulates the general rule: "Une description détaillée de tout ce qui précède le repas, et pas un mot sur le menu: c'est une règle dont l'auteur ne se départ pas. Seulement la formule banale 'assez ont mes à mengier' varie d'un épisode à l'autre." Lozinski then closes his discussion by quoting the passages just cited from *Fergus*: "Et voici que Guillaume le Clerc tranche, à notre avis, la question en se plaçant sur le terrain de la théorie poétique. Le sujet qui nous occupe est un sujet vulgaire, il doit être banni de la poésie."[18]

What Lozinski fails to point out is that *Fergus* articulates this "ironclad" rule and then proceeds to violate it. The transgressive pattern becomes more and more marked: Guillaume le Clerc demonstrates his knowledge of the rules; leads the audience to expect an adequation of genre, social class, space, stylistics and morality similar to that found in the work of Chrétien; then portrays a hero who ignores the conventions of the genre. When Fergus ought to be dreaming of Galiene, he can think of nothing but food:

Fergus vait pensant a sa drue.
Mais fains le destraint et argue
Tant qu'il ne se set consillier.
S'or avoit d'argent un sestier,
Sel donroit il tres tous de plain
Por avoir son seol de pain.
Ne ne fait pas a mervillier,
S'il avoit talent de manger.
Car il avoit deus jors passe
Que il n'avoit de pain gouste.
Or li fait li fains oblier
Le grant cuire de son penser
Qu'il avoit vers s'amie chiere.
(3230–42)

Fergus went on, thinking of his lady-love. But hunger troubled and tormented him so that he did not know what to do. If he had a measure of silver, he would gladly give the whole thing to eat his fill of bread. It is not surprising that he so desires to eat, for he had gone two days without a taste of bread. Hunger makes him forget the great care on his mind, which was his dear lady.[19]

Hunger concludes the dangerous ordeals of Guillaume's *Fergus*. The greater the "aventure," the greater the hero's hunger. As soon as Fergus kills the giant of Mont Dolerous, slays the giant's son, and tames the giant's horse, food is borne in:

> Car durement estoit mal mis
> Et damagies par mi le cors.
> Se n'i pert plaie par defors.
> Les puceles a lor pooir
> Le gardent et servent au soir,
> Et si aportent le manger.
> (4717–22)

[Fergus] was in a very sorry state, and badly wounded internally. But no wound appears on the outside of his body. That evening the young girls protect and serve him to the best of their abilities, and bring him food.

Hunger is the index of valor in the parodic system of *Fergus*.[20] But hunger is not the only bodily joke in *Fergus*; eating is comic, also. Culinary humor, as Ernst Curtius writes, is one of the principal sources of comic invention in medieval literature. It is a constant in the comic tradition, but also in epic, religious, panegyric, and hagiographic literature.[21] *Joca seriis miscere* is not simply an idea in medieval theory, but a practice that, in epic literature especially, relies heavily on food and everything touching it: gluttony, drunkenness, as well as cooks, kitchen scenes, hangovers, and food fights. Curtius cites the example of the ninth-century *Bella Parisiacae Urbus*, by Abbot de Saint-Germain-des-Prés: the abbot, Ebolus, impales seven Normans on a spit in one fell swoop, and laughingly hands them over to the kitchens.[22] But as Curtius's study does not extend to vernacular romance, Lozinski's conclusions on the subject are more pertinent to our discussion of *Fergus*. If hunger and eating are unwonted in romance, food fights and kitchen pranks are even more transgressive as knightly activities in courtly literature.

Fergus, in his hunger, behaves more like an epic figure than the hero of a thirteenth-century Arthurian romance. In one of the best-developed and extended combat episodes of the *Fergus,* the hero fights "comme lion," slaying eleven "bachelers" singlehandedly. It is a glorious moment but for the fact that the altercation is a food fight and the hero wields a wooden spit.

Accustomed to the delicate ellipses propounded by romance tradition, the medieval audience would be jarred (and delighted) by the hero's transgressive behavior as he rides into a camp of knights and wordlessly seizes the bread placed in front of the company's master:

> Un siminel qui ert devant
> Le plus maistre des chevaliers
> (Grans estoit et trestous entiers)
> A pris Fergus qui molt ert preu.
> (3281–84)
>
> A great biscuitlike bread, a whole loaf of it, was in front of the most important of the knights, and the valiant Fergus took it.

As this unexpected behavior continues, the register of the language used to describe it belongs to epic combat:

> Capon tornoient a un feu.
> Je ne sai comment cil s'esforce
> Et a deux mains saissist la broche:
> Onques ne fist noisse ne plait,
> Ains a un des capons fors trait,
> Puis en mangue durement.
> (3285–90)
>
> Capons were roasting on a fire. I do not know how but [Fergus] snatches and with two hands seizes the spit. Without making a single sound or word, he pulled one of the capons off and bit into it voraciously.

The text underscores the hero's ill-mannered eating as a breach of both social and of stylistic codes: even the fifteen robbers are left speechless by such folly. When the bandits finally reproach the hero for eating all their food, the young man from Scotland pretends that he does not hear and snatches another piece of bread:

> Fergus les ot, ne fist sanblant
> Ne nule ciere n'en mostra.
> Trestot son siminel manja,
> Puis entent a l'autre saissir.
> (3313–16)
>
> Fergus heard them, but pretended not to, and showed no sign of it. He ate the whole bread, then began to think about taking the other.

When Fergus finally speaks up, it is to excuse himself on the grounds of his provincial upbringing. He puns on *escot* (part to be paid, bill or check) and *Ecossais*.

> Tels est l'estres de mon pais:
> Quant gent a escot sont asis,
> Il manguent premierement
> Tant com il lor vient a talent,
> Puis si content apres disner."
> (3330–34)

"This is the custom in my country: when people sit down to their share, they eat first of all as much as they like, then settle accounts after dinner."

But Fergus in fact wants to get off scot-free. Having outraged the *brigands*, Fergus engages the mock-epic battle. In a grandiose gesture, the hero seizes the humble spit and wreaks havoc in a show of almost superhuman strength and violence:

> Le broche a tos les chapons prent
> Si a si feru et caple
> Le premerain qu'a encontre
> Qu'andels li fait voler les iels.
> (3347–50)

[Fergus] took the spit with all the capons. He struck and dealt such a blow to the first man he met that Fergus caused both of the man's eyes to fly from his head.

The parodic transgression in this scene is both combinational and juxtapositional. A combinational transgression is one in which the author puts the wrong type of character or discourse in a given genre (combining burlesque characters in an epic text, for instance). In this scene, Guillaume le Clerc has combined chivalric diction with a food fight. A juxtapositional transgression occurs when a scene typical of one genre is followed by a scene or scenes typical of a different literary tradition. In the case at hand, the poet has juxtaposed the space of the romance quest and that of the kitchen. These doughty Arthurian knights bang one another over the head for food.

The medieval intertext of this scene is the "Demoiselle de la Tente" episode in Chrétien's *Conte du Graal*. Chrétien's hero, Perceval, snatches and devours the wine and paté that the young maiden has saved for her love.[23] Once again, Chrétien's well-known work provides a model for the comic errors of the ignorant young hero. In the *Conte du Graal,* the scene is an early comic moment, illustrating the hero's childlike selfishness and the suffering that such thoughtlessness causes others: the Demoiselle de la Tente will be punished cruelly for the theft of the food and drink. In *Fergus,* the scene is not a lesson in a pedagogical scheme. The food-snatching is parodic, generating a mock-epic battle in which the hero proves his strength and bravery by vanquishing thirteen foes at once.

To conclude, in the episodes of chivalric combat, the hero breaks the rules of knightly behavior, just as the text mocks the usual rhetoric of romance. *Fergus* underscores the infractions of social, rhetorical, and spatial codes by first alluding to romance tradition, and specifically to the corpus of Chrétien, and then thwarting the expectations thus created. Guillaume consistently demonstrates his knowledge of the traditional correspondence between genre, social class, stylistic level, rhetorical register, and space, only to introduce comic variations by portraying a hero who has no knowledge of chivalric (and romance) codes.

In the case at hand, to say that *Fergus* is a parody of Chrétien's work does not account for the specificity of *Fergus,* and we now face the question of identifying its interpretant. Humor has been an important hermeneutic guide thus far, and we can return to the initial "jokes" or anomalies of *Fergus* to discover precisely which literary tradition orients the direction of its parody.

"Fergus." What does this unlikely name conceal? Or reveal? Medieval culture found great significance in names and naming. The name of the hero, in medieval literature, is accorded a central position in hermeneutics. Folk etymologies, some quite whimsical, flourished and were considered appropriate methods of glossing a text, deducing scientific facts, and explaining religious mysteries.

Guillaume le Clerc remains silent, concealing as it were the name of his hero, for 738 verses. The audience waits during the opening scenes at Arthur's court, the long stag hunt, the description of Soumilloit's world in Scotland, the hero's comic knighting and first combat, until the hero arrives before King Arthur:

> "De ces sui Fergus apieles
> Qui me connoissent en ma terre."
> (738–39)
> "I am called Fergus by those who know me in my country."

We first understand the unusual, if not comical, praenomen as a guarantee of the hero's Scottishness, a key sign in a constellation of anti-exotic signs in the romance. The queer name is a deliberate "mistake," alerting the reader to a singular textual design.

To a medieval audience, the name Fergus recalls, by homophonic association, the Latin *ferus,* meaning "wild," and also the Latin *ferox,* meaning "ferocious." *Ferus* connotes that which grows wild in a field, as does the hero at the beginning of Guillaume le Clerc's romance. More important from a literary viewpoint, "Fergus" is in fact a morphological variant of the name Ferragut, or Ferraguz, a standard name for Saracen kings in the French chanson de geste.[24] Guillaume le Clerc's romance takes the name of its hero from the Charlemagne cycle of these chansons.[25] Ferragus is the fierce Saracen king in the late-twelfth-century *Floovent* and the early-thirteenth-century *Anseïs de Cartage.* Ferragus is traditionally slain by Roland, as in *Otinel* (second half of the twelfth century), *Girart de Roussillon* (early thirteenth century), and *Hughes Capet* (fourteenth century). The wide range of dates just mentioned indicates a veritable tradition; Ferragus consistently represents strength, fierceness, and the pagan world. Guillaume le Clerc borrows that fearsome name, with all its connotations, and presents it as a Scottish name with a comic ring.[26]

In almost all the chansons de geste mentioned above, the hero marries a Saracen princess and persuades her to convert to Christianity. We must recall that the ideological opposition preoccupying the chanson de geste is not that of vilain and courtois, but of Christian and Saracen. Guillaume's *Fergus* plays with that epic coding of "high" and "low," or civilized and wild, in its choice of the name of its heroine. The name "Galiene" also comes from the Charlemagne cycle of the chanson de geste. As early as the twelfth century, it is the name of Charlemagne's wife, the daughter of a Saracen king.[27]

Thus both hero and heroine bring to *Fergus* markers of wildness and its "conversion," in the literary tradition of the chanson de geste. Furthermore, they illuminate other presumably inexplicable elements in the *Fergus,* signs from the chanson de geste, pointing to the direction of the parodic rewriting. The last parts of the puzzle fall into place. The slivered fragments of the chanson de geste are the visible signs of the interpretant at work, redirecting the romance model.

The literary interpretant is the text or textual model that both effects and, a posteriori, explains the specificity of each parodic production. In medieval literature, the interpretant can be defined as an existing literary tradition, a well-defined literary silhouette; though barely visible at first glance, this silhouette gives shape to the parody, forms its distortion of the intertext. If *Fergus* were simply a composite of Chrétien's five romances, with comic inversions here and there, the relation between the text and the audience would be an easy game of Arthurian hide-and-seek: finding the backwards horse or the cowardly knight. But parody is not the mere inversion of literary elements. It cannot be described by a bipartite model. Guillaume le Clerc does not simply turn the corpus of Chrétien de Troyes on its head. Guillaume rewrites the Arthurian model, giving it a consistent new direction through his systematic use of an interpretant: medieval epic.

The audience of Guillaume's romance senses the presence of another literary tradition in the hero's rule-breaking. Fergus never seems to be a romance hero in the sense of the term *romantic*. He prefers battles and horses, insulting and eating, to the marvelous and amorous events that characterize Arthurian romance.

Once we recognize the onomastic clues in "Fergus" and "Galiene," we find that epic traces, which appear throughout *Fergus*, stand out in relief. One of the more amusing ungrammaticalities, for example—interpreted by critics as a gross mistake—is that Fergus frequently ties his horse to an "olivier," an olive tree. Frescoln, among others, points to the Scottish olive trees as proof that Guillaume le Clerc never visited the Scotland he carefully describes.[28] In truth, the olive tree has nothing to do with the author's horticultural and geographical knowledge. The "olivier" functions as an intertextual sign, referring the audience to what is perhaps the best known chanson de geste, the *Chanson de Roland*:

> Li reis Marsilie s'en fuit en Sarraguce,
> Suz un' olive est descendut en l'umbre.
> (*La Chanson de Roland* 2570–71)[29]
>
> King Marsile fled to Saragossa. Beneath an olive tree, he dismounted, in the shade.

In *Fergus*, the reference to the *Roland* is overdetermined by the Picardian form of the Old French, "olive": "olivier" constitutes a double reference to another of the principal characters in the *Roland,* Olivier.[30] Thus the tree, like the Saracen names of Fergus and Galiene, points to the epic interpretant.

The curious old hag with the scythe, who seemed so out of place in an Arthurian castle and inspired such fear in Fergus, also belongs to epic literature. In the *Chanson d'Aliscans,* the hideous old pagan Flohort charges the Christian army; she reappears in the *Chevalerie Vivien* and *Anseïs de Carthage.* In *Fierabras* we see the giantess Amiete on a bridge, like the hag in the *Fergus,* eyes red with rage as she decimates the French with her scythe.[31]

But what of the vilain father and son? While the literary character of the vilain has an established role in such comic medieval genres as the fabliau, he also holds a precedent role in the chanson de geste, where he is the traditional servant to the epic hero.[32] The puzzling vilain-hero in the *Fergus* will offer the final and fullest proof that the epic tradition rewrites the Arthurian matrix in *Fergus.*

Fergus is the son of a vilain in terms of literary history as well as in Guillaume's romance. He is the descendant of the comic vilain figure in the chanson de geste, a character who is only one of many comic elements in a genre usually taught and read as a "weighty" genre that excludes levity.[33]

The epic vilain plays the role of faithful servant, the hero's good and loyal helper. Huge and strong, this vilain wields a beam or club ("tinel," "massue," or "baston")—which is how Fergus arms himself in the early part of that romance. The language and manners of the epic vilain are rigidly coded as coarse and "low"; he is clearly marked as a member of the lowest social class. His courage, valor, and success as a warrior are unrelated to his social class and manners; he slays massive numbers of Saracens. Furthermore, and equally important for our understanding of the Fergus character, the epic vilain is known for his excessive eating and drinking.

The prototype or model of the epic vilain is Rainouart au Tinel, who serves Guillaume d'Orange in the Guillaume cycle.[34] Notorious for his reluctance to part company with a massive "tinel" and for his drunkenness and gluttony, Rainouart rises to the head of the French troops, thanks to his fierce fighting. The *Chanson de Guillaume* delineates Rainouart as a comic version of the feudal hero.[35] Details and variations of his character and his legendary feats are developed in *Aliscans* (ca. 1165), which retells and expands traditional episodes as well as inventing new ones.[36] The vilain so grew in popularity in the twelfth and thirteenth centuries that he inspired chansons dedicated to himself: the *Chanson de Rainouard* (mid-twelfth century), in which he is a half-heroic and half-burlesque giant, tormented by kitchen scullions, and the *Geste Rainoart* (ca. 1170) which consists of two burlesque epics, the *Bataille Loquifier* and the *Moniage Rainouart*.

But the epic vilain differs from Guillaume's "fils de vilain" in one essential respect: while the Rainouart character is comic *and* heroic, he is not transgressive. A humorous lower-class character does not break the rules of the epic genre; but a ludicrous peasant son definitely constitutes a transgression in romance. Guillaume le Clerc uses this knowledge to achieve his transgressive parody of Chrétien's Arthurian romance. The design of *Fergus* has become clear. The "mistakes" at which we laugh stem from the fact that Guillaume le Clerc has given the role of romance hero to a Rainouart-like vilain who wants only to eat, sleep and do battle.

To conclude our discussion of the interpretant we must raise two further questions. Is there only one interpretant in any given text? And if we must designate one tradition only among several traditions, what criteria does the reader or critic use for determining the real interpretant?

To anchor this theoretical discussion in the specifics of the text at hand, we can step back and ask whether the chanson de geste is the only possible interpretant of the *Fergus* parody.

The reader of French medieval literature is accustomed to finding vilains not in romance but in fabliaux. There, such characters figure prominently, even in titles: *Du Vilein Mire, Du Vilain de Bailleul, Le Vilain Asnier, Le Pet au Vilain, Le Vilain qui n'ert pas de son Estre Sire.*[37] Further, when we learn that the vilain Soumilloit has married an impoverished courtoise, Fergus's noble mother, we wonder whether we have not been plunged into the world of the fabliau, where the courtoise wife and the vilain husband figure frequently.[38]

Could the interpretant of *Fergus* be the ribald *Berenger au Lonc Cul*, a fabliau that presents marked parallels with the first scenes of *Fergus*? There, we find a wealthy vilain, a courtoise who must marry into the vilain's family for money, and a husband who owns a suit of armor and other knightly paraphernalia but would rather pitch hay than joust.[39] In both texts, the "fils de vilain" is characterized as hungry, given to napping, garrulous, and often brutal. These elements appear in a slightly different disposition in the fabliau, where the courtoise marries not the vilain but his socially ambitious son. In *Berenger,* the son of a wealthy vilain leads a rustic existence. The setting is not Scotland, but Lombardy, another anti-exotic joke:

> Que il avint en Lonbardie,
> ou la gent n'est gaires hardie.
> (*Berenger* 11–12)

For it happened in Lombardy, where the people are hardly courageous.

In *Berenger,* the noble wife sees that her husband is lazy, loves nothing so much as eating, and never engages in knightly feats. Like Fergus's mother, this courtoise chides her husband by boasting of her own illustrious forefathers:

> Dont set ele bien sanz doutance,
> a ce qu'il estoit si parliers,
> qu'il n'estoit mie chevaliers
> atrais ne de gentil lignaige.
> Donc li ramentoit son lignaige
> ou tant a vaillanz chevaliers:
> as armes sont hardiz et fiers,
> a sejorner n'amoient rien.
> (*Berenger* 54–61)

She knew without a doubt, from the fact that he was so talkative, that he was no proven knight, nor of noble lineage. So she reminded him of her own lineage and all its many valiant knights: they were courageous and brave in fighting, and cared nothing for staying home.[40]

Offended, the husband sets out to prove his valor. Hidden in the woods, he hacks away at his own shield, breaks his own lance, then returns home to boast. The wife soon notices that her husband is never hurt or spent when he returns. She herself finds armor and horse, dresses as a knight, "Berenger," and witnesses her husband's mad combats. The wife then tricks her husband into submission and humiliates him with the "baiser honteux."[41] She is then free to send for her lover, a true knight, and forces her vilain husband to accept his own cuckolding.

To discover whether we can consider this fabliau to be the, or one, interpretant of *Fergus,* we must hold them up to the light, as it were, at several points. How closely do they correspond, and at what levels? Do they resemble one another only in local narrative features?

In Guillaume's romance, the vilain-courtois thematic remains a literary joke, a formal transgression. In *Berenger,* the question of crossing class boundaries is addressed directly: the noble classes should not intermarry with the peasant classes.

> Ainsi bons lignaiges aville,
> et li chastelain et li conte
> declinent tuit et vont a honte;
> se marient bas por avoir,
> si en doivent grant honte avoir
> et grant domaige si ont il.
> Li chevalier mauvais et vill
> et coart issent de tel gent,
> qui covoitent or et argent
> plus qu'il ne font chevalerie:
> ainsi est noblece perie.
> (*Berenger* 24–34)
> In this way good families are made vile; the squire and the count lower everyone, and come to shame; they marry below themselves for the sake of wealth, and they should feel greatly ashamed for this, as great harm comes of it. Bad, vile, and cowardly knights are born of such people, who desire gold and silver more than chivalry: thus does nobility perish.

Such clear-cut moralizing speaks directly to the changes in feudal structure occurring in twelfth- and thirteenth-century France. Yet Guillaume le Clerc eschews the possibility of commenting on the changes occurring around him; the medieval world's awareness of its own social hierarchy is obvious in *Berenger,* but tacit in *Fergus.*

Considered in this light, *Berenger* is not transgressive; it states that those who marry over class boundaries will suffer, and depicts an unpleasant punishment. The fabliau spells out a social rule: a vilain can never be anything but a vilain. Though *Berenger* shares similar stock comic characters, it does not provide the direction, literary or cultural, used in the parodic rewriting that is *Fergus*.

While *Berenger* is not the most illuminating interpretant of *Fergus* because it accounts for only a small number of local features in Guillaume's text, our comparison of the two texts affords us greater purchase on the functioning of parody. The depiction of Soumilloit, his rustic manners, his courtoise wife, his hungry son, Fergus—all function as a coded literary allusion. The literary character of the "riche vilain" and the "filz au vilain" act as intergeneric signs referring the audience to a comic literary vein, even while holding the attention of the audience on the Arthurian matrix. The medieval listener had only to hear a few verses on the subject of the ludicrous Soumilloit in order to understand that Guillaume's *Fergus* was, like many medieval texts of this period, a mixed text, and that the textual productions to come would be transgressive in character, combining and juxtaposing elements from a variety of literary traditions.

The vilain, hunger, eating, the wild-man hero—these anomalous elements of *Fergus* remind us of another well-known medieval corpus, the *Roman de Renart*.[42] Fergus's fights with animals, his sarcastic language, the savage insults, and other wild elements of Guillaume's romance which seem inexplicable in the Arthurian tradition could be explained if the *Roman de Renart* were the interpretant of the parody. Is the Scots knight in rusted armor a variant of the rust-colored fox who travels through various kingdoms of medieval literature, transgressing its codes and conventions?

Vilain, insults, hunger, eating, animals: *Renart* and *Fergus* draw on the same comic codes. Let us look first at their actualization of the vilain-courtois polarization. The vilains of *Renart* do not fail to remind us of Soumilloit; many of them are "riches vilains" with property and social ambition. The vilain Liétart, in Roques's Branch X, began life in poverty, then in ten years accumulated money, land, and livestock. Liétart marries a demoiselle of nobler birth, and like Soumilloit and the vilain husband in *Berenger,* he tries in vain to please his courtoise:

> Ne li ose dire ne faire
> chose qui li doie desploire;

ele estoit sor le vilain dame
por ce qu'el estoit gentil fame.
(*Renart* x, 10317–20)

He dares not say or do anything lest it displease her; she is the lady who
lords it over the vilain because she is a gentlewoman.

The authors of the different branches of *Renart*, like Guillaume
le Clerc, use hunger as a transition between episodes, and frequently depict food and scenes of eating.[43] Sleepiness, evoked by
the verb *someillier*, plays a role as transition in *Renart*, as it does in
Fergus.[44] Other local narrative configurations, comically treated
in both texts, could lead the reader to see a link between *Renart*
and Guillaume's romance: a family with three sons living in a rustic castle; a lovesome female character; a long hunt scene that
highlights the fear of the hunted animal; the theft of food.[45] The
modern reader will be struck, too, by the cruel, insulting tone of
the sarcastic jibes in *Renart*, and their similarity to the taunts of
Fergus. We find, for example, the same bloodletting joke in *Renart*
and in Guillaume's parody.

Renart lor a gité .II. gas:
"Dant Brun, de Dieu saiez saingniez!
Ieste vos de novel saingniez?
Voste bras bos est escrevez;
je cuit trop tost coru avez."
(*Renart* VIIb, 7171–77)

Renart hurled two insults at them: "Mister Brun, may you make the sign of
God's cross! Have you just had your blood let? Your arm is split open; I
would say you got back on your feet too soon."

Renart turns on the bear again, in another branch, using a familiar doctor joke:

"Alez vos en, Brun, biaux douz sire,
vos avez bien mestier de mire;
gardez ne soit plus respitié:
je ai de vos mout grant pitié."
(*Renart* VII, 7193–96)

Be off, Brun, good and noble sire. You need to see a doctor! take care not to
put it off: I feel very sorry for you.

In *Fergus*, the romance hero dwells on the same bloodletting jokes, and his crowing diction sounds quite like that of the trick-ster fox:

> "Dius vos salt, sire chevalier!
> Mestier avies or de saignier:
> Jel voi molt bien a vostre sanc
> Que pert deseur cel hauberc blanc.
> Il sainne trop, gardes vos viaus!
> Car li sainnieres est nouvials
> Si ne sot pas coissir la vaine.
> Je criem que vos n'en aies painne
> Et dolor de ceste sainnie.
> (*Fergus* 2392–2400)

"God save you, sir knight! You must have needed a bloodletting; I can tell from the blood all over your white hauberk. Look out for your guts, you're bleeding seriously. The doctor must have been in training; he did not know how to find your vein. I fear that you must be in pain from this operation.

When we hold Guillaume's *Fergus* up to the silhouette of the *Roman de Renart,* do we understand the overall shape of its par-ody? Beyond certain local features—vilain characters, animal scenes, food thefts, doctor jokes—the points of comparison be-tween the two works are not as rich or numerous as those shared by the chanson de geste and *Fergus. Renart* cannot account for the specificity of Guillaume's romance parody; Fergus is not a trick-ster. Both *Renart* and *Fergus* draw on the same body of jokes and clichés; both are self-conscious artistic constructions that flaunt their knowledge of a vast array of medieval texts. Both rework and incorporate whole parts of other texts. Such is the mobility of poetic and narrative materials in the Middle Ages. But while *Re-nart* and *Fergus* may share common intertexts, the latter is not a direct response to the former. The epic tradition, on the other hand, is addressed directly in Guillaume's parody. A study of the chanson de geste yields substantial insights into the workings of parody in *Fergus.* The hero is a character from the chanson de geste transplanted to and incorporated in the space of omance.

The answer, then, to the question raised—How does one deter-mine the interpretant?—is empirical. While no one could affirm that there exists one interpretant only for any given parody, it can be shown that one textual tradition is more pertinent than others

to the discussion of a specific parody. And the most pertinent interpretant is quite simply that which yields the most illuminating
and detailed account of transformation of the matrix text in the
parody text.

To conclude our study of Guillaume le Clerc's parody, we must return to the notion of transgression, ascertain the overall project of
Fergus, and ask what it may have meant to the medieval audience.
What is this parody about: a mockery of the chanson de geste? a
subversion of social hierarchy as seen in literature? If *Fergus* is
simply the intertextual transformation of an existing epic tradition, how does it constitute a transgression? Is not all of literature
built on such reworkings of characters from other times or traditions? The character of Fergus differs from other socially anomalous heroes, such as the Wild Man, Orson, or Rainouart, or Her-
cules, in that those other characters are soon revealed to be of
noble or divine birth, and therefore legitimate hero material.
Guillaume le Clerc refuses to justify, explain, or erase his hero's
vilain origins. The peasant's son can hardly be understood as an illustration of the dictate "bon sang ne peut mentir," because
Guillaume le Clerc frequently recalls Soumilloit, even as he allows
the hero's noble mother to be forgotten. Fergus consistently identifies himself as "fils au vilain":

> "Chevaliers sui je, par ma teste!
> Car li bons vilains m'adoba
> Quant a cort servir m'envoia."
> (*Fergus* 1112–14)
>
> "I most certainly am a knight, believe me! For the good vilain dubbed me
> when he sent me to serve at court."

> "Et je vel bien que li dies,
> Se il vous plaist, de moie part,
> Que del fil au vilain se gart."
> (1090–92)
>
> "And I want him to be told, if it pleases you, from me, to watch out for the
> vilain's son."

The text sustains the oxymoron of the vilain hero at the crucial
moment of the character's naming. The dwarf who knows all and
can predict the future hails Fergus thus:

Vilain and Courtois

... "Vasal, bien aies tu,
Li fius au vilain de Pelande!"
(3719–20)

"Young man, I wish you well, son of the vilain from Pelande!"

Guillaume's *Fergus* accomplishes quite a feat: in its representation of chivalry, it simply displaces (the better to maintain) the rigid class boundaries of the Middle Ages, including its transgressive hero in a final gesture of incorporation. Fergus becomes a knight of King Arthur, marries Galiene, and is crowned king of Lodien. All memories of the Scottish farm and the vilain father have been erased; it is as if Fergus were an orphan, now adopted by Arthur's courtly "family."

Can we know how Guillaume's literary transgression was received in the Middle Ages? Frescoln, who summarizes the statements of many critics, claims the romance was unpopular, having neither success nor influence over later medieval literature: "[Fergus] seems to have been mysteriously passed over."[46] But the onomastics of medieval romance tell another story. If we turn to the "Fergus" entry in the indices of Louis-Fernand Flutre, and of G. D. West, we find no less than ten namesake characters in romance texts stretching from 1225 to 1501.[47] In those texts, Fergus is neither Saracen king nor Celtic giant: he is a knight of the Round Table. In the *Livre du Lancelot del Lac,* dated 1225, which is roughly contemporary to *Fergus,* he is "Fergus de la Forest Salvage," son of a king. In the *Prophecies de Merlin,* dated 1276, he is Ferguz, friend of Tristan and seeker of the Grail. In the older parts of the *Roman de Tristan en Prose Française,* dated between 1225 and 1240, Fergus is one of the knights of King Marc. In *Tristan de Leonois,* or *Roman en Prose de Tristan,* dated to the thirteenth century, he is again companion of Tristan, in quest of the Grail. In *La Treselegante, Delicieuse, Melliflue et Tresplaisante Hystoire du Tres Noble, Victorieux et Excellentissime Roy Perceforest, Roy de la Grant-Bretaigne* (commonly referred to as *Perceforest*), from the first third of the fourteenth century, Fergus is a Scottish knight, the son of a vilain.[48]

The integration of the "fils au vilain" in the courtois tradition of the Round Table created a long-lived precedent. The transformation of the fierce pagan Ferraguz into a Scottish knight was accepted and adopted by contemporary and later romance; its presence in the sixteenth century attests to the popularity of this unwonted character. In this sense, the Fergus hero can be studied as a chapter on medieval literary practices of transgression and transformation.

The incorporation in question is thus twofold: that of a character in a specific narrative, and in a romance tradition. Guillaume le Clerc elaborates a practice of literary composition (intertextual transgression) that echoes a paradigm of cultural change (crossing class boundaries). What is remarkable about this parodic practice is that it allows the peaceful coexistence of transgression and integration.

Ultimately, *Fergus* was received as an acceptable variation of the romance tradition. To the later medieval audience, it was as much the final conformity as the initial transgression of *Fergus* that stood out: in adopting the Scottish hero as knight, succeeding poets underscored not the vilain origins but the state of crisis of the institution of chivalry, which had to become flexible and ill-defined in order to survive.

In *Fergus*, chivalry is presented as capable (and in need) of absorbing the lower classes. The members of feudal nobility make the vilain one of their own, thus triumphing over him. The courtois Arthurian romance teaches its hero to accept and conform to its rules. Even when the transgressive hero breaks those rules, they hold fast; the vilain can and must change. The boundaries, though displaced in a comic compromise, are confirmed. *Fergus* devotes most of its tale to presenting a hero who can do no right. Then, in a last-minute twist, the text ceases its playfulness. In the final episodes of the romance, Fergus becomes a courtly, well-spoken, and even dignified hero. These final scenes obey the conventions of romance: Fergus triumphantly raises the siege that threatens Galiene, discreetly wins a tournament at Arthur's court, and solemnly takes on the roles of king and husband. All traces of the Scots vilain have vanished; Fergus is quite indistinguishable from the other Arthurian knights as he accedes to the throne.

In this final incorporation, the project of *Fergus* acquires its full meaning. Fergus was never meant to be a diabolical interloper. The wild Scotsman was not to remain a comic threat to the Arthurian world. *Fergus* portrays the "taming" of the hero, who comes to learn and accept the rules. The boundaries of social class, as laid out in romance, are then displaced. An exception is made in the ideological polarization of vilain and courtois: through compliance with the rules (of class, of language, of morals), the vilain can become courtois.

This symbolic empowerment of the vilain corresponds to political and material changes occurring in thirteenth-century France. The institution of knighthood enters a crisis in the mid-twelfth century.[49] The chivalric classes are forced to allow into their ranks those peasants grown wealthy enough to buy land, armor, or a noble wife. Thus, the literary parody in Guillaume's *Fergus* plays on its own historical context. *Fergus* participates in social discourse, although without becoming satire.

Audigier:
The Courtois Bas-culé

CHAPTER TWO

> If elegance and dignity are qualities of the spirit, then rags
> and garbage are the natural habitat of the aristocrat. . . .
> you may recognize a prince by the way he arranges his few
> filthy rags, by the way he carries a drooping daisy plucked
> from a dunghill.
>
> —Robert Adams, "Rags, Garbage, and Fantasy"

Robert Adams's essay "Rags, Garbage, and Fantasy" is devoted to
the modernism of Joyce, Eliot, and Pound.[1] Yet it could have been
the study of an important aristocrat in medieval literature, Count
Audigier. Born in a warm pigsty, baptized in rags and filth, the
courtois hero of the late-twelfth-century *Audigier* gambols snob-
bishly in Elysian fields of dung.[2]

The briefest synopsis of the Old French text reveals it to be a
parody of medieval epic, or, more specifically, a travesty of the genealogical chanson de geste, a later development of epic in which
the hero's entire life, including forebears and descendants, is cele-
brated in song.[3] *Audigier* is a travesty of courtoisie, because its
world is courtois, its characters are courtois, its verse is courtois.
It actualizes the epic paradigm quite faithfully. The hero's father,
Count Turgibus, lord of Cocuce, one day accomplishes a knightly
feat in the presence of an admiring lady, Dame Raimberge. They
fall in love and are married. Just as their son is about to be born,
Count Turgibus dies in a chivalric fray. A miracle occurs at the site
of his fall, signifying his greatness. All the world rejoices when Audigier is then born. Dame Raimberge has the baby baptized, fed,
and bathed. Little Audigier reaches the age of knighthood and is
dubbed with great celebration. But after the ceremony, a female
enemy, Grimberge, interrupts the festivities to insult Audigier and
his family. The hero rides forth to avenge the insult. After three

combats with Grimberge, Audigier returns to his mother, who presents him with a bride. The young lovers are married; the text closes on the wedding scene.

The student of medieval literature will recognize the basic narrative sequences of the chanson de geste: insult to family honor, war, vengeance. *Audigier* also incorporates scenes reminiscent of the chanson de geste *romancée,* which became popular in the 1120s and 1130s, with the Guillaume d'Orange cycle. At that time, the epic begins to incorporate accounts of the hero's forefathers, of his *enfances,* his courtship and marriage, his *moniage,* or religious conversion, and the miracles which occur upon his death, along with the stories of war.[4]

Jean Rychner, in his seminal work, *La Chanson de geste,* catalogues the epic motifs and narrative sequences travestied in *Audigier*: the dubbing of a new knight (lines 186 ff.), individual sword combat (290–301), an attack with projectile weapons (107 ff.), the pursuit of an enemy in flight (338–55), individual lance combat (217–36), and meals (82–100, 432–43).[5] Even prior to Rychner's 1955 book, Gerald Bertin had examined the ways in which *Audigier* imitates the formulaic composition of the chanson de geste, and the repetition at the start of consecutive laisses:

Audigier chevaucha par grant vitoire.
(*Audigier* 254)
Audigier rode most victoriously.

Audigier chevaucha lez la chauciee.
(261)
Audigier rode along the roadway.

Audigier chevaucha lez une rue.
(285)
Audigier rode along a street.

Audigier chevaucha par grant fierté.
(357)
Audigier rode with great pride.[6]

Audigier constitutes a parody in the strictest etymological sense of that term: *para-odia,* a song sung to the same tune, in a like way, or to a parallel melody.[7] René Louis was the first critic to suggest that *Audigier* and *Girart de Rousillon* shared the same tune.[8] The melody of *Audigier* is in fact the only piece of epic music we possess today, thanks to the manuscript of a thirteenth-century play; Adam de la Halle, who was a well-known musician and poet from Arras, wrote the *Jeu de Robin et de Marion* in approximately 1285, and included verse 746 from *Audigier*: "'Audigier,' dit Raimberge, 'bouse vos di!'" ("'Audigier,' said Raimberge, 'dung in your eye!'"), with musical notation.[9] Jean Beck confidently identifies the musical phrase as "par excellence un thème de récitatif à répétition," the traditional recitative of the French chanson de geste.[10] Whether or not Adam de la Halle faithfully transcribed the original melody of *Audigier*, or of the chanson de geste, is a question that remains problematic, since the *Jeu de Robin et de Marion* is itself a comic play with parodic elements.

Thus, neither doubt nor debate exists concerning the status of *Audigier* as parody of the chanson de geste. It is perhaps the only one of the texts studied in this book that has unanimously been termed "parody." Its imitation of the stanzaic composition, meter, music, characters, rhetorical clichés, characters, narrative, and space of its model cannot be disputed. In fact, *Audigier* departs from the epic model at two levels only: in its hero's adversary, who is a female vilain, a peasant woman, and in its language, its *vilains mots*. The immediate signal that epic is being travestied is the systematic introduction of scatological language. The hero's father cavorts, marries, and dies on a dungheap. The hero is knighted and married on a dungheap. The rituals of feudal life are carried out with scatological props. The vilains mots are transgressive in that they are combined with courtois verse, characters, and space. According to the lexicon used in Gérard Genette's stylistic study of "second-degree" literature, *Audigier* fits perfectly the definition of a burlesque travesty, which "rewrites a noble text, keeping its 'action'—that is to say, both its fundamental content and its movement—. . . but imposes an altogether different *elocution,* which is to say another 'style,' in the classical sense of the term."[11] According to Genette's taxonomy, parody is a semantic transformation, in which vulgar characters are meliorated (as in the case of *Fergus*), while burlesque travesty is a stylistic transformation, in which noble language is degraded.[12] The subject remains courtois; the language becomes vilain.

Vilain and Courtois

The scene of the hero's knighting in *Fergus* merited our attention as a key moment in chivalric texts. That same scene in *Audigier* exemplifies the scatological rewriting of *Girart de Roussillon*, its model or target text.[13] Jean Rychner has demonstrated that the *Audigier* scene actualizes the regular series of epic stereotypes and is comparable to dubbing scenes in the *Chanson de Roland,* the *Chanson de Guillaume,* and *Raoul de Combrai.*[14] In addition to the remarkably similar rhyme scheme, emphasized below, *Girart de Roussillon* and *Audigier* share an unusual caesura division— 6:4, rather than the usual 4:6 in medieval epic:

> Auziretz de quals armas il l'an armat,
> Egal pas l'an poiat en un *solier*
> Et aqui l'an armat cum *chevalier*
> Vestiro lhi ausberc fort e *leugier*.
>
> .   .   .   .
>
> Puis a lassat un elme de fin *acier*
> E a sencha la spaza que fon Disdier.
>
> .   .   .   .
>
> Cel lhi menet en destre son bon *destrier*. (*Girart* 3253–56, 3264–65, 3275)[15]

You are about to hear tell of the arms with which he was armed. Then they led him up to a high chamber, and there they armed him a knight. They dressed him in a hauberk that was strong and lightweight. . . . Then [Pierre] laced on a helmet of fine steel, and buckled the sword that had belonged to Didier. . . . [Acelin] led his strong war horse.

> Seignor, or escoutez tout sans noisier,
> Dirai vos d'Avisart et de Raier
> Qui Audigier, lor frere, font *chevalier*.
> Le vallet amenerent sor un *fumier,*
> Ses armes li aportent en un pannier
> Haubert li ont vestu blanc et *legier*:
> Quinze sols de marcheis costa l'autrier.
> En son chief si lacerent heaume d'*acier*.
>
> .   .   .   .
>
> En la place li traient son bon *destrier*.
> (*Audigier* 183–90, 196)

Seigneurs, listen now and calm your din. I will tell you of Avisart and Raier, who knighted Audigier, their brother. The young boys led him onto a dung-heap; they brought him his armor in a basket. They dressed him in a hau-

berk that was white and lightweight; it cost fifteen sous the other day. On
his head they laced a helmet of steel, . . . There in that place they brought
him his strong war horse.

One key word in the matrix, "acceding to knighthood," is al-
tered in *Audigier*. The stepping-stone to knighthood, the place of
consecration, is transformed from *solier,* the high chamber, or
high place, to *fumier,* the dungheap. The overdetermination of the
rhyme scheme underscores the transgression. *Chevalier, legier,
acier,* and *destrier* are maintained as the guideposts indicating the
simultaneous recreation and destruction of the epic model. The
single changed word, *fumier,* reveals the orientation of the transformation. The high place, locus of epic nobility, becomes a dungheap, which will be the setting for the important events of *Audigier.*

Paul Zumthor points out that the parodic distortions of *Audigier*
indicate the presence of a system: "Even the chanson de geste has
its parody in *Audigier,* which systematically transposes the most
easily recognizable formal techniques of the epic in a scatological
content."[16] But what is the nature of the system? Literary critics
often suggest that *Audigier* haphazardly substitutes stercoraceous
terms for epic words, in a facile and unstudied corruption.[17] The
critic's blunt condemnation would be justified if *Audigier* were a
simple heap of foul language, but that is not the case. Simple word
substitution does not constitute parody. Nor is a parody just a
heaping up of offensive language. Parody is a form of text production. The reader who recognizes the function of the scatological
language in the discourse of this travesty will discover the interpretant which rewrites medieval epic in *Audigier,* and will grasp
an understanding of this twelfth-century "succès de scandale."

Scatology provokes, and has always provoked, a powerful response; it is an extremely stable poetic language. At first glance,
the modern reader may see nothing else in *Audigier.* Yet, without
denying the weight and power of the stercoraceous vocabulary,
objects, and activities in this text, we can say there is another literary pattern at work in the rewriting of the epic matrix.

The following two passages are perfectly characteristic of the
humor of *Audigier,* but they do not depend on scatological language for their comic effect, their distortion, or their transgres-

sion. How is it that they are typical of the travesty, despite the absence of scatology?

Early in the narrative, Turgibus, the father of the (yet unborn) hero, has gone to France to prove his chivalric mettle.[18] There he engages in a battle, the representation of which Rychner lists as an example of a common epic motif, the "attaque aux armes de jet."[19]

> Molt fu quens Turgibus de grant renon.
> Il prist un jor son arc et son boujon
> si en fist un beau trait par avison.
> De l'arc, qui est plus roit que n'est un jonc,
> il entesa la flesche jusqu'au penon.
> A cel cop perce l'ele d'un papeillon
> que il trova seant lez un buisson,
> qui puis ne pot voler se petit non.
> (37–44)

> Count Turgibus was a man of great reknown. One day he took his bow and arrow, aimed well, and shot far. Taking the bow, stiffer than a bulrush, he drew the arrow back to its feathers. In its flight it pierced the wing of a butterfly which was resting near a bush and which then could fly only a little.

The reader hears the parodic distortion in the exaggeratedly minute object of the epic onslaught (the butterfly), the delicate operation of the blow dealt (breaking the butterfly's wing), the inappropriateness of an insect in the context of a chivalric encounter. A break in the syntactical link occurs when one fragment ("papeillon") is subordinated to another, semantically incompatible fragment ("flesche"); a nonsensical effect is produced by that subordination alone, even though "butterfly" and "arrow" contain in themselves, considered separately, no absurdity. The nonsensical precision, or rather imprecision, of verse 44, which states that the one-winged butterfly "could then fly only a little," closes the account of the ridiculous battle.

The second unsullied but comic scene travesties the birth and baptism of the hero in the epic "enfances." Upon the birth of Audigier, a famine spreads throughout the land. Instead of making a joyful noise, Nature raises her voice in the following sounds:

> Quant Audigier nasqui, grant joie i ot.
> Par le pais leva un tel herbot
> roxignous ne oiseaus pas n'i chantot;

laienz ot une asnesse qui rechanot
et une vielle lisse qui lors ulloit,
et une chate borgne de faim braioit.
(135–40)

When Audigier was born, there was great joy. Throughout the land there rose such a famine that neither nightingale nor bird sang; from within one heard a she-ass singing out of tune, an old bitch commenced to howl, and a one-eyed cat brayed with hunger.

While nightingales and cats are not absurd in themselves, they become comic when juxtaposed with the she-ass and the bitch, who strike a discordant note. A break in the expected predicate link between "birds" and "singing" comes in verse 137. The animals, rather than reflecting the harmony of the spheres, have physical deformities, like the one-eyed cat in verse 140. In that same verse the reader finds another apparent break in the predicate link, as the cat howls not with "grant joie" but with "faim," reiterating the contradiction in verses 135 and 136.

The celebration of Audigier's birth, in stanza XII, immediately precedes the introduction of the parish priest, Herbout (from the Old French *herbot*, an adjective meaning "poor" or "wretched," or a substantive meaning "famine," as in verse 136, above), who is to baptize the baby:

L'enfant en aporterent prestre Herbout
qui, devant son mostier, s'espoollot
et a sa destre main son cul gratoit.
Lors est sailliz en piéz quant il les voit.
(143–46)

[The godmothers] carried the infant to Father Herbout, who, standing in front of his church, was picking at his lice, and with his right hand was scratching his ass. He leapt to his feet when he saw them.

The image of a priest scratching and delousing himself is not so much obscene as it is an overdetermined portrait of wretchedness. The audience is shocked and amused by the combination of terms relating to religion (a priest before his church) and an unworthy, because unclean and undignified, task (the scratching of his arse). The text underscores the transgressive combination by having the priest leap guiltily to his feet when the parishioners appear. Then one final example of the comic effect of an absurd specification: he scratches himself with his right (not his left) hand.

In a third moment of this narrative sequence, the priest prepares himself to perform the sacrament of baptism:

Li prestres est entréz en son mortier,
Son soupeliz vesti tout le plus chier,
qui trop bien resanbloit roiz a peschier:
il n'en i avoit pas plain pié d'entier;
si blans estoit venuz du lavendier
com li escoveillons a un fornier.
Les comeres le virent trop atargier;
onques n'i quistrent prestre lirre sautier.
(147–54)

The priest entered his church and donned his very best surplice, which looked for all the world like a fishing net: not a square inch of it was without holes; it had come from the launderer as white as a baker's shovel comes from the oven. The sharp-tongued godmothers saw that he was taking too long. Who needs a priest to read the psalter?

The comic specification of the "very best" surplice is generated by the comparison to a fishing net (newness is contradicted by holes). The surplice is as white as the shovel in an oven: as white as black. Yet another break in the predicate link is generated by the combination of the religious and sartorial, and the humble domestic connotations of the baker's scuffle. The recurring transgression is that produced by the juxtaposition of pure and impure, or clean and unclean, embodied in the character of the man of the holey cloth. Verses 153 and 154 shatter the expectations generated by the priest's preparations: he has taken so long that the godmothers decide they need no clergyman but will perform the baptism themselves.

The celebration of Audigier's birth, and the representation of Father Herbout, are among several passages in *Audigier* that parody epic through stylistic incompatibilities and nonsensical exaggeration. Both features are characteristic of the comic text but owe nothing to the scatological register. Apparently the stercoraceous joke is but one feature of the literary interpretant rewriting the genealogical chanson de geste.

The combination of epic rhetoric ("Never have you seen a

knight as bold as he!") and nonsensical exaggerations ("as brave as a flea!") in these passages does not rely on coprological outrage for its comic effect. The juxtaposition of epic hyperbole and nonsense verse transgresses the rhetorical rules of the chanson de geste. Quite apart from its scatological language, *Audigier* presents epic nonsense poetry, a poetry of "incompossibility": of subject and predicate, of subject and verb, of semantic fragments.[20]

Comic *impossibilia* constitute the semantic, syntactical, and grammatical features of a different Old French genre, the medieval fatrasie: burlesque lyric poems of deliberate nonsense and anomalous word associations.[21] The fatrasie form is highly fixed, composed of a stanza of six pentasyllables, followed by five heptasyllables. The principal device of the fatrasie consists of a communication that is "impossible," grammatically or semantically, despite the comprehensibility of the code, the words themselves.[22] Paul Zumthor has shown that the fatrasie is built upon a "systematic rupture" of poetic meaning, and has documented the workings of this systematic incoherence, demonstrating that a poetic genre which appears to be chaotic nonsense is governed by strict rules of composition.

To the best of our knowledge today, *Audigier* was composed in the mid-twelfth century and the fatrasies in the thirteenth. No one can claim that the fatrasies were the source of *Audigier*. But there are other ways of understanding the interrelatedness of literary texts, traditions, and genres. In fact, the relation of the late-twelfth-century parody to the thirteenth-century poems is not diachronic, but synchronic.[23] The fatrasie genre did not materialize *sponte sua*, but rather as one culmination of an age-old form of literary play. The appearance of the fatrasie in written manuscripts constitutes the formulation and formalization of a literary tradition that, as Ernst Curtius writes, is both "purely medieval" and "of antique origin." The beasts of the field exchange food with dolphins, the wolf flees before the sheep, oaks bear golden apples, and owls vie with swans. The principle of adynaton can be found at the heart of medieval carnival, and also in carnivalesque literature. In the later part of the twelfth century, the famous *Carmina Burana* exemplify the flowering of adynata in Latin medieval literature.[24] The *Fatrasies d'Arras* and the *Fatrasies de Beaumanoir* testify to the success of nonsense poetry in the vernacular.[25] The longevity of that tradition, and its medieval specificity, allow us to reread *Audigier* in the light of the fatrasie tradition. The poetic world of the fatrasie is one of noise and movement, filled with cats, rats, onions, farts, insects, and dung. Animals and things, as well as humans, shout and sing, eat and drink, gallop and do battle. In the *Fatrasies d'Arras* (FA) we find a dismembered butterfly in a passage that could belong to *Audigier*:

Je lor dis en escoçois:
"Des coilles d'un papillon
Porroit on faire craz pois?
Et dou vit d'un limeçon
Faire chastiax et beffrois?"
(FA VII, 7–11)
I said to them in Scottish, "Could you make fried peas from the balls of a butterfly? And from the prick of a snail make castles and belfries?"

In FA XLV, a beetle with greased slippers charges a fishpond, in a stanza that reminds us of the death of Turgibus, assaulted by beetles on a dungheap:

Uns escharbos l'asailli
Qui avoit ces solliers oinz.
(FA XLV, 7–8)
A beetle then assailed it, having greased his slippers.

Chauves soriz l'aissaillent a l'anuitier,
escharboz l'assaillirent en un fumier
et mousches si alerent sor lui chier
tant que il ne se pot plus redrecier.
Audigier 109–12)
Bats attacked him when night fell, beetles assaulted him on the dungheap and flies went to shit on him, until he could no longer get to his feet.

Animal characters are often grotesquely deformed in the fatrasie, as in *Audigier*:

Et quatre asnesses sans piax
Demenoient mout grant feste
(FA XXXIV, 7–8)
And four she-asses without feet were having a high old time.

Human characters, too, are grotesquely exaggerated:

Uns saiges sans sens,
Sans bouche, sans dens,
Ce siecle menga. (FA D, 1–3)
A sage without sense, without mouth, without teeth, ate this worldly life.

Representatives of the church and features of the Christian religion receive the same dubious respect in the *Fatrasies d'Arras* as in *Audigier*:

Uns moines de croie
Faisoit mout grant joie
De foutre un bacon.
(FA XXXII, 4–6)
A monk of chalk made much merriment over fucking a ham.

Crepitation takes on the same fantastic powers and features in the fatrasie as in the travesty. A "pet" can commit suicide:

D'un pet de suiron
Uns pez ce fist pendre
Por l'i miex deffendre
Derier un luiton;
La s'en esmervilla on
Que tantost vint l'ame prendre
La teste d'un porion,
Pour ce qu'il voloit aprendre
De Gerart de Rossillon.
(FA XXVIII, 3–11)
From the foot of a mite a fart hung himself, the better to hide behind a goblin; whereupon all were astounded, for there, to carry off his soul, came the head of a pumpkin, all because he wanted to hear about Girart de Roussillon.

or teach grammar:

Uns pez a deus cus
S'estoit revestus
Por lirre gramaire.
(FA XXIX, 1–3)
A fart with two asses was ordained for the teaching of grammar.

Vilain and Courtois

Scatological objects play an important role in the impossibilities of the fatrasie:

> Estrons sans ordure
> La mer amesure
> Com longue ele estoit.
> (FA XXXVIII, 1–3)
>
> A turd with no filth measured the sea to find how long it was.

In *Audigier,* crepitation can be swallowed, in the form of a beverage, and has restorative powers. The flatulence of the hero's bride, Troncecrevace, has the magic power to protect Audigier from enemy swords:

> Se vos avez beu de sa fumee,
> ja mais n'auriez garde de coup d'espee.
> (*Audigier* 482–83)
>
> If you have drunk of her smokey odor, never again need you fear the blow of a sword.

Excremental odors perform similarly outlandish deeds in the fatrasie:

> Li flairs d'une poire
> D'un pet de provoire
> Lor chantoit d'Audain.
> (FA LIII, 4–6)
>
> The smell of a pear of the fart of a priest sang to them of Audain.

Arbitrary mathematical specifications often render the scatological objects more absurd: "a fart and a half" (*FA* II, 6); "four farts on his face" (*Audigier* 77); "three turds and one half" (*Audigier* 322).

Among the inanimate objects most common to the fatrasie, we find the same onions, eggs, prunes, ham, and beans we find in *Audigier*:

> Uns oingnons pelez
> Estoit aprestes
> De chanter devant,
> Qant sor un rouge olifant
> Vint uns limecons armes
> Qui lor aloit escriant:

"Fil a putain, sa venez!
Je versefie en dormant."
(FA LIV, 4–11)

A baldheaded onion was making ready to sing on when, atop a red ele-
phant, came an armored snail who was shouting at them: "Sons of bitches!
Get over here! I'm versifying in my sleep."

Kitchen utensils, like the cook's mortar in *Audigier* (449), instruments of religion, and everyday articles of clothing and furniture
are put to ludicrous use, as in the epic travesty:

Une viés kemise
Eut s'entente mise
A savoir plaidier,
Et une cerise
S'est devant li mise
Pour li laidengier;
Ne fust une viés cuillier
Qui s'alaine avoit reprise.
(*Fatrasies de Beaumanoir* X, 1–8)

An old shirt put her whole heart into the study of law, and lo, a cherry came
and stood before her with a mind to insulting her, were it not for an old
spoon that had just caught her breath.

A comparison of *Audigier* and the fatrasies yields the conclusion that the texts are linguistically similar. A like formal principle
governs both: the semantic disassociation of subject and predicate, a disassociation achieved by selecting subject and predicate
from a series of incompatible terms, frequently but not always
scatological in nature. What Paul Zumthor writes of the fatrasie
holds for *Audigier*: the two principal results of this technique are
nonsense and outrageous scatology.[26]

What of the differences between *Audigier* and the fatrasies?
The chief difference lies in the fact that one is a narrative, and the
others are not. There is also a marked dissimilarity in the degree of
coherence of the communication: the grammar and syntax of the
fatrasie are so broken as to be incomprehensible, destroying the
possibility of mimesis. The *impossibilia* of *Audigier* do not
threaten the mimesis of the epic narrative, despite their absurdity;
the story of Audigier and his family remains perfectly coherent.
The images of the fatrasie verge on the incoherent because of their

extreme incompatibility and because of the short lyric format. Thus, the fatrasies themselves could not be classed as parodies: they do not offer the consistent reproduction of a recognizable matrix. Finally, the fatrasies supply poetic elements but without supplying any systematic opposition. There is an absolute lack of polarization in the fatrasie, whether moral, social, spatial, or rhetorical, while *Audigier* is a strongly polarized text, morally, socially, spatially, and rhetorically. Here the interpretant teaches us something about the parody and its functioning. The fatrasies show us another way of reading the paradigmatic signs of *vilain* and *courtois* in *Audigier*. *Vilain* and *courtois* function as a moral polarization (that of high and low, or "good" and "not good") that is projected in terms of a class opposition. *Audigier* uses the courtois-vilain nexus in order to tell its story in terms of contemporary social discourse. The fatrasies make no attempt to tell a story despite their occasional use of a vocabulary that alludes to contemporary society.

While some critics will doubtless continue to regard *Audigier* as a careless "chanson de merde," other readers will consider its scatology in the context of the medieval nonsense tradition exemplified by the thirteenth-century fatrasie, and understand that the "careless" scatology enables us to follow the direction of this parodic rewriting of the genealogical chanson de geste.[27]

Stercoraceous objects and activities recur throughout *Audigier* in a kind of catalogue not unlike Freud's list of the child's uses of feces. The characters of *Audigier* and the children Freud studied have in common something significant. In both groups one recognizes a dramatic split or cleavage among the functions of scatology: in both worlds there is a sharp polarization of positives and negatives. In Freud's study, for instance, the child uses feces in negative ways: as a weapon, to commit aggressions.[28] The same child also uses them in distinctly positive ways: as a gift, to obtain love; as property, to assert independence; and as toy, to obtain narcissistic pleasure in play. An identical bivalence exists in *Audigier*. The enemy, Grimberge, understands body wastes as weapons. She disrupts Audigier's celebration with an aggressive insult:

Molt li desplot la joie du chevalier
et, por lui faire honte et courroucier,
se descouvri la dame sanz atargier,
tres enmi les quaroles ala chier.
(215–18)
Greatly does the knight's joy displease her, and to shame and enrage him,
the lady bares herself without further ado, and goes to shit right in the middle of the dancing.

Grimberge triumphs over the hero on three occasions, and upon
each victory she and her daughters mete out scatological punishments:

"Audigier," dit Grimberge, "bouse vos di.
De trois de mes estrons et un demi
vos desgeüneroiz demain matin
si baiseroiz mon cul et l'aubatri."
(321–24)
"Audigier," says Grimberge, "dung in your eye! Of three and a half of my
turds you will make your breakfast tomorrow morning, and then you will
kiss my cunt and the crack of my ass."

Quite to the contrary, the hero's father, Turgibus, uses dung as
his favorite toy. The count hides when the battle cry sounds, so
that he may continue to play at his preferred game:

Et quant il a chié plaine s'aumuce,
ses doiz boute en la merde, puis si les suce;
puis ne li fait mal riens que il menjuce.
Et quant l'en crie as armes, il se muce.
(12–15)
And when he had shit into his furry cap until it was filled, he stuck his fin-
gers in the crap, then sucked them; after that, nothing he eats can harm him
in any way. And when the call to arms sounds, he hides himself.

To obtain love, the hero's mother, Raimberge, unfailingly gives
excremental productions as gifts, as in her own wedding scene:

Rainberge li aporte plan poi[n]g de beuse,
puis prent de son pissat si l'en arreuse.
(69–70)
Raimberge brings him a fist full of shit, then takes some of her piss and
showers him with it.

Vilain and Courtois

Scatological objects constitute the dowries exchanged between bride and groom:

> De quinze estrons de chien li fist doaire.
> Adonc se porpensa la debonnaire;
> quatre pez li a fet sor le viaire.
> (75–77)

Of fifteen dog turds he made his dower. Whereupon the lady of good breeding gave the matter a good deal of thought and farted four times in his face.

Goatdung is used as money (property) at the hero's wedding:

> Il i ot juglëors bien jusqu'a cent
> lendemain sont venuz au paiement
> et Audigier lor donne molt lieement:
> trent crotes de chievre a chascun tent.
> (513–16)

There were well nigh one hundred performers who came the next day to be paid, and Audigier gave them [their pay] most gaily: thirty goat turds he hands each one.

Defecation is not only a gift, meant to obtain love, but is also the purest expression of affection:

> Audigier prist la dame par le mantel
> si l'en a enmenee en un prael,
> puis la fist acroupir enz el plus bel;
> en chiant li a mis el doi l'ennel.
> (486–89)

Audigier took his lady by her mantle and led her into a meadow, then had her squat there in the most beautiful spot; while [she was] shitting, he placed the ring on her finger.

Finally, excrement is maternal nourishment:

> "Souviengne vos de boivre, et savez quoi,
> que vos n' bevrez ja se ge n'i poi."
> (473–74)

"Remember to drink, and you know what, for you will have nothing to drink if I do not fart."

At this point in the analysis we begin to understand fully a scene in Adam de la Halle's 1285 play, the *Jeu de Robin et de Marion*. Several peasant characters are having a party. One of them, named Gautier, offers to entertain Robin and Marion with a chanson de geste. Barely has he sung one verse (321) of *Audigier,* when Robin interjects with great indignation:

> "Ho! Gautier, je n'en voeil plus. Fi!
> Dites, seres vous tous jours teus?
> Vous cantes c'uns ors menestreus."[29]
>
> "Now Gautier! I'll have no more of that! Fie! Tell me, will you ever grow up? You sing like some filthy minstrel."

The indignant Robin prefigures the Victorian medievalist and his twentieth-century grandson, the modern critic, who exclaim over *Audigier* with outrage:

> . . . a coarse parody, but amusing. (Paul Meyer, 1884)

> . . . a rather witty poem, but extremely filthy. (Ernst Langlois, 1902)

> Upon reading this obscene work, one wonders in what class of society it could have been acceptable, for *Audigier* does not even merit such adjectives as *lusty, hearty, ribald,* or *earthy.* . . . With justice to the poem it must be admitted that there are moments of bright wit, but these glimpses of humor are almost completely besmirched with the basest form of scatology. (Gérard Bertin, 1953)

> In daring to take up *Audigier,* this filthy work, my only excuse is that it is not useless to study a parody of the chanson de geste. . . . Let us strip this filthy work of all its nauseating details, of its excremental seasonings and revolting stews, which in another time delighted listeners whose senses seem not to have been aggravated by sights, smells, and tastes of an uncommon bestiality. Scraping them off is not difficult. And behold, after a meticulous and thoroughgoing disinfection appears a skeleton that we can decently exhibit. (Omer Jodogne, 1960)

> Scholars have heaped abuses on [*Audigier*], as well they should . . . because the defecations do not lead anywhere or prepare for anything but instead just lie there. (Thomas Cooke, 1978)[30]

Curiously, the men who pen these protestations of shock and disgust are, at the very same time, reading *Audigier,* presumably speaking about *Audigier,* publishing articles on, devoting chapters to, and even editing *Audigier,* so that others might read it. Their scholarly activities bespeak an interest in the text that their disclaimers do not entirely hide. Of all the parodies included in this book, it is *Audigier* that, when recounted to an audience, never fails to provoke pleasure and comprehension.[31] The same group that listens to a summary of the *Chanson de Roland* or the *Roman de la Rose* with slight confusion and some indifference will listen to *Audigier* with immediate understanding and undivided attention (whether in the form of horrified repugnance or enjoyment). Furthermore, an audience who has never read or heard of *Girart de Roussillon* will nonetheless grasp the parody in *Audigier* with no difficulty. The consistency of the audience response also teaches us something about forbidden language. Since we all recognize and, to some extent, fear authority, we are delighted to see a text defy authority and rebel against the rules of proper language.

On the other hand, the negative reaction of literary critics teaches us something about the limits of critical language, which is ultimately a closed and constrained language. While professors might gleefully summarize *Audigier* for a group of students, colleagues, or friends, they do not feel entirely free to publish such enthusiasm in a scholarly journal. It is that lack of freedom that makes the telling of the forbidden tale such a pleasure. We are bound not to enjoy scatology, and therefore we are bound to enjoy it.[32]

Scatological words and texts elicit a dual and divided reaction: we are both pleased and put off. Even those critics who acknowledge the positive qualities of *Audigier*—notably the older generation, such as Paul Meyer and Ernst Langlois—must couch their appreciative judgments in exceptive clauses: "mais." From such official doubletalk we learn that scatological language is taboo, a taboo still functioning today exactly as it did in the twelfth and thirteenth centuries. These words were not vilains in the Middle Ages alone; they remain so today. The closer the critic comes to vilain texts, the more esoteric the metalanguage becomes: "excremental ingestion," "scatophagy," "coprophagy," "stercor-

ary."[33] The modern literary critic has no choice but to maintain
the taboo.

The explanation of formal features in *Audigier* identifies the tradition from which the parody's interpretant comes but leaves the
reader with still other questions about its cultural meaning. The
world of the fatrasie seems nonhistorical, or historically un-
marked; it appears to be a universe in which mimetic oppositions
and distinctions are introduced only to be destroyed in the utter
nonsense of the fractured image. Thus, if a fatrasie speaks of a
courtois vilain, the reader does not seek any sociopolitical meaning in the character, but rather accepts it as one more example of
adynaton, or as a deliberate oxymoron:

> Ez vos sus une papoire,
> Criant, un cortois vilain:
> "Chiens, ne m'abaie;
> Mie tien de mon pain."
> (*Fatrasies d'Arras* DIII, 10–13)
> Behold behind a bearded mask, a courtois vilain crying, "Dog, don't bark
> at me; have a crumb of my bread."

Audigier, however, has carefully constructed a courtois kingdom, in which all values and codes of behavior are marked and
opposed by the vilain-courtois nexus. When the story begins, the
audience is shocked (and delighted) to hear of courtois characters
happily playing in excrement, joyfully defecating in concert, and
cheerfully exchanging gifts of turd. When the enemy, Grimberge,
appears at the midpoint of the narrative, her gestures and attitudes contradict those of Audigier's family at the opening of the
travesty: no longer signs of celebration and well-being, scatological objects and activities now signify opprobrium and pain. By the
end of the travesty, however, scatology has regained its initial,
positive status.

In representing a scatology of a dual and opposed nature, *Audigier* sets itself apart from most stercoraceous literature, which
represents the scatological life of the body as shameful and uses
offensive language as a figurative weapon. Such is the scatology of
the theater of Aristophanes and of Attic comedy.[34] Throughout

Aristophanes' work, scatology is dysphoric, whereas sexuality is euphoric, a pendant sign of peace and well-being. Jokes stem principally from the ignominy of dealing with the unacceptable life of the body in an acceptable fashion and avoiding unpredictable accidents. Scatophagy appears only as a figurative insult directed at homosexuals. As Freud was to note, scatological humor in literature is chiefly tendentious.[35] Yet the audience of *Audigier* (whether medieval or modern) has no difficulty grasping and following the shifts from positive to negative. We understand immediately that in scenes of courtship and wedding, at mealtime and bathtime, during mating and birth, defecation, urination, crepitation, and scatophagy signify pleasure, and that in scenes of war (the midpoint of the narrative), they take on the traditional connotations of pain and humiliation. *Audigier* communicates these shifts through its cast of characters and their spatialization. When Audigier and his family speak and perform *vilains mots*, the act seems as innocuous as making mudpies. When Grimberge, the enemy, and her family speak and perform the same *vilains mots*, the act is presented as loathsome and opprobrious.

Audigier creates two imaginary spaces within its story, each space replete with characters, buildings, furniture, and other props. In the epic space of Count Turgibus we find houses, a church in which infants can be baptized, horses and armor, silk cloaks and jewelry, fields for dancing, a kitchen in which the cook awaits orders, and meadows in which jongleurs perform. At the midpoint of the story, however, Audigier must leave the paternal space of epic and ride out into the unfamiliar space of his enemy, Grimberge, and her three daughters. In that space we find chicken coops and poultry, but neither horse nor armor; a hundred toothless hags, but neither cook nor priest; a stall, but no dungeon; and fields not intended for dancing, in which Grimberge herself industriously cleans goat guts. The formidable enemy inhabits a rural space. Grimberge is presented not as a Saracen hag, an evil fairy, or a sorceress, but as a peasant, the peasant who lives on the farm down the road from the local nobleman. The word that is conspicuously absent from the text, but overdetermined by everything that surrounds Grimberge, is *vilain*. And because the scatology is spatialized along class lines, the audience can agree to believe that the scatology of Audigier, no matter how outrageous, is indeed courtois.

How does the anonymous poet create these two spaces? The text charts out a geography that separates one world from another. Audigier must travel to reach the rural space of Grimberge:

Jusques a prime chevaucha.
(244)
[Audigier] rode along until six o'clock.

Audigier chevaucha lez une rue.
De ce jour estoit ja none venue.
(285–86)
Audigier rode along a pathway. On this particular day three o'clock had already passed.

After each day of battle the hero returns home; the following morning, he must set off again:

Audigier chevaucha par grant fierté
et vint a son ostel tot abrivé.
(357–58)
Audigier rode with great pride, and reached his home with rapidity.

Time is carefully marked out to show that noblemen and peasants live in different areas:

L'endemain au matin, a l'einzjornee,
est levez Audigier, la matinee.
(372–73)
On the following morning, at the break of day, Audigier rose at matins.

By means of such spatial and temporal strategies, *Audigier* deliberately portrays the enemy as a vilain, yet never uses that particular vilain mot. In the initial encounter, for example, the hero knows immediately how to take revenge on Grimberge:

Il ira a la vielle son huis brisier
et, se il peut trouver le gelinier
il s'en vorra otout les hués aler.
(222–24)
He will go to the old lady and break down her door, and if he can find the henhouse, he will make off with all the eggs.

Vilain and Courtois

As in *Fergus,* with its portrayal of the vilain father, *Audigier* refers to the fact that Grimberge owns land, whereby she has obtained status:

Grinberge n'ert pas riche d'or ne d'argent,
mais ele avoit un pou de tenement
dont ele se vivoit trop noblement.
(280–82)
Grimberge was not rich in gold or silver, but she owned a little property, and lived off of it very nobly.

Like the *vilains* we will see in the *Roman de Renart,* Grimberge must protect her chicken coop at all costs. The skirmishes between Grimberge and Audigier are located in the vilain space and plotted along a description of that world, as if to leave no doubt about the enemy's true condition:

Quant li vassaus l'entent, molt fu marri.
Il a sachié du fuerre le branc forbi,
envers le gelingnier tantost guenchi.
Quant la vielle le vit, tout en pali.
(325–28)
When the vassal heard [these words], great was his wrath. He drew his gleaming sword from its sheath, and straight away turned toward the chicken coop. When the old woman saw him, she grew deathly pale.

The three ugly daughters advise their mother to join them in surrounding the hero. The horrific Bougise is chief military advisor:

"Alez par dela, lez ce mesnill
et g'irai par deca lez cel cortill."
(331–32)
"Go on over that way, next to the farmhouse, and I will go this way, along the garden."

The battle rages on in the agricultural space, until "la vielle l'ateint en une aree" (340; "The old woman catches up with him in a plowfield."

On the second day of the travestied war, Audigier espies his mighty enemy occupied with an uncouth chore:

Si a veü Grinberge ou a lavee
les boieaus d'une chievre et la couree.
(382–83)

There he saw Grimberge where she was washing the guts and innards of a she-goat.

When Grimberge finally takes the hero prisoner, she locks him up in her stall and specifies a vilain ransom that sounds very much like the stuff of the fatrasie: a bushel of beans, a side of pork, a fat capon, a kiss on her "cul" and one on her "con" (399–404).

As the hero moves from one space to another, the meaning of the scatology shifts simultaneously, sometimes from one stanza to the next. In stanza XXXVI, for example, Grimberge sits on Audigier's face and inflicts a humiliating scatological punishment:

Sor sa face li a son cul assis.
Quant Audigier se sent si entrepris,
par un seul petitet n'enrage vis.
"Quar ostes, pute vielle, ton aupatriz."
Grinberge se leva si en a ris.
(420–24)
On his face she sat her ass. When Audigier felt himself surrounded thus, he came very close to going mad with rage. "Hey, get your crack off of me, stinking old bag." Grimberge got up and laughed at him.

In the very next stanza, only a few verses later, Audigier's doting mother offers him a scatophile fiancee in a gesture of love:

Molt fu dame Rainberge joianz et lie
quant Audigier commence chevalerie.
"Beaus (filz)," ce dit Rainberge, "vels tu amie [?]" . . .
ainz ne lava ses mains jor de sa vie
si n'ot onques la roie du cul torchie:
ja ne l'en souvenra quant el[e] chie.
(456–58, 462–64)
Greatly does lady Raimberge rejoice when Audigier enters knighthood. "Dear son," says Raimberge, "do you want a sweetheart? . . . never once in her life has she washed her hands, nor ever had the crack of her bottom wiped; she can never remember to do it when she shits."

The same body parts, wastes, and hygienic habits that mortified Audigier in Grimberge now cause him to fall madly in love:

"He Dieus!" dit Audigier, "quel compaignie!
Or sachiez que g'en vueil faire m'amie.

Vilain and Courtois

Dame," dist Audigier, "monstrez la moi.
Ge sui ja por s'amor en grant effroi;
ge me desverai ja se ne la voi."
(465−69)

"Good God!" said Audigier, "what company for me! Let me tell you right
now that I want her for my sweetheart. My lady," said Audigier, "I am already in great dread of losing her love; I will go quite mad if I don't see her."

It would be difficult to determine whether the audience reacts
more strongly to the "positive," courtois scatology (joyful prox-
imity, filial scatophagy, marital coprophilia) of *Audigier*, or to the
"negative," vilain scatology (bepissing, besmirching, and the immemorial "baise-cul"). While we are more accustomed to finding
negative scatology in literature, the kindnesses bestowed by Lady
Raimberge have no less power to shock than the indignities in-
flicted by Grimberge. In French medieval literature, and indeed in
most literature, scatology and scatological humor are commonly
mediated through the representation of social class.[36] The fabliaux offer a perfect example of this strategy. In the *Jeu de Robin
et de Marion,* for example, the audience can accept the naughty
stories in good conscience because they take place in the lower
class of society, among lower-class characters. The anonymous
Audigier poet manages to go the fabliaux authors one better. Out-
Heroding Herod, he places foul acts and words in the mouths of
noble characters, defying his audience to protest such filth—or
more accurately, enabling his audience to enjoy such entertainment. Even in the fabliaux, in which the lower-class space functions as a "garde-fou," scatology must be mediated with representations of disgust. But in *Audigier,* apologies or disclaimers
become unnecessary through parody; the socially low is recoded
as morally high.   Excrement also carries a metatextual meaning
in *Audigier,* for it is linked to the very nature of parody itself: parody ingests texts that have already been "digested," that are inert
and fecal matter. Metaphorically speaking, parody is *a priori* scatological, a point that medieval authors and audiences, accustomed to yearly expressions of the link between excrement and
parody in Carnival rituals, could not have missed.[37]

What was the medieval consensus concerning *Audigier*? Literary history reveals that medieval authors and critics regarded sev-

eral features as the salient traits of the unquestionable popular parody.[38]

One group of medieval texts shows us, not surprisingly, that the very name "Audigier" was synonymous with indecent language. We have already seen that Adam de la Halle's *Jeu de Robin et de Marion* presents us with a staging of this aspect of the consensus. In much the same way, a fabliau by Rutebeuf, *Le Pet au Vilain,* presents the land of Audigier as a scatological purgatory. Rutebeuf's text also illustrates the implicit association (in medieval literature as in modern criticism) of peasant characters and *vilains mots*: since a vilain can enter neither heaven nor hell, he must do penance

> En la terre au pere Audigier
> c'est en la terre de Cocuce
> ou Audigier chie en s'aumuce.
> (*Le Pet au Vilain,* 74–76)[39]
>
> In the land of Audigier's father, which is to say in the land of Cocuce, where Audigier shits into his furry cap.

A second group of medieval texts reveals that the name "Audigier" signified a ludicrous hero and a poverty-stricken knight: ill-equipped, inept, and cowardly. Ernst Langlois referred to this connotation when he wrote "Audengier or Audigier is the Don Quixote of the Middle Ages."[40] The twelfth-century *Aiol,* a romance that shares many comic elements with both *Audigier* and *Fergus,* and is dated 1173, uses the name to jeer at a rattletrap knight in rusty armor:

> Car chi nous est venus uns chevaliers
> qui samble del parage dant Audengier."
>
> .   .   .   .
>
> Trestout le porsievent par la chite.
> "Vasal, chevalier, sire, a nous parles!
> Furent ces armes faites en vo resne.
> Fu Audengiers vos peres, qui tant fu ber,
> Et Raimberghe vo mere o le vis cler?"
> (*Aiol* 952–53, 989–93)[41]
>
> What have we here! A knight who seems to be of the lineage of Mister Audengier." . . . They pursue him all through the inner walls of the town. "Vassal, knight, sire, speak to us! Was this armor made in your kingdom? Was

the brave Audengier your father? And Raimberge, of the shining counte-
nance, your mother?"

Here, as elsewhere, to call someone a "son of Audigier" is to call
him a coward, as in the romance *Octavian,* dated between 1229
and 1244.[42] The use of the name as a degrading epithet is not re-
stricted to literature. In March of 1304, Edward I of England re-
proached his captain, Patrick Dunbar, with the activity of Scottish
marauders, and accused him of being like Audigier: "Quant la
guerre fu finee, si treste Audegier s'espee." (When the war was
over, then did Audigier draw his sword).[43] Edward I's dispatch indicates that the literary character had become a stock cliché in the
military language of the Middle Ages and that *Audigier* was
known for features other than its scatological language. The *Roman de Renart* and the *Roman de la Violette,* by Gerbert de Montreuil, use the proper name in the same way as Edward I: to qual-
ify an incompetent knight.[44]

A third group of texts reveals that *Audigier* was considered a
canonical performance piece, a part of the jongleur's repertoire.
Doon de Nanteuil, a romance dated in the second half of the
twelfth century, refers to *Audigier* as a popular and frequently
performed song:

> Or n'i a mes garçon, s'il set ung vers rime,
> quant a clerete voix et est bien desree
> d'Audegier qui fu cuens.[45]

> Nowadays there is not a single boy who, if he knows a song, has a clear
> voice and gets a little carried away, will not sing to you of Audigier, who
> was count.

Audigier gives his name to a metric form, considered a fixed poetic formula by the literary critics of the Middle Ages: "laisses
douzainnes, qui sont nommees audengieres." An anonymous
fifteenth-century *Arte de Seconde Rhetorique* reveals the "Laisse
audengiere" to be a monorhyme stanza of twelve dodecasyllabic
verses.[46] Thus, by the fifteenth century, the name has become synonymous with a form of epic.

Literary history indicates that the Middle Ages remembered
Audigier as a particular metrical form, a popular song, a poor
knight, a cowardly soldier, and a synonym for dirty words. The
medieval audience understood the scatological humor of *Audigier*

as one part of the epic joke. The various comic and formal features were not crushed by the weight of the stercoraceous vocabulary. Medieval critics did not feel obliged to apologize for their interest in the text. Does this bear out the time-honored prejudice that men and women in the Middle Ages were coarser, more accustomed to bawdy vulgarity than we are? If the modern critic sees little else than a "chanson de merde" in this work, is it because he is more civilized than the medieval listener, or perhaps because there is some aspect of the text that escapes him altogether? Scatological humor, though we know it to be eternal, may well have been charged with a historically specific meaning in the Middle Ages, a cultural meaning lost to a modern audience, which is left to puzzle over the offensive outpouring of indecent language in *Audigier*.

The term *scatology,* of nineteenth-century coinage, today suggests psychiatric disorders, or perversions. Julia Kristeva has voiced this specifically modern perspective in a way that underlines its fundamental difference from the medieval mentality:

> These body fluids, this defilement, this shit are what life withstands, hardly and with difficulty, on the part of death. There, I am at the border of my condition as a living being. My body extricates itself, as being alive, from that border. . . . Excrement and its equivalents (decay, infection, disease, corpse, etc.) stand for the danger to identity that comes from without: the ego threatened by the non-ego, society threatened by its outside, life by death.[47]

It might seem that Turgibus and his kin suffer from arrested psychological development, like incorrigible children at the anal stage, unaware of the threat posed to their ego.[48] But Bakhtin's Marxist study of Rabelais's work and its relation to medieval culture places scatological humor in quite another light, situating this form of grotesque realism in the medieval carnival culture.[49] Rabelaisian scatology, themes, characters and narrative sequences constitute a Renaissance "flowering" of the medieval traditions visible in *Audigier*. In the medieval life of carnival, the scatological vision of *Audigier* takes on greater acceptability.

In the Middle Ages, Bakhtin argues, excrement has not only a vulgar physiological significance; but also contributes to men's and women's awareness of their corporality and their undeniable link to the life of the earth. As such, it is an occasion for rejoicing: "O belle matiere fecale!"[50]

Food and cooking belong to the images of medieval carnival, where, as in *Audigier,* they overlap with excrement. Erasing the boundaries between the eating body and the eaten, scatophagy destroys finality in a comic image of movement and change. The chicken turd casserole and the cowdung patties served at Audigier's wedding feast, an example of what Bakhtin calls the "carnivalo-culinary," are not negative images. They express the truth that life is in constant "movement," unfinished, teetering between what has fled and what is to become.[51]

Even in the most ancient scatological figures, excrement is linked to virility and fecundity. It fertilizes the earth; it unites the living and the dead, the cradle and the grave. The reader recognizes this association throughout *Audigier,* where the heroes fall in love and marry for the fecal production of women. Both Raimberge and Troncecrevace are important, attractive, and revered because of their symbolic fertility. Grimberge, the enemy, represents the ambivalence of the medieval images of carnival. When she defecates on the hero, and her daughter bepisses his open-mouthed face, they perform fertility rites. They also embody the threatening power of female fecundity: the power to humiliate and to renew.[52] In their frightening ugliness and their larger-than-life stature, these female characters raise more questions about male attitudes toward the female in medieval culture, and from these loathesome giantesses, man-eaters, and Saracen hags, we could perhaps learn more about attitudes toward women in the Middle Ages than from all the ladies of courtly love literature.[53]

In the opening scene of the text, Turgibus, avoiding war and death to play in a dungheap, constitutes the picture of virile life. And at the very moment that Turgibus is overcome and lies dying, the infant Audigier is born. The weddings of both father and son are strewn with excrement. The noisy joy and comic ebullience in those nuptial scenes evoke not only fertility and virility but also the refusal of fear, an effort to conquer the terror of night and death. Suffering and fear pull us lower; joyous scatology bespeaks victory over our terrors.[54]

For Bakhtin, both medieval carnival and the work of Rabelais form a whole and obey a single narrative logic: the comic drama of life, death, and birth. In this sense, *Audigier* offers a comic version of the feudal play of life, at each of its significant moments.[55] In this corporeal drama, however, it is Grimberge, the vilain enemy, who plays the most significant role. As the *vieille,* the old woman, she represents the threat of death, but that death also implies the perpetual metamorphosis which is life. Grimberge enacts this truth, performing the symbolic killing and rebirth of the hero. While the hero's mother, Raimberge, signifies the celebrative side of life, her counterpart, Grimberge, posits the death necessary for rebirth. The homophony of the two female names is not without importance.[56] Grimberge is the figure of paradox and of the crisis that are at the heart of all holidays. She posits the death necessary for renaissance. Death, in medieval carnival, was often portrayed as an old woman great with child and about to give birth. The importance of the old woman to the *Audigier* story becomes evident in a startlingly comic scene at the midpoint of the narrative. Having pulled Audigier from his horse, Grimberge swallows him:

> Ausi le tranglouti com une oublee.
> Et quant ele senti qu'el fu enflee,
> a terre s'acroupi, li cus li bee.
> Audigier s'en oissi, criant: "Outree!"
> (*Audigier* 344–47)
>
> Then she gobbles him up like a pastry. When she feels herself swell up, she squats down on the ground, her ass wide open. Out comes Audigier, crying: "Over there!"

Two symbolic events transpire. Grimberge has actually given the hero death, and transformed him into yet another piece of excrement. Audigier has changed roles from eater to eaten, from life to waste. Conversely, Grimberge has given birth to the hero, renewing him in a scatological renaissance not unlike that of Pantagruel. The scene dramatizes one of the central arguments of Bakhtin's study: that carnival, the life of the body, scatological acts, and language are all ambivalent. The swallowing of the hero and his journey to the carnival underworld are grotesque and funny, threatening and reassuring.

The stercoraceous comedy of *Audigier* overwhelms and shocks the modern reader because its representations of scatology go far beyond the familiar jokes concerning unwilling acts. Excrement appears in conjunction with moments we hold sacred: eating, drinking, kissing, loving, marrying, and dying. It is precisely in this extension of scatological humor to the whole of life that we catch a glimpse of what *Audigier* evoked for a medieval audience: the powerful bonds between men, women, and earth; the unfailing exchange of life for death; the inseparability of the rotten and the fertile; and the tangled struggle of terror and joy in the brief space of our lives.

Le Roman de Renart:
The Courtois Bes-tourné

CHAPTER THREE

Parody and satire have been wed, divorced, subdivided, opposed, and generally confused for centuries.[1] In medieval literature we find no better example of this confusion than the late twelfth- and early thirteenth-century branches of the *Roman de Renart*. In 1887, Charles Lenient classed the *Roman de Renart* as both satire and parody: "L'oeuvre satirique par excellence, celle qui domine toutes les autres par l'importance et la popularité, c'est le *Renart*, vaste parodie qui se joue, se parle, s'écrit."[2] The critical tradition of reading the *Roman de Renart* as satire can be understood by examining the place of Renardian material in the literary history of the Middle Ages.[3] In medieval Europe there existed a pool of literary material made up of the stories of the fox, the wolf, and the lion and their friends, adventures, and tricks played on one another. This body of characters and stories is in itself neither satirical nor parodic, but neutral. The twelfth- and thirteenth-century branches of the *Roman de Renart* came after a satiric use of the Renardian material—the characters and stories of an ecclesiastical Latin satire, the *Ysengrimus*—in which social abuses and religious practices were mocked and chastised.[4] Such are the literary antecedents of the twelfth- and thirteenth-century romance branches. In the mid-thirteenth century, authors discovered that the animal tales lent themselves to a new literary use: political satire.[5] The ease with which history appropriated the animal characters for satirical purposes is eloquently illustrated by the *Mémoires* of Philippe de Novare. Under siege, Philippe wrote his own Renart text, drawing on the well-known characters for political allegory. The author described how he used the material to write a satire:

> Et puys qu'il ot comencié a escrire les letres, li prist il talant
> de faire les en rime. Et por ce que sire Heimery Barlais estoit

plus malvais que tous les autres, il le vorra contrefaire a Renart, et por ce que, au romans de Renart, Grimbert, le tais-
son, est son cousin germain, il apela messire Amaury de
Betsan Grinbert, et por ce que sire Hue de Biglet avoit la
bouche torte, et il faisoit semblant que il feïst tous jors la
moe, Phelippe l'apela singe.[6]

And once he had started to write the letter, he felt like writing it in rhyming
verse. And because Sir Heimery Barlais was the worst man of all, he gave
him the role of Renart, and because in the romance of Renart, Grimbert, the
badger, is Renart's first cousin, he named Amaury de Betsan "Grimbert,"
and because Sir Hue de Giblet had a twisted mouth and always seemed to
be pulling faces, Philippe made him be an ape.

It is not that the *Roman de Renart* is satiric in and of itself, nor
even the Renardian material, but rather, the satirical impulse
seizes upon the *Roman* tradition. In other words, the modern critical habit of reading the romance branches as satire is closely related to the medieval tendency to appropriate the romance material in order to satirize society. This satiric impulse both preexists
and postdates the *Roman de Renart,* which is why modern
readers have been led, mistakenly, to interpret the Renardian
characters as satirical every time they appear. This chapter will
show that the twelfth- and thirteenth-century branches of the *Roman,* unlike the earlier Latin and the later Old French texts, constitute parody.

Far from satirizing medieval society, the *Roman de Renart* parodies twelfth-century epic literature, in its cultural high-
mindedness, in its celebration of social order, and in its fixed, elevated poetic language. Rather than presenting themselves as so
many attacks on feudal institutions, the branches of the twelfth-
and thirteenth-century *Roman* are playing with the codes of the
Vergilian wheel, pulling at its spokes and disobeying its rules.

The critical confusion of parody and satire deserves our full attention, for in sorting out its whys and wherefores we will learn
more about medieval literature in general and a great deal about
the medieval *Roman de Renart* in particular.

Can we distinguish parody from satire on formal grounds? In
Palimpsestes, Genette defines parody structurally as a "détournement de texte à transformation minimale," then goes on to characterize four categories of parody according to their function,

"régime fonctionnel." Genette touches on the relation of satire to parody when he classifies three types of parody as satiric: "parodie stricte," in which a noble text is adapted to a vulgar subject; "travestissement," in which the style is degraded without modifying the subject of the text; and "pastiche satirique," the imitation of a noble style applied to a vulgar subject. Only one form of parody is, according to Genette, nonsatiric: the "pastiche," a technical imitation, neutral in intent.[7] Genette's classification of parody and satiric parody is limited in its usefulness for our study of medieval literature for two reasons. His categories cannot account for the variety of forms of medieval parody, which do not always obey the classical restrictions. Genette's definitions do not, for example, account for the fact that in *Fergus,* the parody ends before the story is finished. Nor do they account for the complex shifts between "noble" and "vulgar" in a text such as *Audigier,* with its constant *glissements* between courtois and vilain. Secondly, Genette's definition by intention, in which "régime satirique" is explained indirectly as the author's attitude—"intention agressive ou moqueuse"—is unwieldy when dealing with the texts of medieval authors, whose intentions and attitudes are difficult to know or verify with any precision across the centuries. Was the author of *Audigier,* for instance, feeling playful or angry in writing his scatological travesty? Modern critics could make a case for either interpretation.

More useful for the study of medieval literature is the definition that distinguishes parody and satire according to their respective targets. Parody plays with aesthetic models; it is a mocking of codes or of codifiable forms. Linda Hutcheon locates the difference between the two not in the intention of the author or in the attitude toward human behavior, but in the targeted "text": parody's target is intramural or literary; satire's target is extramural or societal. Parody's "intent" can range from genial to biting, but, Hutcheon maintains, its target is always another form of coded discourse. Satire chastizes moral or social abuses. Its intent can be destructive, reforming, or ameliorative.[8]

What about the differences between parody and satire in medieval French literature? Do the same definitions yield helpful distinctions? The notion of target proves itself pertinent to our discussion of medieval texts. For many decades medievalists read any comic exaggeration of social-class categories to be a marker of satire. No distinction was made between the exaggeration of literary images of social class, and social classes themselves.[9] The critical work of recent years has reversed this trend. Per Nykrog, in his landmark work *Les Fabliaux,* was one of the first to argue that the literary imagination of the Middle Ages was given to playing with artistic constructs, rather than to criticizing real institutions. Nykrog demonstrated that the target of the fabliaux, in their comic distortions of social class categories, is neither aristocratic society nor peasant society, but courtly literature. In a more general way, Paul Zumthor has argued that many medieval characters and texts which have commonly been identified as satirical are frequently parodic actualizations of literary stereotypes. In one of the latest readings of the Old French fabliaux, R. Howard Bloch takes Nykrog's demonstration still farther to show the highly literary character of these comic texts, their extreme self-consciousness and acute awareness of the role of language.[10]

Turning from the issue of target to the thorny question of function, which has received the lion's share of attention in critical discussions of medieval satire and parody, there too we witness a recent reversal in past trends. Since the work of Freud on humor, it has generally been held that humor is critical and aggressive, if not hostile, and that parody is a form of attack.[11] In other words, Freud viewed all of parody as satirical parody, committing the error Genette refers to as the confusion of parody and satirical pastiche. A revision of the opinion that parody is negative has been made possible by Mikhail Bakhtin's work on Rabelais in the history of laughter.[12] The Russian formalist stressed the positive function of laughter in the Middle Ages. As we saw in *Audigier,* the scatological parody that seemed so negative to the nineteenth and early twentieth centuries bore positive cultural functions in medieval France. In short, recent trends stress both the ubiquity of parody in medieval literature and its playful, not satirical, nature. Medieval parody ranges from *ludique* to neutral and even respectful. Quite often it is a way of paying homage to past traditions and of invoking the continuity of past and present.[13]

The twenty-odd branches of the twelfth- and thirteenth-century Old French *Roman de Renart* do not fulfill the function of satire, particularly that of political satire.[14] Polemical by its very nature, satire seeks to influence the opinion of an audience by attacking someone or some practice. Satire must then be clear. It must make its point, or it has no raison d'être. Satire names a precise target, aims at a specific abuse; it is partisan, hurling insults at the "other side." The *Roman*, however, neither attacks vices nor articulates a program of reform. It in fact enables the reader to distinguish between an attack on society and a play on cultural constructs.

Is there a practical kind of indexing that can be used to distinguish parody from satire? Medieval parody, like medieval satire, teaches us how it is to be read. The texts themselves enable the reader to formulate an empirical definition. Satire wants nothing better than to be recognized and thus invites its own identification. In medieval satire, the text heightens and underlines its references to reality. It leaves specific markers and precise clues, frequently onomastic: names, places, dates, events. The referential becomes dominant, as the comic distortions refer quite obviously to the outside world.[15] Medieval parody, on the other hand, contains elements which hold the critical impulse in check, preventing it from reading references to social class as references to reality.

It is because the *Roman de Renart* depicts twelfth-century social categories and pays careful attention to the mimesis of social hierarchy at the king's court, as well as to feudal law and legal procedures, and because later actualizations of the *Roman* material are satiric, that literary historians have traditionally indexed the *Roman* as satire.[16] The fact that the text uses the feudal structure for the cohesiveness of its animal fiction has until recently been used to justify this reading.[17] Critics put forth additional a posteriori arguments to shore up the satire interpretation.

What has constituted proof of the author's satirical intention? Satire names people, places, or moments. But how topical, how recognizable, is the humor generated by specific characters in the *Roman*? The data on which the assimilation between characters and historical figures has been based are so general as to be inconclusive. Similarities between the "personality" of Noble, the lion and king in the *Roman de Renart,* and that of Louis VII of France constitute a major block upon which the satire argument is built. The fictional lion is said to satirize the king who reigned from 1137 to 1180.[18] King Noble is identified as Louis VII because he is weak-

1. King Noble holding court. BN Fr. 12584, fol. 3r.

willed, indecisive, irascible, and vacillating. How many heads of
state would not fit that description? If the portrait of the lion were
meant to be satirical, it would, by virtue of its own design, contain
allusions to Louis VII (proper names referring to certain scandals,
for example, or place names, referring to military debacles) that
would inform the audience that it is listening to satire. But as the
following analysis will show, the *Roman*'s portrait of the lion
points to no target in reality. *Le Roman de Renart* draws on the
same Renardian material as texts that can properly be called satires, like the antimonastic satire in the *Ysengrimus*, by Nivardus,
or texts that teach a pragmatic morality for everyday life, such as
the *Ysopet* fables of Marie de France.[19] All three twelfth-century
texts relate a common story, the time-honored tale of the lion's
share. Only the *Roman*, the supposed satire of feudal life in
twelfth-century France, reveals an absence of any moral discourse
and thus resists a reading as satire.

We are familiar with Aesop's version of the tale, and a medieval
audience would doubtless have heard the Latin translation of
Phaedrus, or the vernacular version of Marie de France. Aesop
uses the story to draw a universal lesson. Briefly, a lion, a fox, and
a donkey go hunting. When they have taken their game, the lion
tells the donkey to divide the booty. Seeing that the donkey has divided the prey into three equal parts, the lion angrily devours him.
The lion then instructs the fox to divide the portions and is delighted to see the fox collect nearly everything into one pile (for
the lion), leaving only a few scraps for himself. The lion asks,
"Who taught you to divide things in that way?" "What happened
to the donkey," answers the fox. Aesop's moral: we should gain
wisdom from the misfortunes of others.

In Marie de France's *Fables*, each narrative ends with a "Mor-
alité," a didactic message, for which the audience listens. In Fable
XI, the tale is told almost as succinctly as the moral: the lion-king
is hunting with a buffalo and a wolf, when they catch a stag. The
wolf and buffalo wonder how they will divide the prey, but the
king announces that the first share will be his because he is king,
the second share will be his because he killed the stag, and the
third portion will be his because he is the third party in the group.
The moral of the story: when a poor man keeps the company of a
rich man, the poor man will lose all. For Marie, the story warns us
about the insatiable greed of the wealthy.

2. Renart jousting with King Noble. BN Fr. 12584, fol. 148v.

The same tale appears in Magister Nivardus's *Ysengrimus,* a Latin satire of the mid-twelfth century. *Ysengrimus* is a key intertext of the *Roman de Renart,* not only because they were composed during the same period, but especially because they share the same cast of characters: Isengrin the wolf, Reynard the fox, the rooster, the ram, and so forth. They share twelve identical narrative episodes, including that of "the lion's share." In the Latin version, Ysengrimus the wolf, Reynardus the fox, and Rufanus the lion-king hunt down a heifer. At the king's command, Ysengrimus is about to divide the game—into three equal parts. Seeing this, the king grows furious and slashes the wolf with his claws. The king orders Reynardus to divide the food. The wily fox makes one pile of the choicest morsels (for the king), one pile of lesser quality (for the queen), and puts the bones in a third pile (for the lion cubs). Delighted, the king asks the fox who taught him to divide so well. Reynardus points to Ysengrimus and says, "My uncle has taught me not a little." The king then asks why Ysengrimus cannot divide things if he has taught Reynardus to do so, and the fox quips: "Propter Belvacos non fuit ausus idem" (*Ysengrimus* VI, 290; He didn't dare to do it because of the people of Beauvais).

The reference to the inhabitants of Beauvais alludes to an embarrassing quarrel between Louis VII and his brother, Henri.[20] Their dispute concerned a genuine division, the carving of France into shares. When Henri managed to appropriate the episcopal see of Beauvais in 1149, King Louis rashly assembled an army in order to march on and raze Beauvais. As Sigebert de Gembloux relates the event in his *Historia Pontificalis,* only the intervention of Suger, the abbot of Saint Denis, Adelaide, the queen-mother, and Joscelin, the bishop of Soissons, kept the people of Beauvais from seeing their city destroyed. The fox's sly allusion to the greed and rashness of Louis VII indicates the aim of the satire. Magister Nivardus easily adapts the tale to his satirical purpose, and his satirical purpose is made manifest through a specific reference to Beauvais and an implicit reference to Louis's refusal to share with his brother, Henri.

The author of this branch of the *Roman de Renart,* in telling this tale, has available to him at least two moral satirical tacks. Were the intent of the *Roman de Renart* to criticize Louis VII, or kingship, or twelfth-century France, this fable of brutal injustice would afford the perfect vehicle for satire. But resolutely eschewing satire, the *Roman* closes its version of the tale with a joke, an old and well-known joke, found throughout medieval French literature.

Here is what the poet of Branch 18 does with the fable. Renart, Isengrin, and Noble go hunting and espy a bull, a cow, and a calf. The king assigns the task of dividing the booty to Isengrin, who assigns the bull to the king, the cow to the queen, keeps the calf for himself, and tells Renart to make himself scarce. Angered by the three-part division, the lion deals a terrible blow to the wolf, bloodying his head, then orders Renart to redistribute the booty. Renart gives the bull to the king, the cow to the queen, and the calf to their newborn lion cub. Noble leaps with joy: "Who taught you to divide shares?"

> "Sire," fait il, "par sainte Luce,
> cil vilains a la rouge aumuce,[21]
> je n'en oi onques autre mestre;
> ne sai s'il est ou clerc ou prestre
> qui si porte roge corone,
> mais bien sai, se il est persone,
> qu'il est ou pape ou cardonaus."
> (*Roman* XVIII, 16769–75)
> "Sire," says he, "by Saint Lucy, it was this churl with the red cap; I have never had a teacher. I do not know whether he, who bears this red crown thus, is cleric or priest, but I know full well, if he is anyone at all, that he is a pope or cardinal."

Rather than draw any moral on the lessons we can learn from injustice, or from the greediness of monarchs, the *Roman de Renart,* brandishes this "red riding-hood" joke, ubiquitous in medieval literature from the *Fecunda Ratis,* a Latin fable of the late tenth century, to works owing nothing to the fable tradition, including twelfth- and thirteenth-century chansons de geste.[22] Any time an animal or a knight suffers a bloody head-wound, this punch line reappears: "You must be a cardinal, you with the red cap!" The *Roman,* again, shows no interest in reform or in satire, and interpolates an intertextual joke rather than a moral or a message. The humor is Gallican, to be sure, which may explain its longstanding

success with an audience that had seen a good deal of trouble between kings and popes. Yet political content (and in this case the
opposition of secular and sacred power constitutes a medieval
topos) and polemical position are not the same thing; this is a
joke, not a political lesson.

Critics have extended their literary fingerprinting of the lion to
yet other characters, in order to show that the entire *Roman* can
be understood as a satire of twelfth-century France. The camel,
for example, because he speaks French with an Italian accent, has
been positively identified as Cardinal Pierre de Pavie, Pope Alex-
ander III's legate to Louis VII. Is this reading authorized by the
text itself? How can we tell whether such "play" is a satirical attack or simple entertainment? We cannot fail to note that the *Roman* names no names, even when it is free to do so. Other French
poets of this period name names, such as Pierre de Pavie, quite
openly. A well-known Goliard poem, "Propter Sion non tacebo,"
repeatedly attacks the Italian legate whom modern critics have
recognized behind the pompous camel in the *Roman*.[23] This Latin
text goes about its satirical business quite methodically and blatantly, first alluding to a certain "legistam" (stanza 10), then pun-
ning coyly on the name and word "petrus" (Peter, a man of stone,
in stanzas 16 and 18), and finally (In stanza 27) launching an all-
out attack:

> Petrus enim Papiensis,
> qui electus est Meldensis.[24]
>
> First it's Pierre de Pavie, elected bishop of Meaux.

In the Latin text, the bishop of Meaux is openly charged with corruption, simony, and the unforgivable crime of failing in generosity toward poor Goliard poets. The *Roman*, however, eschews
the possibility of a satirical attack, choosing once again to play
with language. The camel character is remarkable not for corruption or stinginess, but for his speech:

> "Qare, mesire, me audite.
> Nos trobat en decret escrite
> legem expresse plublicate
> de matrimoine vïolate."
> (*Roman* VIIB, 6269–72)

Vilain and Courtois

"Prego, prego, Signore, listeneth up to me. We findeth in written decree laws that expresseth forbidding of matrimonial violation."

The *Roman* accuses no one of injustice or malpractice but plays with the comic effect obtained by combining the exotic foreignness of a camel in France with the exotic foreignness of learned legalese.

The portrait of the Italian camel is no more satirical than play with language, and we find countless examples of wordplay in the *Roman,* as in the following exchange between Renart and Tibert the cat:

"Deauble Renart; ies tu ivres?
Que feraies tu de mes livres?

.   .   .   .

Sez tu riens de dïaletique?"
"Oïl, tote quiqueliquique."
(*Roman* XI, 12173–74, 12179–80)

"By the devil, Renart, are you drunk? What would you do with my books? ... Do you know anything about dialectics?" "Yes, all kinds of quick-quackalectics."

The passage is not criticizing the increasing intellectual prominence of dialectics as a branch of knowledge at the twelfth-century university of Paris or the phenomenal popularity of Abelard's classes; it is playing with the comic novelty of a polysyllabic Latinate word that carries serious sociolectic connotations of academia, erudition, and high-brow pretentiousness.

Why has the critical fate of the *Roman* been so different from that of the other parodies studied thus far? Guillaume le Clerc's *Fergus* has never been interpreted as satire because it does not refer to any specific event, person, practice, or attitude; its representation of knighthood, though comic, remains in a realm akin to that of fairy tales. In *Audigier,* the kingdom of Cocuce, the count named Turgibus, and his son, Audigier, bear imaginary names that permit of no historical identification, thus preventing a satirical reading. The scatology of *Audigier* has almost always been understood as parodic, for it certainly invites no identification with actual practices or abuses in twelfth-century France. Its comic exaggerations target the nature of language and language substitution in literary codes. But the *Roman de Renart* draws on a body of material so frequently used for satire that critics applied a satirical reading to a text that in fact uses that material parodically.

It is one thing to ascertain that the *Roman de Renart* is a collection of parodic stories, quite another to define and describe the specific features of parody's system in this group of texts. Most modern criticism agrees that the *Roman* takes as its matrix the medieval épopée, examining the epic language as comically rendered in the beast fables.[25] The epic intertext explains the feudal structure of this animal world and enables the reader to understand its cast of characters: seneschal, gonfalonier, vassals, ladies-in-waiting, queen, and court physician. The epic narrative paradigms—treason or insult followed by a "conseil de barons," war, revenge, and victory—constitute the frame of these branches, which do not form one extended narrative but are loosely related through the characters.

It is the presence of the animal characters themselves that prepares the listener or reader to laugh, and deftly circumvents any lofty feelings. The expectations awakened by the epic matrix are interrupted first by Renart's name, then by the perception of a foreign presence that stirs expectations not of the epic system but of another textual system. In other words, it is the presence of animals in this mimesis of the feudal world that clues us in to the interpretant as it orients the deformation of the epic model. The interpretant is not an interfering language, as it was in *Audigier,* a parody that obeyed the narrative grammar of the chanson de geste throughout, simply rewriting it in a scatological lexicon. Rather, it is a literary space.

Unlike the courtois in *Audigier,* the courtois characters in Noble's kingdom are repeatedly sidetracked from the epic space of the text. They stray from their struggle for honor and their duties as knights and vassals into another space and another type of struggle: the rural space and the struggle for food and safety. It is this literary construct of the rural space that constitutes the interpretant of the *Roman de Renart.*

Let us see how this occurs in the text itself. In Branch VIIB we find a passage frequently identified as a heartless satire of peasants.[26] The vilains have armed themselves with pitchforks and

Que il eussent. j. peu cessé
Tant que mieussies confesse

A cest mot li prebstres pris ha
un baston que il auisa

3. Vilains pursuing Renart. BN Fr. 12584, fol. 53r.

clubs, and rush to protect their homes and larders from the famished animals who search for food. The conflict becomes a full scale *ruée épique,* and leads to a mock-epic battle. The comic names of the vilain characters—Tiegiers Brisefouace, Hodeberz Brisebraciee, Rogiers Briseglace, and Femeris Voideescuele—and their rustic weapons, consisting of clubs, whips, and arrows, have been cited as proof that the passage is a mordant satire on the brutish nature of the medieval peasantry. But if we reread the scene, we realize that the vilains are scarcely depicted in the passage. No attention is drawn to them *as peasants,* to their manners, appearance, values, or language. These vilains are not the object of satire, for they are not at the center of the textual project; rather, they are the marker of the literary space of the medieval beast fable, collections called *Ysopets.* For what is being played with in this scene is the overblown style of epic battle scenes: the thronging rush of horsemen, the enumeration of their elaborate patronyms, the pretentious description of their arms. This passage parodies the glorious clichés of epic literature by transposing them in the peasant space:

Es vos poingnant sire Frobert
et dant Costant, et dant Nobert.
(*Roman* VIIB, 7049–50)
Behold galloping before you Sir Frobert and Mister Costant, and Mister Nobert.

Or ça, baron, or ça, a l'ors!
(7061)
Onward, great lords, onward, follow that bear!

ça .X., ça .V., ça .VII., ça .IIII.
(7090)
Behold ten, over here five, there seven, and here four.

The text does not mock rural patois; it comically rewrites the epic battle descriptions of the chanson de geste, transgressively juxtaposing it with the space of the beast fable tradition.

In the *Roman,* the courtois animal frequently wanders into the world of the vilain, with its cabbage patches and its smoked hams unfailingly hung from barn rafters. In this collision with the vilain, the courtois undergoes a curious transformation. It is here

4. Renart jumps from a window and falls into a vat of yellow dye. BN Fr. 12584, fol. 20r.

that the reader perceives the narrative tension or contradiction that accounts for the "redirection" of epic. It is here that we discover the interpretant. The courtois of Noble's court periodically relapse, fall from grace, to their animal status. No longer barons and knights, they are hungry foxes, wolves, and bears, prowling for a meal.

The stereotypical vilain, the sole human character in the animal hierarchy in the *Roman,* stands at the liminal position between the matricial intertext, the space of the epic, in which animals are knights, and the parodic interpretant, the space of the *Ysopet* tradition, in which animals are creatures with tails and claws (not horse and armor), scrapping over sausage or tricking one another for a coveted fishtail.

While the characters find themselves at the king's court, their language and preoccupations comply with the epic matrix. Questions of peace and war, loyalty and treason, prevail.[27] Quarrels and disputes continue to structure the narrative when the courtois animals leave the space of the court, but their concerns and behavior change. The epic structure (built on the story of war) weakens; the cohesion of the initial frame gives way to the briefer, recurring structure of the trick.[28]

In Branch VIII, "Le duel judiciaire," as in other scenes at Noble's court, Renart shows a perfect mastery of courtly language:

"Biau sire, sauve vostre grace,
onques ne fui de tele estrace
c'a mon saingnor face contraire,
ne chose que ne doie faire.
Ge suis voz hom et vos mes sire."
(VIII, 7382–87)

"Good sire, God save your grace, I was never of that ilk who go against the will of their lord, or do things they ought not do. I am your man, and you, my lord."

But when, in a later passage, Renart is intent upon seizing fowl in the vilain Berthold's barnyard, the fox speaks quite a different language:

"Taissiez," dist Renart, "ne ganglez,
fil a putain, traïtres sers,
que, par les os et par les ners,

je vos metrai en male paine."
(XVIII, 15806—9)

"Shut up," said Renart, "don't squawk, you son of a bitch, you sneaky
peon, lest I put you in danger of your life by mangling your bones and
nerves."

Such sharp transgressions of rhetorical register underscore the
movement from epic to fable space throughout the different
branches of the *Roman*. This technique of shifting language has
been deplored by critics as a regrettable mistake. Scholars point
out similar inconsistencies: in the epic space, the animals actually
ride horses; in the fable space, they go on all fours; when they
move from the royal court to the woods, their steeds vanish mysteriously as the characters themselves return to their animal form
and begin to gallop on their own legs.[29] Gabriel Bianciottoi was
perhaps the first to understand this metamorphosis as a deliberate, fictive strategy.[30] While Bianciotto underscores the use of this
fusion to translate the animals' "états d'âme" in Branch I, we can
also read this marvelous transformation as a sign marking the
characters' passage from the literary space of the feudal court to
the literary space of the forest.

When the animals proceed to the court of King Noble in
Branch I, for instance, they are knights, in a "grande chevauchée":

> Or s'an vont li baron ensanble:
> Diex! com la mule Grinbert amble;
> mais li chevax Renart acoupe.
> Li flans li bat desoz la croupe:
> mout crient et doute son seignor,
> onques paor n'ot mes greignor.
> Tant ont erré, a plain, a bos,
> et l'anbleüre et les galos,
> et ont tant la montaigne alee,
> Qu'i sont venu a la valee
> qui vers la cort le roi avale;
> par le pont entrent en la sale.
> (*Roman,* Roques ed., I, 1209—20)

Then the barons ride off together: God, how Grimbert's mule ambles! But
Renart's horse stumbles. His flank beats hard beneath his croup; greatly
does he fear his lord, never has he felt such fear. They ride through so many
woods and plains, both ambling and galloping, and cross the mountains

until they reach the valley where the king holds court. They cross the draw-bridge and enter the palace.

Clearly, those characters are knights on horseback. But when hunger drives the same characters to roam in search of food, they enter the rural space on all fours:

> Et Renart cele part s'adresce
> tout coiement, le col baissié
> entre la soif et la plaissié.
>
> .   .   .   .   .   .
>
> ne puet müer, ne puet tapir,
> n'a geline ne puet venir.
> Acroupiz est en mi la voie;
> mout se defripe, mout coloie.
> Porpanse soi que se il saut,
> que se il chiet auques de haut
> et il est veüz des gelines,
> ficheront soi par les espines,
> (*Roman*, Roques ed., IIIa, 4090–92, 4097–4104)

And Renart turns very stealthily in their direction, his head bent low, be-tween the hedge and the gate. . . . he cannot move, he cannot hide, nor can he reach the hens. Down he crouches in the middle of the path; in great ag-itation, he watches closely. He tells himself that if he leaps, and if he falls from this height, and is seen by the hens, they will throw themselves into the thorny thicket.

Suddenly, the hero is a quadruped carnivore, with pointed muz-zle, erect ears, and a long, bushy tail.

The importance of the rural space to the *Roman de Renart* has not been recognized by critics. Nor have the shifts from courtois to animal. Once the animal characters find themselves in the peas-ant world, they cease to be parodic actualizations of courtois knights. On the contrary, the comic paradox of these episodes lies in the fact that the vilain peasant character here takes on the role of courtois lord. In the rural space, it is the benighted vilain who signifies order, prosperity, even leisure, all that is usually signified by the noble human characters. The text presents courtois ani-mals and vilain animals, courtois vilains and animal vilains. It does not, however, present any genuine courtois characters, only animals and peasants. The absence of the traditional courtois fig-ure creates a gap, an open space in which animals and peasants alternately take on the role of the missing courtois, the epic noble-man. The parodic humor points implicitly toward the figure con-spicuously absent from these stories, the courtois character as traditionally represented in twelfth- and thirteenth-century litera-ture. That is not to say that the *Roman* satirizes the French aris-tocracy of the time; it parodies the courtois characters and codes of epic literature.

Thus, these humble little tales of trickery offer us new insight into the medieval "opposition" of courtois and vilain. Tradition holds that their roles and characteristics are stable and unchanging. In-deed, the very table of contents of the only book on the subject—Stanley Galpin's *Cortois and Vilain*—imposes a static immobility that belies the complexity of medieval texts:

Ch. III   "The *cortois* has polished manners; the *vilain*, rude manners"
Ch. IV   "The *cortois* is gentle in speech; the *vilain*, rough"
Ch. V   "The *cortois* has 'mesure'; the *vilain* lacks 'mesure'"

and further:

Ch. IX   "The *cortois* is good; the *vilain*, bad"
Ch. XVIII   "The *cortois* is intelligent; the *vilain*, stupid."

Galpin's categorical ordering of an enormous mass of texts (and characters) is useful. He must be credited with pointing out that medieval poets strove to establish a fixed and coded literary sys-tem and that this coded system had nothing to do with historical realities.[31] What Galpin does not study is the corpus of texts by medieval authors who sought to transgress the prescriptions that others worked to establish. It is the medieval parodists who show us both the law and its transgression.

In the poets' transgression of such a static opposition of vilain and courtois we discover the coherence of the *Roman*'s parodic project. The humor is directed not at twelfth-century peasants who aspire to knighthood or nobility, nor (less probably still) at animals who are tried in court as humans.[32] Parody is pulling the Vergilian wheel from the rut of its fixed rules.

Parody's system, in the *Roman*, is cohesive and visible. The epic matrix is repeatedly interrupted, transgressed, and juxtaposed to the *Ysopet* tradition, in which animals fight both among themselves and with peasants in a struggle for physical survival, and in which the ostensible moral of the story is never really a moral, but an example of quick-wittedness.[33] Just retribution does not exist in the space of the *Ysopet*, nor do heroic deeds or virtues; there is only the virtue of being more clever. In recognizing the absence of any moral telos in the animal fable we can finally and fully understand the parody at work in the *Roman de Renart,* a collection of texts whose amorality has baffled literary critics as much as it has delighted audiences.

The *Roman de Renart* offers no critique of feudal kingship, no critique of judicial systems or injustices, of peasants or of nobles. Given this absence of a moral, social, or political orientation in the *Roman*, some readers have inferred that it is devoid of any literary ideology, that it is purely gratuitous language play. Marie-Noëlle Lefay-Toury has concluded, for example, that the structure of the *Roman* is so loose as to be incoherent, and that the only meaning generated is as "gratuité de l'écriture."[34] But can we fail to distinguish here between episodic structure and gratuitous structure? We have just seen that neither structure nor writing is gratuitous in the *Roman*. The text is a systematic and complex play of textual traditions. Its references to the heroic literary tradition of the twelfth century do produce meaning. The *Roman* ties and unties the literary manifestations of courtoisie, thus creating a new and rather well-defined system of its own. These texts establish a tradition of their own, through the dismantling of old ones. They reinvest the epic matrix with a new cast of characters and with a series of amoral comic tricks, undermining the epic celebration of a fixed moral and social order, the epic ethos of just retribution (war and vengeance), and the literary assumption that justice is necessary, if only as a narrative pattern.

Having cited the practice of compositional transgression in the *Roman*, we should now study some specific examples of this practice. As we saw in *Fergus* and in *Audigier*, it is the parodic interpretant that rewrites the matrix. Once we see that the epic matrix, in the *Roman*, is "interpreted" by fable material (space, rhetoric, and characters) we can then make sense of textual elements that had at first seemed literary errors or textual flaws.

Turning to the characters in the *Roman*, we note first of all the transgressive combination of courtois and beast. The courtois in these texts misbehaves because he is an animal character; his behavior in the epic space is quite noble, but he repeatedly returns to the rural space of fables, where trickery and deceit are the rule. Rather than understand the *Roman* as a satire on the bestiality of medieval nobles, the reader can understand it as a play upon two literary traditions.

Thus, the reader's task becomes that of determining the nature of the tricks played not on animals (for the animals conform to their proper literary roles) but on literature, and then that of determining whether the degree of these literary transgressions is like or unlike those of other medieval parodies, such as *Fergus* and *Audigier*.

Many of the transgressive combinations in the *Roman* will remind us of those in *Audigier*. Both texts are epic parodies. Both dwell on transgressive topics such as the body (eating, sex, scatology). Both present heroes who fail to conform to the codes of courtoisie. Yet the resulting texts are quite dissimilar. Parody's undertaking is always the same; the parodic production is ever different.

The *Roman de Renart* is transgressive with respect to its matrix, and thus with respect to literary tradition: its characters engage not in heroism but in tricks. They trick one another principally in order to steal, to hurt, or to rape. The failure to trick is punished; the ability to trick is rewarded.[35]

The tricks of the *Roman* fall into the same categories that we will discover in another medieval parody by Douin de Lavesne, *Trubert*: sexual tricks, food thefts, sadistic tricks that inflict physical pain and tricks of humiliation. Such tricks constitute the sine qua non of much comic medieval literature, such as the fabliaux, and are the stuff of which beast fables are made. So the rapes, thefts, scatological humiliations, and murders in the *Roman* are in themselves conventional; they do not transgress but conform to rules of the beast fable. It is the combination of tricks (and of transgressive acts in general) and characters representing feudal nobles that constitutes a literary transgression.

The *Roman de Renart* represents a world ruled not by justice but by injustice. It disassociates vilains from *vilenie,* and implies that vilenie is universal. Further, it presents this widespread vilenie not as serious but as comic. It celebrates the disjunction of evil and punishment as a great joke. By loosening the equation of vilain and vilenie, by making the trickster Renart a courtois, a noble baron, the *Roman* discovers a new source of transgression in the possibilities of playing with the infinite permutations of the courtois-vilain polarization. Studies of the *Roman de Renart* have focussed on the animals as courtois feudal subjects. Little attention has been paid to the many vilains and rural scenes in its branches. In point of fact, there are more vilains in the *Roman de Renart* texts than in any other French work of the twelfth century. Most of them have proper names. Four of them have recurring roles.[36] Twelve narrative episodes center on a vilain.[37] More important still, these vilains do not always maintain the same status with respect to the animal characters, but are caught up in a seesawing of social roles. Therein lies the genuine transgression of the *Roman*'s parody.

The *Roman de Renart* presents the reader with a multiplication of juxtaposed and combined characters. This form of literary transgression differs markedly from that practiced in *Audigier,* a text in which the courtois alone occupies the epic space, where no vilains dwell. The social-class oxymora of the *Roman* guide the audience, first tripping it up, then pointing it in a new direction.

Examples of the courtois animal abound in the space of Noble's court, where truth and justice are mere chimeras. The animal knights struggle to maintain order in a kingdom threatened from without and certainly from within. Tardif, the snail who is King Noble's brave gonfalonier, exemplifies the courtois animal at the royal court. Chantecler is another and familiar example of the intelligent and well-spoken animals in this animal world; just and benevolent, the rooster reigns over the courtoisie of the "basse cour" with his lady, Pinte.

Equally numerous are examples of the vilain animal. Their wrongdoings occur both in the epic and in the rural space: Hersent, the unfaithful and lecherous wife; Ysengrin, the greedy and dull-witted wolf; and the hero, Renart, who is the principal villain and worst subject, lying, cheating, sowing chaos in the kingdom. Renart commits heinous crimes (perjury, treason, rape, and murder) with gleeful hilarity.

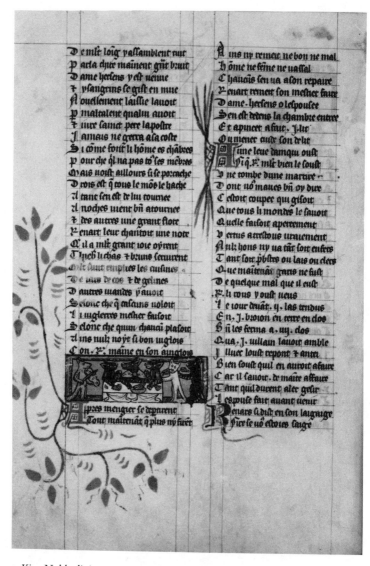

5. King Noble dining at court. BN Fr. 12584, fol. 25v.

In several episodes of the *Roman* one particular permutation of these oxymora, the courtois vilain, stands in the interstice left vacant by the text. The courtly peasant protects the weaker animals against the vilains animals. In Branch IIIa, Constant de Noes leaves his leisurely game of "choule" (medieval bowling) to defend the animals on his prosperous farm. In Branch X, the wealthy Liétart must also defend Chantecler against Renart. In Branch I an affluent vilain is well-known for his refinement and his skill in playing the "vielle" (viol).

One final combination in the *Roman,* the vilain vilain, or vile peasant, bears a marked resemblance to the vilain of the Old French fabliaux: base, hungry, and benighted. The episodes of the "Femme du vilain," in Branch v, and the "Bacon enlevé," in Branch xvII, represent such vilains and vilaines in contest with the animals. As in the *Ysopet* fables, men, women, and animals engage in tricks that consist essentially in the theft of food.

In Branch xvIII, during the course of an extended fight, Renart takes on traits that are more and more markedly human, while the vilain Berthold is described as taking on the features of an animal. In pitting vilain against fox, the *Roman* offers a new version of the archetypal struggle between giant and knight. As in the epic, where the knight conquers the giant despite the latter's physical stature, so too in the *Roman* the fox reduces the peasant to begging for mercy: Bertold offers to become Renart's vassal. Only the archetypal opponents have shrunk. At the start of this fight between peasant and animal, Bertold masters the situation, leaving the little fox helpless. Even Bertold's language reveals the strength of his position:

"Ha! ha!" fait il, "mar i venites,
fil a putain, lierres traïtres,
par ça saudroiz par saint Germain!"
(xvIII, 15683–85)

"Ha! ha!" says [Bertold], "you'll be sorry you came, you son of a bitch, you thieving traitor—by Saint Germain, you'll pay for this!"

Meanwhile the small animal struggles in silence:

[Renart] si se fiert en un des reseus,
s'il en eschape, c'est merveille:

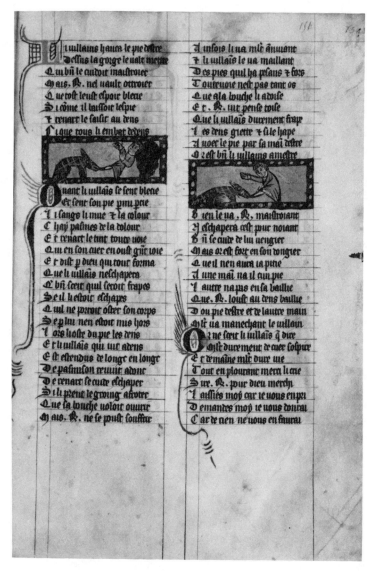

6. Renart caught in the net of the vilain Bertold. BN Fr. 12584, fol. 154r.

la roiz entor lui s'entortoile,
pris est et par groing et par piez;
or a il esté engingniez
ne li a riens valu sa guile.
(15693, 15697–701)

[Renart] finds himself caught in one of the nets, it will be a miracle if he can
escape: the net wraps itself around him, he is caught by the snout and by the
feet; now he has been tricked and his guile was of no use to him.

As the scene continues, however, Renart seems to grow before our
very eyes. The fox suddenly escapes from the trap and overpowers
Bertold. Renart seizes the man's throat not with his "patte," but
with his "pié destre," then bites him not with his "goule," but with
his "bouche." It is the peasant who is endowed with a muzzle:

Renart a sa goule saisie
del pié destre et de l'autre main;
mout va menacent le vilain.
(15774–76)

Renart seized him by the muzzle with his right foot and his other hand; he
threatens the vilain menacingly.

The "giant" human is soon reduced to pitiful tears:

Des iauz plore, dou cuer soupire

.   .   .   .

tot en plorant merci li crie:
"Sire Renart," fait il, "merci!"
(15784, 15786–87)

He cries his heart out, he sighs profoundly . . . as he cries he begs for mercy:
"Sire Renart," says he, "mercy!"

and Renart appears to tower over him:

"Fiz a putain, vilains engrés,"
fait Renart, "qu'alez vos querant?"

.   .   .   .

Cil qui ne se puet revanchier
si pleure et crie et fait grant duel:
(15792–93, 15802–3)

"Son of a bitch, you stubborn vilain," says Renart, "what is it you want?"
. . . [Bertold], who can not avenge himself, weeps and cries and noisily be-
wails his fate.

Vilain and Courtois

By the close of this scene, Renart has been transformed from a small fox to a knight. This is signalled by a shift in rhetorical register, from vulgar to epic:

> "Voil que tu me bailles ta foi
> que mes par les tuens ne par toi
> n'avrai ne honte ne domage,
> et que tu me feras homage
> si tost conme laissié t'avré
> et trestout a ma volanté
> metras et ton avoir et toi."
> (15863–69)

"I want you to pledge your word that neither you nor any of yours will disgrace or harm me, and that you will do homage to me as soon as I let you go, and that you will place your person and your possessions at my disposal."

In yet another way, the *Roman* has transgressed the codes of genre and character, transforming a beast-fable archetype (a peasant sets out to trap the animal who is stealing his food) into an epic combat between courtois and vilain (the triumphant combatant forces the loser to become his vassal). The twist in the parodic version is, of course, that the role of the noble courtois is played by the faithless trickster, Renart.

Although there are many such epic scenes in the *Roman*, it does not actually obey the matrix of epic (treason, revenge, victory), for there are no wars. "Guerre" is waged to punish or to interrupt a trick; war is in fact replaced by the trick structure. The text's pretext, as invoked in one of the initial branches, is the age-old war between Renart and Isengrin: "La guere, qui mout fu dure de grant fin, entre Renart et Isengrin" (III, 3742–44). But the "war" shifts and becomes an opposition between Renart and all the other characters, whether situated in King Noble's court or on the farm of a peasant. Yet despite this polarization of trickster-"hero"and the other characters, the fox does not become a peasant, and the *Roman* does not adhere to the epic ethos or the moral code of the chanson de geste. The *Roman* texts transgressively juxtapose the trappings of the epic's socionarrative codes with a foreign moral code. In the epic tradition, a ruthless trickster would be punished for acting against the rules of the community. Epic heroes are admired for their tricks only when they harm the enemy and favor the French cause, as in *Le Charroi de Nîmes,* for example. In the *Roman,* that moral code is replaced by the trickster ethos. The successful traitor is rewarded. Cunning, slyness, and stealth triumph.

The medieval equation between character, social rank, and moral codes depicted by the Vergilian wheel breaks down completely, or rather is broken down in the *Roman.* Any character, courtois or vilain, can initiate a trick and harm any other character. The juxtaposition of human and animal characters is used to blur even more the social and ethical poles of literary tradition. Nothing is exempt from the *chassé-croisé.* In Branch I, a vilain animal successfully tricks a courtois vilain into saving his life; a group of courtois vilains successfully wages war on a vilain animal; and one vilain animal successfully tricks a courtois animal. In Branch IIIa, a vilain animal fails to trick, and is then tricked by, a courtois animal. In Branch V, a vilain vilain and his wife succeed in outsmarting two vilain animals who had initially tricked them.

Branch X exemplifies the interchangeability of roles in a series of tricks, as well as the absence of any narrative pattern of moral order or principle of justice. This branch also provides the clearest example of the role of the beast-fable interpretant (cunning animals fighting humans for food) as it informs the epic frame, replacing traditional pretexts for, and forms of, war. Brun the bear, a courtois animal, tricks Liétart, a courtois vilain (that is to say, a wealthy peasant with the civilized lifestyle of a feudal lord). Renart, a vilain animal, joins sides with Liétart in order to trick the courtois bear, Brun. Liétart, however, becomes something of a vilain vilain when he tries to double-cross his ally, Renart. Thus a lengthy "war" breaks out between Liétart and Renart, in an episode that parodies the repeated attacks of enemy armies. After countless upheavals (their war occupies no less than 1.790 verses) Renart takes the final trick and Liétart becomes his vassal. The peasant then wins the fox's friendship by inviting him to dine from a well-stocked larder.

The shifting roles of vilain and courtois prevent the audience of the *Roman* from feeling social or moral allegiance to the characters; there are no real sides to be taken. We laugh at the loser, and then laugh again when the victor meets with defeat. The arbitrary assignation of essentially antisocial acts to any social type or

7. Renart saying a mass. BN Fr. 12584, fol. 56r.

moral role, or to any stable language, defies the tightly coded laws organizing the chanson de geste. Gone are the guiding poles of honor and shame, righteousness and guilt, Christian and Saracen. In the absence of such moral frameworks, the audience finds itself free to laugh, without regard for the conventions of high and low, noble and ignoble.

The *Roman de Renart* portrays all manner of vilains and villainy, but posits no necessary relation between social class and moral behavior. This transgression, which may seem ideologically radical to a modern audience, is a function of trickster literature, or rather of the decision to choose a trickster hero: knight, animal, and trickster.[38] Although a knight, the fox is blatantly indifferent to the good of society which knights swear to defend. More exactly, Renart desires nothing more than to satisfy his own illegitimate desires. Further, the trickster-knight frequently succeeds in his unjust causes.

But Renart the trickster is not the sole transgressive element in this parody. Like the characters of the beast-fable interpretant, the *Roman*'s characters live in a world ruled by injustice, by "le droit du plus fort." In showing the repeated failure of courtoisie and justice, the *Roman de Renart* implies that vilenie is universal.[39] That implication in itself is not transgressive: many are the didactic sermons and allegories that declare as much in the Middle Ages. The ultimate transgression of the *Roman* resides in its comic presentation of universal vilenie and its jubilant representation of the reign of injustice.

The reader now learns what can be gained from the understanding that the *Roman de Renart* is parody, not satire. The textual representation of a society in which injustice reigns can signify something other than (or in a way other than) a mirroring of contemporary society.

Conversely, we learn from the *Renart* that no discourse, not even a parodic discourse, is ahistorical. The humor of the *Roman* may be literary play, but it is actualized in a meaningful cultural context. The rural space of the *Roman* is populated by vilains who have grown wealthy enough to buy their own land and livestock. The authors portray rich peasants who enjoy their newfound leisure by playing the lute. At the same time, these wealthy vilains often function as the ludicrous foils of the animals. The real empowerment of French peasants at the turn of the thirteenth century is both mirrored and undercut by their comic denigration in the *Roman de Renart*.

Parody's presence indicates the acute medieval awareness of society as construct, of culture as representation, and thus as subject to re-creation and recreation. The success of parody indicates that laughter was one of the cultural resources of medieval France, a response to tensions in problematic domains of social life.

Trubert:
The Courtois Trompé

CHAPTER FOUR

Once upon a time a boy lived with his poor mother. To earn a little money, he bought a pig. While returning home through the forest, the boy was persuaded to sell the animal to a hermit, who promised to pay in two weeks.

When two weeks passed, the boy disguised himself as a girl and went to the hermitage. Alone with the hermit, the girl brought forth a club from beneath her skirts and beat the monk until he made partial payment.

After a week the peasant boy disguised himself as a doctor and returned to the hermitage. The doctor beat the monk again and took the price of the pig. Disguised as a priest, the boy returned yet again and attended to the invalid. The youth pummeled the hermit one last time, and again took the price of the pig.
—"The Youth and His Pig"

A poor hero, the pursuit of justice, the triumph of the weak over the powerful: such is the stuff of folktales.[1] And indeed, the synopsis above is that of a Lorraine version of a universal folktale (Aarne-Thompson type 1583), known as "The Youth and His Pig."[2] The matrix, or invariant, of the tale: a have-not is cheated by the powerful, then avenges himself three times, using three different masks. Other versions or subtypes are found in Breton ("The Monks and the Poor Lad"), in Kirghiz ("Eschigueldi"), and in Norwegian ("The Boy Who Wanted to Be a Merchant"). The stories present several variants. The initial disguise is often that of a carpenter, for instance. In Norway, the hermit monk is a pastor. But the invariants remain the peasant, the sale of an animal, and three disguises.

What happens when a sophisticated medieval author decides

to change this folk material into something that will suit the tastes of a thirteenth-century audience, well versed in the latest literary trends? Douin de Lavesne rewrites the folktale in his thirteenth-century *Trubert*, with two important substitutions: a new kind of hero and a new set of tricks.[3] The central character has been re-colored as a trickster.[4] Consequently, the moral intention of the narrative has been utterly transformed. Justice does not prevail, even though the weak triumph over the powerful. The three masks no longer correspond to a three-part vengeance. The restitution of money wrongfully gained no longer motivates the protagonist's actions. The masking has become tricking, an end in itself. Furthermore, the tricks are of an extremely obscene and unusually violent nature—far more violent, dirty, and cruel than the tricks of the fabliaux, the *Roman de Renart,* or other medieval trickster stories. Sexuality is now linked with cruelty. The pig in the first version, a reference to peasant life and rural economy, has become a goat, a medieval symbol of lechery.[5]

In the folktale, the struggle for justice organizes the story, and the happy ending fulfills the reader's expectations of narrative closure. The poor boy is wronged: a figure of power and authority bilks him of his pig. In the Lorraine version recorded by Emmanuel Cosquin, the authority figure is a monk. The poor boy refuses to be cheated, and works both to right a wrong and to obtain vengeance. When the youth recovers his money, he punishes his persecutor by taking additional payment and by pummeling him three times. Thus the story satisfies the reader artistically, with its neat closure, and emotionally: the good peasant family can survive as the evil bachelor hermit succumbs. Nature reclaims its rights over culture; the savage *cru* asserts its power over the civilized *cuit.*[6] *Trubert,* though ostensibly telling the same story, does not provide a similarly uplifting ideational structure. Trubert is no little David, saving his people from the Philistines. There are narrative elements which could lead us to that interpretation at the start of *Trubert,* but the text eschews that possibility and guides the audience to quite another conclusion.

I have been using the term *trickster* to describe the new hero. Literary critics adopt the term and the concept from anthropology and psychology. Both sly and stupid, a figure of cruelty and of lib-

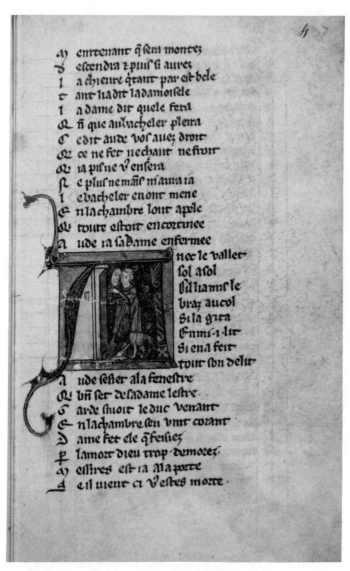

8. Trubert exacts payment from the duchess of Burgundy for the striped goat. BN Fr. 2188, fol. 4v.

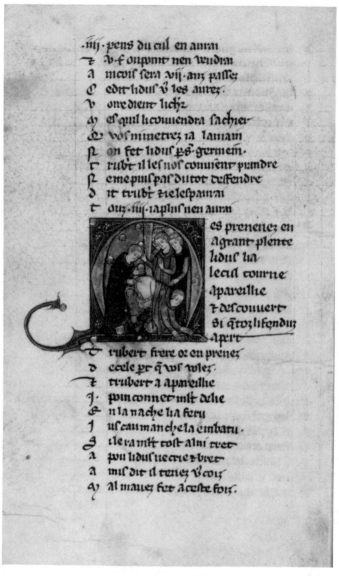

9. Trubert exacts payment from the duke of Burgundy for the striped goat. BN Fr. 2188, fol. 5v.

eration, the trickster acts on and acts out the traits repressed in the conscious personality of society.[7] The trickster is the collective unconscious that is inimical to boundaries. He is notorious for his infinite disguises, his insatiable hunger, his unbridled sexuality, and his scatological obsessions. Obeying no rules, the trickster refuses the constraints of established society; in so doing he renders helpless those who obey the rules and subscribe to society's values.[8] Furthermore, the trickster represents the life of the body, the sphere that a strict social order constantly attempts to control.

In literature the trickster functions, as Karl Kerényi describes it, "to render possible, within the fixed bounds of what is permitted, the experience of what is not permitted."[9] Like the trickster, Trubert is an amoral figure of disorder, a breaker of rules, and an exponent of the life of the body. Trubert is also a trickster in that he is oblivious, an unconscious fool, yet at the same time a masterful manipulator of disguises. Trubert punishes the powerful and unleashes the repressed sexual drives of the community but appears to act without reflection.

The recasting of the hero brings in its wake a change in lexicon. Common narrative syntagms are not necessarily the crucial element upon which the audience relies in comparing texts or stories. We do not read for plot alone; we also read vocabulary. Contrary to traditional assumptions, which hold that a reader gives priority to the narrative and quickly skims the descriptive, we realize here that as readers we look to the lexicon in order to determine what we will make of the text. We quickly seek out the semic cornerstones that tell us whether the story will be comic or tragic, religious or bawdy, moral or sentimental. We instinctively note whether the text says "peasant" or "knight," "farm" or "castle," "feat" or "trick," "love" or "goat." And we rely heavily on those initial signs, allowing them to guide our reading and interpretation of the ensuing story. In short, it is often the language, not the narrative, that tells the tale.

Audigier, with its scatological lexicon and its epic structure, offers an example of the importance of vocabulary to the reader. In many texts, the apparent difference between "unrelated" traditions is a difference of vocabulary. We think, for example, of the Tristan texts as wholly unrelated to the *Roman de Renart* texts. Yet, as Nancy Regalado has ably demonstrated, they actualize

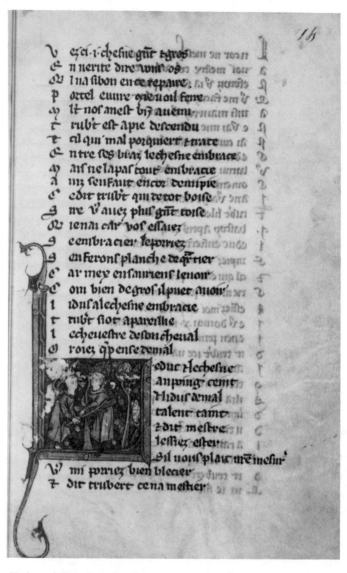

10. Trubert, disguised as a carpenter, ties the duke of Burgundy to a tree and administers a beating. BN Fr. 2188, fol. 14r.

nearly identical narrative structures.[10] We give the same events an utterly different interpretation because the vocabulary of each suggests a different genre tone, constructs a different reader. Thus, while the critics of *Audigier* pen indignant statements couched in terms of esthetic or moral judgment, such responses merely obey the scatological vocabulary in the most predictable fashion; they fall into step with the project of *Audigier*, which is to shock. Furthermore, *Audigier* exemplifies the story that is read not for plot but for vocabulary.

In *Trubert* too it is the lexicon that characterizes the protagonist, showing the reader how to understand his acts. Trubert is a trickster. The text calls him "fou" and "glouton." He is filled with "guile" and "vilenie"; his actions are described by verbs such as "engignier," "boiser," "gaber."[11] The text need not offer any psychological motivations for his behavior, for they are implicit in his identity as a trickster.

Beyond considerations of lexicon and of character—areas of transgression in all medieval parodies—lies the category of space. *Trubert* functions similarly to *Fergus, Audigier,* and *Le Roman de Renart,* in that it transgressively juxtaposes two languages (one vilain, the other courtois), in that it transgressively combines two literary genres, each with a distinctive ethos or moral register, and in that the "hero" effects a series of passages between two mimetic spaces, thus illustrating the virtual tension between two spaces of the medieval imagination. *Fergus* presents a hero who makes one journey, leaving the wilds of Scotland behind forever and passing into the civilized world of King Arthur. *Audigier* presents its hero's passages between the epic space of Cocuce and the rural space of Grimberge, but Audigier and his family belong to the epic world of courtly ceremony. *Le Roman de Renart* depicts the animal hero as he moves between the rural landscape of the fable and the epic space of Noble's court, but Renart, like Isengrin and the other animals, is drawn back incessantly to the wild forest, his natural habitat. *Trubert* depicts the folk space of simple characters in ragged clothes on their way to the market, juxtaposing it to the romance world of the Duke and Duchess, a space of wealth and luxury. Unlike the other heroes, however, Trubert is caught between two spaces because he belongs to neither ethos. The trickster hero cannot remain wild in the woods (like Renart), nor can he be assimilated to the court (like Fergus). Trubert reminds us of Spider, the African trickster, who is destined to spin a web of tricks between two worlds.

Can our formal model of parody cope with this type of parodic transformation? This is no longer parody of stylistic form, but of the underlying moral purpose of the story. The dramatic change in the hero is something that would escape the structuralist grids of Genette and of Riffaterre, for Douin reaches deeper than form, style, or setting to intention, and as the intention of the hero shifts, the entire story line shifts.

Literary critics have accounted for the transgressive humor in *Trubert* by calling it a fabliau, echoing the text's own first lines.[12] Indeed, the Old French fabliau is known for its comic tricks, its representation of sexuality, and its obscene language. To the extent that *Trubert* moves from one erotic mystification to another it resembles a kind of extended fabliau. But the fabliau is not the interpretant of the *Trubert* parody. The transgressive nature of *Trubert,* a text that takes the trickster from the "indecorous" realm of fabliaux, animal fables, scatological farce, and so forth, introducing him into a "decorous" literary tradition, indicates the interpretant that rewrites the folk tale: chivalric romance. *Trubert* practices combinational transgression, joining the roles of the wily trickster and the chivalric hero.

Tricks and characters who trick constitute an identifiable tradition within decorous medieval romance. Tristan, after all, has been identified as an adulterous trickster. Chrétien's Cligès is another trickster lover and hero. In the *Roman d'Enéas,* both Paris and Dido employ deceptive strategies to achieve their ends.[13] A certain vein of chivalric romances incorporates tricks in the form of masks and disguises, a decorous way of describing tricks. Tristan dons a series of disguises: pilgrim, leper, fool, Tantris. In *Aucassin et Nicolette,* the heroine masks first as a man, then as a jongleur. *Gautier d'Aupais* relates the story of a courtois knight, Gautier, who masks as a simple domestic in order to prove his courtoisie to the lady of the castle.[14] In short, the mask is a common romance device which facilitates passages from the safe courtois space to the dangers of a foreign space. It also legitimizes trickster behavior in decorous characters, saving them from the amoral status of trickster.

"Byzantine romance" is the name loosely given to a group of twelfth- and thirteenth-century texts which often incorporate trickster-like heroes.[15] Yet these texts manage to remain within the boundaries of respectable romance, never seeming to transgress romance codes. In one of them, *Guillaume de Palerme*, the hero disguises himself in bearskins to trick the emperor of Greece and to escape with his mistress. In Raoul de Houdenc's *Méraugis de Portlesguez*, the hero is a trickster knight in an extended tale of successive disguises. Méraugis dons the mask of fool to gain admission to his ladylove. Like Trubert, Méraugis plays a transvestite scene in which he successfully parades as a coy courtly lady.[16]

The tricks, masks, erotic farce, and obscene humor of the transgressive *Trubert* all appear in a Byzantine romance composed between 1180 and 1185, Hue de Rotelande's *Ipomédon*.[17] The *Ipomédon* stands out as the interpretant of the relation between "The Boy and His Pig" and *Trubert*, as it accounts for most of the features in *Trubert* that do not belong to the folk matrix. While other texts might account for certain local features in *Trubert*, allowing specific textual elements to take on new meaning, it is in the light of *Ipomédon* that we gain the fullest understanding of the literary forces at work in *Trubert*.[18]

But *Ipomédon* is not an interpretant in the sense prescribed by our tripartite model of parody. *Ipomédon* is itself a parody. Like Douin de Lavesne, Hue de Rotelande uses folk material as a way of processing sophisticated romance material. Rather than an interpretant, in Riffaterre's sense of the word, *Ipomédon* is a *parallel* parodic text; it enables us to understand how Douin manages his folk and romance material. Studying *Ipomédon* and highlighting its differences with *Trubert* will enable us to understand the transgressive project of Douin.

Ipomédon is a gangly account (10.580 verses) of a series of adventures in which the hero, variously disguised, tries to prove his courtoisie without revealing that he is the son of a king, a true courtois by birth. Ipomédon desires to win the love of La Fière through noble deeds alone. He takes on a series of masks: cowardly huntsman, white knight, red knight, black knight, foreign mercenary, fool, and even Indian king.[19] The masks function structurally as an indefinite deferment of closure, and thematically as an expansion of the chivalric valor ethos. In *Trubert,* the masks function as a deferment of closure, too, but in an expansion of an opposing ethos, showing how vile and cruel a character can be.

If we take *Ipomédon* as the likely interpretant of *Trubert,* we gain new insights into the transformation of the folktale model and its relation to questions of literary genre. *Trubert* no longer actualizes the three-trick structure of "The Boy and His Pig" tale, or the two-trick *trompeur trompé* structure of the *Roman de Renart* branches, or even the one-trick structure of many fabliaux. In Douin's parody we find an astounding multiplication of tricks. *Trubert*'s form is that of a heaping up of tricks upon tricks, a feature determined (and explained) by its interpretant. When the simple yet clearly motivated tricks of the folktale are rewritten and redirected in a trickster romance, the result is a cascading series of tricks. Trubert is the joker, a wild-card figure whose presence in the folktale model authorizes any form and number of literary tricks adapted and adopted from Byzantine romance.

To demonstrate the wild proliferation of tricks generated by this parodic conflation of folktale and trickster romance, we will focus on one central episode (derived from one of the three initial tricks of "The Boy and His Pig") and show the way in which it spins out tricks.

In "The Boy and His Pig," the second ploy is a transvestite disguise: the boy dresses up as a girl and goes to the hermitage in order to gain access to the ailing hermit and exact payment for the stolen pig. In *Trubert,* this disguise is developed in what can be called the "Couillebaude sequence": Trubert dresses up as his sister and takes on a female identity. The sequence consists of approximately eight tricks—"approximately" because it is impossible to begin recounting this or any sequence of *Trubert* at a starting point, since every trick is interwoven with those of a preceding series. In Douin's text, the Couillebaude sequence is triggered by the Hautdecoeur or "Sir Belch" sequence, in which Trubert has disguised himself as a knight and tricked the duke of Burgundy into thinking that the enemy king has died at the hands of Trubert. In his anger at being duped, the duke sends his men to find Trubert, who attempts to save himself by dressing in his sister's clothes. So the first trick in this sequence is an effort to avoid punishment for a previous trick: Trubert dupes the soldiers into taking him (literally) for a young girl. The comic element in this first trick is the humor of the transvestite disguise: we laugh at the dull-witted soldiers who find the "girl" to be charming and carry her off to the duke's court.

The second trick in the Couillebaude *noyau* is a sexual joke. The duke and duchess declare the young peasant woman so lovely that she is assigned to be the attendant of their young daughter, Rosette. When all the damsels retire to Rosette's chamber, the false girl has the voyeurist privilege of watching the ladies-in-waiting undress:

> Les damoiseles vont couchier;
> devant leur lit sont desvestues
> et Trubert les vit toutes nues.
> (2450–52)

> The young ladies go off to bed. Before their beds they stand undressed, and Trubert sees them all quite naked.

As Jeffrey Henderson writes in *The Maculate Muse,* involuntary nakedness is a time-honored and reliable joke.[20] Douin de Lavesne avails himself of this comic resource at various points throughout *Trubert.* This particular scene satisfies the voyeurism of the audience, who identify with the hero as he contemplates a room full of naked girls all unaware of the presence of a man.

The third trick is also sexual. Young Rosette is quite taken with the travestied Trubert, who calls himself Couillebaude ("Gayballs"). Couillebaude has won the privilege of sharing Rosette's bed and tricks her into playing with his "little rabbit" every night, until Rosette becomes pregnant.

Having tricked Rosette into sexual intercourse, Trubert must now find a way of keeping his gender a secret. He consequently tricks the duke and duchess into believing that Rosette has participated in an immaculate conception and is filled with little angels. This trick is played at the expense of the Holy Ghost:

> "Par foi, dame, toute nuit vient
> a nostre lit uns colons blans;
> il m'est avis, et bien le pans,

que ce soit un angre enpanez."
(2586–89)

"By my troth, lady, every night a white dove comes to our bed; in my opinion—and I really am convinced of it—it is an angel with wings."

Coillebaude jure la mort
et quanque de Dieu puet jurer
qu'elle n'a cure de gaber.
"Mes sachiez bien, n'en doutez mie,
dou saint Espir est raemplie!
Trestoute est plaine d'angeloz."
(2596–2601)

Coillebaude swears by death, and by any part of God on which she can swear, that she is not jesting. "On the contrary, believe me, you must not doubt at all; she is filled with the Holy Ghost! She is entirely filled with little angels."

The joke here is religious, or rather sacrilegious, a strain of humor that recurs throughout *Trubert* in parodic prayers and jokes about the crucifix. Such impiety is part and parcel of the vilain stereotype. As Galpin has documented, the courtois is religious, the vilain impious.[21]

But the tricks do not stop there. Rosette, we learn, is engaged to marry the king. Having learned that their daughter has been elected by the Holy Ghost to be filled with little angels, the duke and duchess decide she is too precious to be taken from them. As a result, the lovely Couillebaude must take her place as the king's bride.

The false bride travels to the king's court. Before the wedding she must make confession to the royal chaplain. Here Trubert pulls off the fifth trick in the series, which incorporates the humor of transvestitism, nudity, anticlericalism, and violence (the comic "coups"). Beatings, tortures, genital mutilation, rape, and murder are presented as part and parcel of the general hilarity of obscene humor in *Trubert*. The trickster's triumph over the guardians of female sexuality is usually double: violence is the insult added to injury. Moreover, the tricks of violence serve to underscore the violent nature of sexual tricks. While the folktale relied on a series of three beatings to tell its tale of revenge, saving sex (in the form of the false girl who pulls a club from under her skirts) as one comic thread in the trick, the relation between the two is reversed in *Trubert*: the violence only seconds the transgressive humor of the sexual trick. Thus, in the fifth trick, Couillebaude must go to confession before marrying the king. Hoping to shock the chaplain, Trubert gleefully lifts his skirts. Douin underlines the exposure of the male organ by playing heavily on the obscene "vit":

> Trubert si a fors trait le vit,
> si que li chapelains le vit:
> "Sire prestes," ce dit Trubert,
> "vos öes ont eles teus bes?"
> Quant li prestre vit le vit grant,
> cent foiz se seigne en un tenant.
> (2693–98)
> Trubert pulled his prick out, so that the chaplain saw it. "Sir priest"—this is how Trubert talks—"does your flock have such beaks?" When the priest saw the big prick, he crossed himself a hundred times without stopping.

The chaplain shrieks. The guards arrive. Couillebaude accuses the chaplain of making sexual advances. The priest is beaten to death by the guards.

Duping the king into having his chaplain executed is not a necessary part of Trubert's narrative agenda; this violent joke typifies the gratuitous heaping up of tricks in what was once a tightly directed and motivated narrative sequence.

When Couillebaude finds herself in the king's bed, on their wedding night, she must trick her bridegroom into believing she is a virgin. Couillebaude arms herself with a purse. When the climactic moment arrives, she pulls the drawstrings in a mock deflowering, and the king faints with pain:

> "Par foi, ainz mes ne vi tel con,"
> fait li rois, "ne sai dont ce vient."
> Et Trubert qui mout bien le tient:
> "Sire, c'est un con de biais;
> sifet con ne verroiz jamais."
> (2848–52)
> "By my troth, I have never seen such a cunt," says the king, "nor do I know how such a thing can come about." And Trubert, who really has him, re-

plies: "Sire, it is a crooked cunt; you will never see another cunt made in this way."

This tranvestite trickery, in its conflation of sexual transgression and violence, reminds us of the archetypal trickster of anthropology. Trubert is not unlike the Winnebago trickster described by Kerényi: "His nature, inimical to all boundaries, is open in every direction. . . . he does not even observe the boundaries of sex. His inordinate phallicism cannot limit itself to one sex alone: in the twentieth episode he cunningly contrives to become a bride and mother—for the sake of the wedding feast and also, no doubt, for the fun of it." Kerényi continues by recalling that classical audiences relished the sight of men dressed up as brides, "as in the Casina of Plautus, or the Atellan farces of Pomponius, not to speak of similar disguises in Aristophanes."[22]

This transgression is all the more striking as medieval texts do not as a rule represent the intimate activities of royalty or the bodily functions of monarchs. They do not portray kings in the throes of passion. As Per Nykrog reveals, the fabliau genre carefully excludes any representation of royal characters. The fabliau may be recounted to august characters, but it cannot engage them in the action, and certainly not in erotic triangles: "C'est une question de style."[23] Style, by its very definition in the Middle Ages, means a strictly coded adequation between genre, social class, spatial setting, ethical behavior, and linguistic level.

How does Douin de Lavesne get away with such scandalous transgressions? He first informs his text with a historical content: vilain and courtois. Whatever the peasant achieves in the world of the courtois must be understood, therefore, in terms of medieval ideology as well as in terms of narrative structures. Douin then limits the direction of the transgressions; the tricks are always played by vilain on courtois. This is quite unlike the *Roman de Renart,* in which any character, vilain or courtois, could trick any other character. Douin mediates the extreme and offensive nature of his tricks by using them to affirm the moral hierarchy of the Middle Ages: the vilain is bad, the courtois is good.

If the sheer number of masks taken on by Trubert and by Ipomédon is surprising, even for a trickster story and for Byzantine romance, the eroticism and obscene language of the two parodies are still more unwonted. The sexual preoccupations of *Ipomédon* enable us to understand the erotic transgressions of *Trubert* and to place them in a broad literary context. A comparison of sexual language in the two parallel texts will highlight their specificity.

Ipomédon lays bare the erotic scaffolding of medieval chivalric romance. It does so periodically and gradually at first, but with increasing persistence throughout the text, building to its infamously obscene climax in the epilogue.

> Se il i ad dame u pucele
> U riche vedve u dameisele
> Ne voille creire ke jo l'ai,
> Venge la, jo li musterai;
> Ainz ke d'iloc s'en seit turné
> La chartre li ert enbrevé.
> E ço n'ert pas trop grant damages
> Se li seaus li pent as nages.
> (*Ipomédon* 10573–80)
>
> If any lady or virgin or rich widow or young woman does not want to believe that I have the charter of absolution, let her come to my house and I will show it to her; before she takes her leave, the letter will be inscribed on her, and it will not be any great shame even if the seal hangs from her ass.

Hue de Rotelande's romance disingenuously depicts the heroine as sexual object, as a body to be possessed—sooner or later, and preferably sooner—by the hero. It portrays the effort of the hero as an effort to earn an erotic treat: sexual possession of La Fière.

The portrait of the heroine instructs us in the text's libidinous project. The traditional romance portrait is highly conventional and coded, a set piece with infinite but minute variations.[24] The descriptive movement of the portrait is a descent, from head to toe. *Ipomédon* explodes the coy suggestiveness of that downward inventory. The text rewrites the traditional head-to-waist portrait, refusing to obey the rules of romance decorum:

> Quant si beaus out les membres tuz,
> K'en dites vus de cel desuz
> Ke nus apelum le cunet?

Je quit qe asez fut petitet.
Vers le rei vait, un poi ruvi,
Ki estrangement la enbeli.

(2267–72)

Seeing how all of her body parts are so beautiful, what do you say of that part down below, which we call the pussy? I think that it was quite a tiny little thing. Moving back toward the lips, it took on a slight blush, which rendered it curiously more beautiful.

Even though the narrator boldly draws our attention with the arch "K'en dites vus?" and the graphic language, modern critics have tended to ignore Hue de Rotelande's transgression.[25] Why is it that readers are so punctilious with *Audigier,* a wholly chaste text in which babies could well be brought by the stork, and so forgiving of the deliberate lubricity of *Ipomédon*? Recent revisionist studies by feminists are revealing the mystified misogyny of the representations of sexuality in medieval romance.[26]

The obscene metaphor used to describe the queen's distinctly sexual yearnings for the hero has attracted scarcely more critical attention. The narrator likens Ipomédon's body to a healing herb which the queen would like to press close to her thigh:

Cele erbe mut pres de sun flanc
Eüst mut volenters liee,
De ren ne serreit si hetee.

(5454–56)

She would most happily have moved this herb close against her thigh; nothing would have made her more ecstatic.

If the medical language were not clear enough, it is repeated in the same way in a later passage, thus overdetermining its sexual suggestiveness:[27]

Quant la reïne aveit mangé,
E li chevaler sunt drescé,
Sis druz en la chambre la meine,
Si la besa de bon' estraine;
Cument ke il fust, a la reïne,
Ffust le beser bone mecine,
Mes il le prist trestut a gabs.
Certes, jo nel fereie pas,

Einz i mettreie mut grant peine,
Tant ke tastee fust la veine
Par unt le mal si la teneit.
(5509–19)

When the queen had eaten, and the knights had risen, her lover led her into
the bedchamber, made her a present of a kiss; however, it came to pass, the
kiss was good medicine for the queen, but to him the whole thing was a
joke. Believe me, I would not take it as a joke, but would go to great lengths
until I had touched the vein that was making her ill.

The description of Ipomédon's wedding night moves pur-
posefully from the lexicon of love to a more earthy language:

Chescun de cez ad ben gardé
A autre sa virginité
Or se entreaiment tant par amur
Ke il se entrefoutent tute jur.
(10513–16)

Both of them had carefully saved their virginity for one another. Now they
love one another with such true love that they fuck one another all day.

At the very apogee of the love story, then, Hue de Rotelande ban-
dies unmistakably obscene language.

Finally we reach the epilogue, a key moment in any text. Like
Le Bel Inconnu, by Renaut de Beaujeu, *Ipomédon* closes with the
narrator's message to a female audience.[28] But where Renaut
spoke earnestly of courtly love, Hue de Rotelande speaks lech-
erously of sex. This "splendidly obscene allegory" is a caricature
of the farewell to lovers in *Tristan.*[29] Holden, *Ipomédon*'s most recent editor, notes that the reader cannot mistake the striking con-
trast between the solemn declarations of the prologue and the indecent taunting of the end, and states that it is here we can
recognize the author's true intentions. Holden lists nearly all the
instances of obscenity and erotic titillation in *Ipomédon.*[30] They
suffice to convey the transgressive nature of this supposedly
"straight" romance as contrasted to the chastity with which other
Byzantine romances depict their heroines and recount their love
stories. *Ipomédon* typifies one strain of medieval romance, in
which an erotic ethos refuses the high-minded euphemisms pre-
dominant in much twelfth-century romance.

The narrator of *Ipomédon,* a trickster in his own right, plays at covering and uncovering the sexual motivations of the courtois romance characters. Repressed preoccupations are made to break through the highly formalized paradigm at curiously regular intervals. This open acknowledgement of the life of the body in a trickster romance enables us to place the unveiling of the erotic world of the courtois in *Trubert* in a broader literary context. From reading *Ipomédon* we learn that the very presence of sexual euphemism in courtly romance invites its own reverse side, the use of obscenity.

In *Trubert* we find two types of sexual language: obscene and euphemistic. In its direct representation of erotic activities, the text alternates between vilain four-letter words and courtois metaphors. In its transgressive use of pointed obscenity, *Trubert* establishes and reaffirms a limit that it respects throughout: only the narrator and Trubert use vilains mots, or obscene language. The duke and duchess cannot bring themselves to speak in Trubert's language. The duchess, for example, when propositioned, persists in replacing the word *foutre* with *croïstre*, "to creak," "to crack," "to break," an Old French euphemism for coitus. Similarly, the duke, while bargaining over the goat, cannot bring himself to say *cul*. Nor does the chaplain use the word *vit*, although the narrator repreats it several times in Couillebaude's confession scene.

In a variant of this courtly reticence, euphemisms are placed in the mouths of courtois characters who do not understand what they are saying; their ignorance heightens the transgressive joke. During the seduction of Rosette, the innocent young girl coins her own euphemism: *cunnetiaus*, or "bunny rabbit," is a conflation of *cunet* (the diminutive form of *con*) with *conin* (a diminutive of *lapin*), adding the diminutive suffix, *-iaus*. The humor of the neologism is augmented by the length and insistence of the dialogue in which it is repeated by Rosette, who unwittingly narrates foreplay, climax, hiatus, and resumption for the laughing audience. Rosette's naïve questions and ingenuous exclamations of pleasure are tantamount to graphic depiction, and we can imagine the gestures and vocal mimicry of the medieval performer as he acted out the part of sweet Rosette:

"So what is that?"
(2485)

"What do you do with it?"
(2489)

"Would it like to come into mine?"
(2492)

It is the courtly Rosette, not the seedy Couillebaude, who expands upon the extended bunny-rabbit metaphor:

"Certes mout l'avez or bien duit,"
fet Roseite; "ja me connuit;
il ne me mort ne esgratine."
(2501–3)
"You certainly have trained him very well," says Rosette; "he already
knows who I am; he doesn't bite or scratch me."

The joke, like the obscenity, is twofold: Rosette understands neither the double significance of her words, nor the significance of
her acts. To underline her naive delight in the sexual act, Douin
extends the scene still further to show Rosette's postcoital panic:

Le vit a sesi par la teste:
il ne li joe ne fet feste.
Dis Roseite: "Ci a mal plet!
Je cuit nos li avons mal fet;
assez estoit ore plus forz,
certes je dout qu'il ne soit morz."
(2549–54)
[Rosette] seized the prick by its head. It does not greet her or play with her.
Says Rosette: "Something has gone wrong here! I think that we have hurt
him; a little while ago he was much stronger, but I am afraid that now he is
dead."

Douin de Lavesne forges the bunny-rabbit neologism not for its
discretion but as a way of heightening the transgression of directly
representing sexual acts by attributing such representation to the
young daughter of the duke. The sexual offense is multiplied by
putting the words in Rosette's sweet and pure mouth.

To better understand the nature of obscene language in *Trubert*,
we can compare this scene to an important Latin intertext,
Guillaume de Blois's *Alda*. Traditionally, one scene in the *Alda* is
commonly considered to be the "source" of the Rosette scene in

Trubert.[31] The Latin play uses the term *cauda,* a standard phallic euphemism, to tell the story of a man, travestied as a woman, in bed with a virgin. Guillaume de Blois surrounds the *cauda* euphemism with other, nonobscene euphemisms, to avoid the direct representation of sexual acts:

> Sumpta satis Pyrrus post oscula cetera sumit.
> Defloratus abit uirginitatis honor.
> (*Alda* 465–66)
> After having taken his fill of kisses, Pyrrhus took the rest, and the flower of virginity was plucked.

> Inque uoluptatem Veneris resoluta uolutat
> Secum quid sit ea cauda uel ille tumor.
> (469–70)
> While she abandons herself freely to the voluptuous pleasures of Venus, she wonders, what is this tail, this swelling?

The humor of the Latin text is in fact generated by Phyrrus's "ludicra ficta," which relates the purchase of his "cauda" at the marketplace:

> Impar erat precium pro ponderis imparitate;
> Magni magna, minor cauda minoris erta.
> Est minor empta michi, quoniam minus eris habebam.
> (495–97)
> The prices vary according to weight; large tails cost a great deal, small tails cost less. I bought a small one because I did not have a lot of money.

While Guillaume de Blois, like Hue de Rotelande at the start of *Ipomédon,* trusts to the titillation of coy euphemism, Douin de Lavesne signals and italicizes the obscenity of his graphic sexual euphemism.

One liminal scene in *Trubert* incorporates both types of language, obscene and euphemistic, and their mediation through and of vilain and courtois. When Trubert wishes to pass himself off as Couillebaude at the court of Burgundy, he changes not only his clothes, but his language as well.[32] It is no longer he who uses obscene language. To mask as a courtois character, he must appear to be uncomprehending of direct obscenities. Yet, trickster that he is, Trubert cannot resist using the sexual travesty as an occasion for obscene euphemism. When the duchess's lady-in-waiting asks his name, Trubert forges a scandalous name that hints at his true gender:

> "Comment avez vos non?" fet Aude.
> "Dame, en m'apele Coillebaude."
> Quant Aude l'ot si en a ris
> et toutes les autres ausis.
> "Comment? comment? dites encor!"
> (*Trubert* 2403–7)
> "What is your name?" asks Aude. "My lady, people call me Gayballs."
> Upon hearing the name Aude laughed aloud, and all the other ladies as well.
> "What? What? Say it again!"

The false courtoise pretends to be shocked by the prurient titters of the well-bred ladies:

> "Par foi, je nel dirai plus or;
> je voi bien que vos me gabez!"
> (2408–9)
> "I swear, I will not say it anymore. I see clearly that you are making fun of me!"

Another of the ladies, Dame Coutance, then instructs the tittering ladies in the proprieties of courtly language:

> "Entre vos ainsi l'apelez;
> quant i avra autre mesnie,
> si ait non dame Florie."
> (2418–20)
> "Among yourselves you can call her that; but when other household members are about, let her be called Lady Flowery."

To become courtoise, the obscene "Couillebaude" must be transformed to a flowery euphemism, "Florie." Through language, the trickster has managed to transgress another rule of propriety, and the text must mediate that transgression through this transparent fiction. The game of the text is to allow its audience to hear the obscenity and to witness the transgression. Douin de Lavesne corrects the obscene "mistake" only once it has occurred, thus underlining the error, and doubling the pleasure of the audience. The group of courtly ladies-in-waiting who hear "Gayballs" and cry out "Say it again!" is an inscription of the implied audience of the text, an audience that exults in hearing the repetition of vilains mots which it cannot use but can enjoy, thanks to the trickster vilain. The obscene lexicon of *Trubert* reveals the systematic playing with the limits and taboos of language and social class, language and moral decency, language and literary genre.

Such was not the case in *Audigier*. In comparing these two parodies, we discover a distinct difference between scatological vilains mots and obscene vilains mots, a difference that remains noticeable in the twentieth century. While it is difficult to make any general or theoretical pronouncement as to whether scatology is less offensive than obscenity, or vice versa, it is possible to make the following empirical observation: *Audigier* is a text that can be summarized and told to a variety of audiences, in its entirety, while *Trubert* contains certain passages and episodes that are scarcely repeatable. The epic parody is almost child's play, and while it may offend an audience it would do so by virtue of its "juvenile" humor. Douin's obscene parody reaches the limits of what can and cannot be told, and many of its scenes could be summarized only with some discomfort on the part of teller and listener. *Audigier* can be repeated in baby-talk; one could substitute infantile language for the scatological vocabulary. The teller could be castigated for puerility but not for immorality. There is, however, no safe substitute language in which to recount the scenes of castration, cuckolding, sexual mutilation, and defloration in *Trubert*. It reads like a catalogue of dirty jokes and is informed by all the violence that dirty jokes can contain.[33] It is here that we touch upon the element that sets *Trubert* apart from the other parodies studied: its violence. The force of the *Trubert* transgression lies in the brutal nature of its tricks. While the most violent act of *Audigier* occurs when Grimberge sits on the hero's face to perform a scatological indignity, *Trubert* represents the gamut of cruel crimes, from rape to castration and murder. This violence is inextricably interwoven with obscene language. In *Trubert* violence is obscene, and obscenity is violent. Further, Douin crosses the *garde-fou* of class lines, which usually contain brutality by depicting it among the lower classes. The author heightens the text's transgressiveness by placing obscene violence in the world of dukes, duchesses, and kings.

Douin de Lavesne has been patiently working his way to a

transgressive crescendo throughout the text. And once inside the king's bedroom, Douin heaps up still more trickery. After the mock deflowering, and having convinced the king that she is a virgin, Couillebaude tricks him into believing that she must leave the bed:

> "Sire, je me vueil relever
> por pissier, que mestier en ai."
> Dit li rois: "Avec vos irai."
> "Sire, ce seroit vilenie,
> Se m'en creez, n'i venroiz mie."
>
> Li rois une cordelle prent,
> au pié li lie estroitement.
> (2874–80)
> "Sire, I want to get up and pee; I really need to go." Says the king: "I will go
> with you." "Sire, that would be naughty, believe me. Don't come along."
> The king takes a string and ties it tightly to her foot.

Not content with one false bride, Douin must introduce a second one. In the final development of the sequence, Trubert goes to the antechamber, where he tricks a serving-girl into believing that he is the king, deflowers her, ties the string to her toe, and sends her back to the king's bed:

> "Demain vos ferai coroner,
> de mon reaume serez dame;
> onques ne fu si riche fame!"
> "Sire," dit ele, "grant merciz!"
> (2978–81)
> "Tomorrow I will have you crowned queen; you will be the reigning lady of
> my kingdom. Never was there such a rich woman as you will be!" "Sire,"
> says she, "thank you so much!"

In *Trubert* we see the king in his bed, and sexually engaged, first with a vilain, then with a serving-girl. And at that very point, the text ends:

> Atant est li rois endormiz
> et la damoisele avec lui.
> Braz a braz se dorment andui.
> (2982–84)

Thereupon the king fell asleep, and the damsel with him. Arm in arm the two of them sleep.)[34]

The thirteenth-century parody comes to a close because its episodic structure must find some form of closure. Trickster romance shares at least one property in common with trickster narrative and romance: both are endless. The accumulation of tricks is the goal of trickster literature; endless wandering is the goal of romance.[35] Having guided the audience along this cascade of tricks to the climactic point of every folktale, which is to say marriage, and of every romance, which is to say a coronation and royal wedding, Douin can lay down his pen in a virtuoso triumph. Douin de Lavesne has transgressed the rules of social, moral, and literary adequation, has even duped and "castrated" the king before an audience for whom authority is held to be tutelary;[36] he must seek a resolution that is appropriate from a literary or generic viewpoint. *Trubert* mediates its final transgression (castrating the king) and ends its (potentially unending) trickster story by introducing the traditional happy end of the folktale tradition: the king has found a bride. Douin cleverly pirouettes away from the tension generated by the encounters of vilain and courtois, handily devising a conclusion that is aesthetically acceptable, because from a formal viewpoint it is true to its folk matrix, and yet transgressive still, because it sustains the social oxymoron it has repeated throughout: the vilain and courtois embracing:

Arm in arm, the two of them sleep.

How fitting that this text should close on a bedroom scene, as sex is the *vis comica* of Douin de Lavesne's parody. In the late-thirteenth-century manuscript of *Trubert,* the scenes chosen for illustration in the capitals are the scenes of sexual trickery (see Figs. 8, 9, and 10).[37] Indeed, to speak of *Trubert,* today as in the thirteenth century, is to speak of sexual obscenity.

In its predilection for the unseemly, *Trubert* can well be described as "drastic entertainment," an expression used by Kerényi to refer to the point at which archaic mythology passes over into scatological comedy.[38] Douin de Lavesne's unclassifiable text explores all manner of formal and ideational transgression: parodic combinations and juxtapositions of social, ethical, spatial, and linguistic codes. *Trubert* toys with most of the forms of transgression we have seen in *Fergus, Audigier,* and the *Roman de Renart*.[39] In fact, a brief summary reveals that *Trubert* incorporates more transgressive material than the other parodies. Douin manages to include the heroic failure of *Fergus* and *Audigier*; the trickster behavior of the hero of the *Roman de Renart*; the vilains mots of *Audigier* and the *Roman de Renart*; the scatological jokes of *Audigier* and the *Roman de Renart*; the humor of sexual violence of the *Roman de Renart*; the kitchen humor of *Fergus* and *Audigier*; the transgressive preoccupation with money of *Fergus*; and the anticlerical humor of *Audigier* and the *Roman de Renart*.

Such a heaping up of drastic transgressions might lead a modern audience to view *Trubert* as a subversive text. Does this scene in which the king and the serving-girl sleep peacefully together authorize us to read this thirteenth-century parody as a revolutionary text? Manoine, Badel, and Amaury Duval, among other critics, have interpreted the acts of Trubert as the acts of a progressively enlightened good conscience, culminating in the final bedroom trick, which they unde ʌ̣ʌ̣ʌ̣ʌd as beneficial to society.[40] While it might be so in a nineteenth-century novel, it is anachronistic to say that the substitution of a deflowered servant is a high-minded act in a thirteenth-century text. Trubert's final gesture is as roguish as any of his earlier tricks. Douin de Lavesne's parody is neither a radical cry for social revolution nor a scandalous call to sexual revolution. Douin's text was not banned or censored, it remained popular throughout the Middle Ages, and its manuscript has been handed down to the twentieth century. From this we infer that *Trubert* was not a heretical or revolutionary text. The ideological status of the transgressions in *Trubert* is a complex one, and to understand it we must inquire into the meaning of transgression in medieval French literature.

In my initial presentation of the Vergilian wheel, I pointed out the strict medieval adequation of literary genres, ethical hierarchies, social-class categories, rhetorical registers, stylistic levels, and spatial configurations. I stated that vilain and courtois are literary characters, not representations of social reality, and that the transgressive representations of vilain and courtois in these parodies are not sociopolitical but literary.

But to say "literary" is not to imply "value-free," or purely formal. Medieval literature is by definition ethical, and therefore ideological.[41] Indeed, if the literary characters of vilain and courtois have one fundamental underlying signification it is a moral one. To speak of *Trubert* as a text filled with literary transgressions is not to say that those transgressions fall shy of any ideological meaning. By virtue of the fact that Douin de Lavesne deliberately transgresses the codes and norms of the Vergilian wheel, he transgresses the medieval law of hierarchy.

What is the meaning of Douin's transgressive parody? While parody is a transgression, a "crossing over" by its very definition (*para-odios*), it is also, in medieval literature, conservative. Even *Trubert* has a conservative side. It is a reappropriation of older literary traditions.[42] In subverting the authoritarianism of the Vergilian wheel, *Trubert* recognizes and incorporates that very authority.[43] This is what Kristeva called parody's principle of "law anticipating its own transgression."[44] *Trubert*'s wild transgressions are authorized by the rules they break and the norms they mock; conversely, *Trubert* guarantees the ongoing existence of those norms and rules. In the very act of drawing on anterior models and established paradigms, Douin's *Trubert* enjoys authorization and legitimacy. Douin challenges but also pays homage to law and hierarchy. "Parody is the custodian of the artistic legacy, defining not only what art is, but where it has come from."[45]

We have seen the ways in which real and symbolic empowerment play off of one another in medieval parody. In closing this final chapter, let us look once more at the various parodic treatments of the literary paradigm of chivalry.[46] In *Fergus*, the mockery of the hero's accession to chivalry is mild. Fergus sports rusty armor and vilain weapons, but he rides and fights with great success. Fergus is an ignorant rustic, but he is not an unmitigated failure, and he eventually becomes a king.

Fergus may have the misfortune of being suited up by a vilain in Scotland, but Audigier is dubbed on a dungheap, in the scatological land of Cocuce. When Audigier rides out to punish his first opponent, a peasant hag named Grimberge, he fails to display equestrian skill and falls into a hedge, where he hangs for hours until the wind blows him to the ground. And although Fergus looked silly throwing a rock at a harmless statue, Audigier is ludicrous when he takes revenge on the hedge in question:

Isrieement s'en vait vers le buisson
Si a coupez trois ronces et un chardon;
molt s'est bien esprouvez li gentius hom.
(251–53)

Angrily he sets off toward the hedge, and cut from it three brambles and a
thistle; well did he prove himself the noble man.

Whereas Fergus quickly triumphs over the loathsome hag at Dunostre Castle, Audigier, pitted against another hag and her three daughters, struggles gallantly but is defeated three times. The ignominy of the three separate failures is measured by three correspondingly ignominious scatological punishments. Briefly, though Audigier is a courtois character with an undeniable knowledge of the rules of chivalry, and though his failure seems more drastic, and transgressive, he remains a courtois count to the end.

Sir Renart, Noble's unfaithful subject, is such an accomplished knight that he and his mount become one, quite literally. Though an animal, Renart is perfectly skilled in chivalry.

In *Trubert,* the vilain hero makes an appearance in the role of Hautdecoeur. Sir Belch is knighted by the duke of Burgundy himself, in the solemnity of mass in the duke's chapel. Unlike that of Fergus, Trubert's armor is truly vermillion, not rusty. Unlike that of Audigier, Trubert's horse is a handsome steed, not a scrawny nag. The chief transgression, in Douin's version of the hero's knighting, is Trubert's unwillingness to ride a horse:

Trubert s'en ist parmi la porte
de la vile et vint au sentier;
grant paor a de trebuchier,
(*Trubert* 1822–24)

Trubert rides forth through the gate of the city and reaches the road; great is
his fear of falling off.

Not only can this vilain not ride, but he also cannot see; the visor of his helmet has fallen, and the helmet has slipped around his eyes:

Mauveisement li fu fermez
ses hiaumes qui li est tornez;
par derrier en sont li oillier,

les eulz samble qu'il ait derrier!
(1843–46)

His helmet was not properly closed, and slipped around; the visor has
slipped behind, and he seems to have eyes in the back of his head!

Paradoxically, whereas Count Audigier's comic ineptitude caused
him to lose to a peasant woman, Trubert's uncontrolled riding,
backwards helmet, and clanking shields bring about a comic victory by causing the enemy army to let the hero flee unharmed. In
fact, the backwards helmet functions as yet another trickster
mask. It remains a mask to the end of the scene; Trubert never
learns to ride, and never shows his face.

In each of the four parodies, we find the same comic archetype,
caricaturally distorted in different ways. None of these transgressive parodies of the cultural icon of chivalry is a direct or literal
comment on contemporary society, yet each reflects in its own
way the fact that the institution of knighthood finds itself in crisis
from the second half of the twelfth century.

All this literary fooling around, all these *vilains mots,* all this
transgressive crossing of class lines was tolerated, and enjoyed, in
the Middle Ages. Even *Trubert,* with its obscenity and violence,
engendered literary progeny: in the fourteenth century Eustache
Deschamps was to write the *Farce de Maître Trubert.*[47] Trubert's
very name became a household word in the late Middle Ages. *Trubert* evolves, in the course of the fourteenth and fifteenth centuries, into a common noun and adjective, meaning "a debauched
man," "debauched."[48] Thus medieval culture accepts and contains the figure of the violent trickster who poses as a knight. The
very word *trubert* comes to constitute a marker of limits, the limit
after which excess becomes transgression.

CONCLUSION

The use of a postmodern theoretical model conceived of to account for modern parody affords new and greater purchase on medieval parody, and especially because of the questions and difficulties raised by the use of such a model. Some readers may be surprised at the choice of a semiotic linguistic model, which was developed for use with literary texts. Yet the triadic model of text, intertext, and interpretant renders an astonishingly accurate account of the triple nature of medieval parody. For, as we have seen, medieval culture was everywhere informed by the idea of the semiotic trinity and by triadic paradigms.

Furthermore, the four parodies on which I have focussed effected their own, specifically medieval corrections of the theoretical model. The medieval texts teach us that intertextuality always contains a historical dimension, however universal the literary nature of parody. Intertextuality is, of course, quite distinct from the business of dating sources and influences. Nevertheless, intertextuality does not function in a historical vacuum; its manifestations are always marked by the time, place, and subjects that create them. We see examples of this in all of our parodies, for they rely heavily on the French medieval figures of vilain and courtois to produce their comic distortions of matrix texts.

As for the intertext, our medieval parodies have allowed us to define it differently than do modern critics, and that is for historical reasons. Most studies of parody have attempted to explicate nineteenth- and twentieth-century texts, and have posited the existence of a single intertext motivating any given parody. But the literature of the modern period is a literature dominated by the notion of originality: the original author, the original text. The twelfth and thirteenth centuries give less thought to personal invention, and far more thought to tradition and its reworking across the ages. Thus, in medieval parody the intertext is not likely to be a single work signed by a particular author, but rather, a central and identifiable literary tradition. An example of this can be seen in Guillaume le Clerc's *Fergus,* a parody in which the intertext is the epic tradition of the chanson de geste and, more specifically, of one traditional character in the Old French chanson de geste: Rainouart au Tinel.

The notion of the interpretant contributes richly to the study of medieval parody, for it explains the ever-varying parodic manifestations of one genre or one theme. All parodies of medieval romance obey the same structural rules, yet each is quite unique. All the texts studied here play on the same thematic of vilain and courtois, yet each does so in different ways. What can explain the wealth of this comic vein? The fact that parody is not simple structural overturning (high to low, or low to high) but the complex rewriting of the intertext through the interpretant. So, with respect to the interpretant, the medieval texts again made their own comment, as it were, on the postmodern model. The interpretant in the Middle Ages can itself be a parody or the parody of a literary tradition, as we found in the case of Hue de Rotelande's *Ipomédon,* the parodic interpretant of Douin de Lavesne's *Trubert.*

In describing transgressive parody, I spoke first of formal or literary transgression. By this I meant texts that break the rules of genre, or rather disobey the medieval adequation of genre and several corresponding areas: character, setting, lexicon, rhetorical level, stylistic register, and moral ethos. In medieval literature of the twelfth and thirteenth centuries, each genre is assumed to adhere to a certain level of social class, of language, of subject matter. The best-known paradigm that illustrates this adequation is the Vergilian wheel. Medieval parody is transgressive to the extent that it practices inappropriate or unwonted combinations and juxtapositions. In *Fergus,* for example, Guillaume le Clerc juxtaposes romance love scenes with burlesque food fights. *Le Roman de Renart* juxtaposes animal fables with lofty epic battle charges. Aristocratic characters are combined with scatological lexicon in *Audigier.* In *Trubert* Douin de Lavesne combines episodic trickster tales with the setting of Byzantine romance.

The examination of medieval texts teaches us that parody is not a purely formal practice. If the semiotic model of medieval parody is triple, accounting for its text, intertext, and interpretant, parody is triple in another way, also: formal, ideological, and historical.

Parody is not without an ideological dimension. The parodic text always bears a relation to the cultural text of its day: a relation of questioning, mockery, transgression, or opposition. Even though parody's purpose is not to criticize society, it nonetheless has a discursive status, and as discourse it cannot remain neutral but enters into the discursive production that is ideology.

The stuff of which literary transgression is made appears to be universal and age-old. Five recurring areas of study emerged from our medieval parodies. All five areas of comic literary transgression can be found in the theater of Aristophanes or Plautus, of Shakespeare or Molière, the texts of Cervantes, Voltaire, or Swift. They do not constitute formal categories only. They also reveal the point at which formal transgression is inextricably intertwined with ideological transgression, for they all represent cultural taboos that have existed and remain very much alive in many societies. It is impossible to draw a neat line dividing the fictional from the historical, the artistic from the social: all of those discourses participate in the structure of ideology.

Language taboos, bearing on the rhetorical level of the text parodied, are transgressed most commonly through the use of obscene and scatological language, as in *Trubert* and *Audigier*. Rhetorical level can also be broken down by combining hostile insults with decorous romance diction, as we see in *Fergus*.

Dietary taboos, or questions of culinary etiquette, appear frequently in transgressive texts: gluttony, scatophagy, food fights—all are popular tools for parodic rewriting of traditional models. Food taboos take center stage in *Fergus* and in *Audigier*.

Sexual taboos are equally common sources of transgression: adultery, cloacal intercourse, homosexuality, and sexual relations between members of different social classes constitute age-old fields of literary play. These sexual taboos are underscored most heavily in *Trubert*.

Trickery is an infraction of the moral ethos of many high-minded literary genres. Masks, disguises, and fraud of all sorts constitute the obvious transgression of romance and epic models in *Le Roman de Renart* and *Trubert*.

Finally, violence, and violent acts of humiliation, often linked to sexual taboos, are as familiar to transgressive comic literature as they are ancient. Beatings, rape, castration, sodomy, and murder are moral taboos that seem to provoke laughter when used in the "safe" domain of parodic literature. Their staging, combined with or juxtaposed to the serious features of the traditional target text, signal the presence of parody.

Transgressive literature is found throughout the Middle Ages in France, and seems to have been both tolerated and cultivated. The Middle Ages have often been misrepresented as a time of monolithic fear of and respect for cultural law. Our study of parody belies the image of simple medieval men and women quaking in the face of all authority, both worldly and divine. Irreverence, intelligence, rebellion, and fun are hallmarks of our texts, their authors and audiences.

Although the transgressions studied verge on the unacceptable because of the very serious taboos with which they toy, they are, to a greater or lesser extent, handily mediated in medieval literature. The use of animal characters is one method of mediating serious transgressions, as in the *Roman de Renart*. One of the most common forms of narrative mediation is that of the happy ending, and in particular the use of a marriage as closure. Marriage closes *Fergus, Audigier,* and *Trubert*. It is the poet's way of reassuring the audience that all the naughtiness was in good fun, and that all is well that ends well in any fictional tale. This recuperative closure is of course complicated in *Trubert,* in which the "marriage" is the dubious and fraudulent coupling of king and serving-girl; it is not without significance that Douin de Lavesne alone cannot desist from his compulsive trickery and stops on a transgressive note, only partially mediated by the suggestion of a forthcoming marriage. In short, the manner in which ideological transgressions are handled varies widely in medieval parody. Guillaume le Clerc's *Fergus* stands as an affirmation of the cultural law, while Douin de Lavesne's *Trubert* firmly establishes the borders of law and the limits of decency, only to claim the status of outlaw for itself.

Many mines of literary transgression are as old as they are deep. Five have just been highlighted as they appear in our parodies. There are, however, other fields of transgression, equally common in our medieval texts, that do not date from time immemorial but are favored subjects in the cultural text of France in the late twelfth and thirteenth centuries. Five popular themes or configurations recur in our parodies. Their transgressiveness is historically specific: interclass marriage, peasant land-holding, peasant wealth, interclass conflict, and the institution of knighthood.

Marriage between members of different social classes, and particularly between wealthy peasants and daughters of impoverished noblemen, becomes a frequent narrative arrangement in comic literature of this period. The issue is explicit in *Fergus,* and implicit in *Trubert.* Historical records show that such interclass marriages were not rare by any means. Parody thus draws on current social questions and tensions, just as it avails itself of archetypal comic themes, in order to rewrite literary tradition.

The phenomenon of peasant land-holdings is mentioned overtly and in a fairly detailed manner in *Fergus, Audigier,* and the *Roman de Renart.* The literary image of the peasant who apes the noble lord of the manor points to a historically specific political situation, the result of changing patterns in prosperity and taxation in thirteenth-century France. In much the same way, the issue of peasant wealth is a source of humor in *Fergus* and in the *Roman de Renart;* the character of the *riche vilain* makes its appearance in French literature at the precise moment that a growing portion of the peasantry had become affluent.

Hostile interclass conflict is a ready source of parodic distortion in *Audigier, Le Roman de Renart,* and *Trubert.* From the very outset, parodists had enjoyed burlesquing epic battle scenes. In the Middle Ages, the literary representation of hostility between *vilain* and *courtois* offers a perfect vehicle for transforming serious epic charges into bathetic comedy.

Finally, the institution of knighthood itself offers the richest vein of humor to the parodist of twelfth- and thirteenth-century France. As a joke it is clearly contextualized: it flourishes during the decades in which the institution of chivalry is in material crisis and must decide whether to open its doors to the lower classes. The ridiculously inept knight appears to be a constant and stable source of parodic distortion in most of the comic literature of the period, and especially in Old French parody.

The pervasive presence of these five themes clearly demonstrates the contextual nature of parody, or rather the parodist's desire to draw on social reality as a vehicle for his literary game. But despite his references to social reality and to history, the parodist is not to be confused with the satirist. While the latter draws on literary paradigms to effect a critique of society, the former mines the social context in order to play his joke on literature. The satirist quarrels with real empowerment (or disenfranchisement), while the parodist toys with the relation between images of real and symbolic empowerment and disenfranchisement.

Guillaume le Clerc, Douin de Lavesne, and the anonymous authors of the *Roman de Renart* and *Audigier* take up the contradictions of twelfth- and thirteenth-century feudalism in order to polarize their characters and shape their parodic rewriting. Transgressive parody in medieval France constitutes a form of cultural play that seems to be an integral part of that society. Rather than posing a direct threat to social-class structures or to feudal institutions, transgressive parody participates in the composition of the identity of these structures and institutions. Medieval culture expresses and defines itself in these comic texts. In literary parody, medieval society stages its own tensions, rehearses its own dilemmas, and plays with its own worst fears.

Scholars have examined the distant Middle Ages, the autumnal Middle Ages, the Middle Ages of sorrow and persecution. It is to be hoped that we can now become better acquainted with the laughter and play of medieval culture.

NOTES

INTRODUCTION

1. See Eugene Vance, *Mervelous Signals: Poetics and Sign Theory in the Middle Ages* (Lincoln: University of Nebraska Press, 1986), for an invaluable study of Augustine's poetics and its relation to medieval French literature.

2. Jean Daniélou, *From Shadows to Reality: Studies in the Biblical Typology of the Fathers,* trans. Wulston Hibberd (London: Burns & Oates, 1960). See also Fredric Jameson, *The Political Unconscious: Narrative as a Socially Symbolic Act* (Ithaca: Cornell University Press, 1981), pp. 30–31.

3. Georges Duby, *Les trois ordres; ou, l'imaginaire du féodalisme* (Paris: Gallimard, 1978).

4. The model is from Edmond Faral, *Les arts poétiques du XIIe et du XIIIe siècle* (Paris: Champion, 1971), p. 87, reproduced by permission of Editions Slatkine. In each of the concentric circles are found the indication of social status, proper names, instruments, residence, and plants that can be attributed to the characters appropriate to each of the three styles.

5. Perhaps the work of Saint Augustine best expresses this feature of medieval epistemology, and especially his *Confessions,* trans. R. S. Pine-Coffin (New York: Viking, Penguin Books, 1961), and *On Christian Doctrine,* trans. D. W. Robertson, Jr. (New York: Bobbs-Merrill, 1958).

6. Augustine, *Confessions* XIII.24, pp. 336–37.

7. Paul Lehmann, *Die Parodie im Mittelalter* (Stuttgart: Hiersemann, 1963). Philippe Ménard, *Le rire et le sourire dans le roman courtois en France au moyen âge* (Geneva: Droz, 1969), provides a useful catalogue to romance parody but does not offer any definitions of parody or satire. Armand Strubel, "Le rire au moyen âge," in *Précis de la littérature française du moyen âge,* ed. Daniel Poirion et al. (Paris: PUF, 1983), pp. 186–213, devotes four pages to parody, and several more to satire. The bibliography on medieval satire dwarfs the list of works on medieval parody. See also Hans Robert Jauss, Erich Köhler, et al., *Grundriss der Romanischen Literaturen des Mittelalters,* 13 vols. (Heidelberg: Carl Winter, 1968–70).

8. *Aucassin et Nicolette,* ed. Mario Roques (Paris: Champion, 1975). For a summary of the debate, see the work of Tony Hunt, "Precursors and Progenitors of *Aucassin et Nicolette*," *Studies in Philology* 74 (January 1977): 1–19, and "La parodie médiévale: Le cas d'Aucassin et Nicolette," *Romania* 100 (1979): 341–81.

9. Mikhail Bakhtin, *Rabelais and His World,* trans. Helene Iswolsky (Cambridge: MIT Press, 1968). Bakhtin's study has given rise to a term and a marked trend in literary criticism: "carnivalization" is used widely to describe texts, medieval or modern, in which one finds reversions, inversions, or disguises.

10. R. Howard Bloch has demonstrated this ably with respect to the medieval fabliau, in *The Scandal of the Fabliaux* (Chicago: University of Chicago Press, 1986).

11. Sigmund Freud, *Jokes and Their Relation to the Unconscious,* in *The Standard Edition of the Complete Psychological Works of Sigmund Freud* (London: Hogarth Press and the Institute of Psychoanalysis, 1953–74), 8:201.

12. See Gilbert Highet, *The Anatomy of Satire* (Princeton: Princeton University Press, 1962), p. 69, and Northrop Frye, *Anatomy of Criticism* (Princeton: Princeton University Press, 1957), pp. 233–35, 321–24.

13. Vladimir Nabokov, *Strong Opinions* (New York: McGraw-Hill, 1973), p. 75.

14. For an excellent presentation of structuralism, see Terry Eagleton, *Literary Theory: An Introduction* (Minneapolis: University of Minnesota Press, 1983), Ch. 3.

15. Gérard Genette, *Palimpsestes: La littérature au second degré* (Paris: Seuil, 1982), pp. 11, 8, 33–34.

16. Ibid., pp. 34–36.

17. Linda Hutcheon, *A Theory of Parody: The Teachings of Twentieth-Century Art Forms* (New York and London: Methuen, 1985), pp. 85, 21–28, 33 and 1, 35 and 97, 69–83.

18. "That for which [a sign] stands is called its *object,* that which it conveys, its *meaning*; and the idea to which it gives rise, its *interpretant.*" Charles S. Peirce, *Collected Papers* (Cambridge: Harvard University Press, 1931–58), 1:171, par. 339. See also Vance, *Mervelous Signals,* p. xi, and Umberto Eco's discussion of the interpretant in "Peirce and Contemporary Semantics," *Versus* 15, no. 4 (1976), 49–72, and idem, *A Theory of Semiotics* (Bloomington: Indiana University Press, 1976), 68–72. For further commentary on the tripartite paradigm, see Jacques LeGoff, "Note sur société tripartie, idéologie monarchique et renouveau économique dans la chrétienté du IXe au XIIe siècle," in *Pour un autre moyen âge,* pp. 80–90.

19. Michael Riffaterre, "Interpretants," in *Semiotics of Poetry* (Bloomington: Indiana University Press, 1978), pp. 81–114, and idem, "Sémiotique intertextuelle: L'interprétant," *Revue d'Esthétique*, n.s., 32 (1979): 128–50.

20. Michael Riffaterre, "La parodie à la lumière de la théorie de l'intertextualité" (Paper presented to the Colloquium on the History and Theory of Parody, Queen's University, Kingston, Ontario, 10 October 1981). Riffaterre elucidates the nature and functions of parody as a system of textual production, proposing a model of parody as triple, structured like Peirce's model of the sign: text, intertext, and interpretant.

21. Hans-Robert Jauss, "Littérature médiévale et théorie des genres," *Poétique* 1 (1970): pp. 79–101, esp. p. 92.

22. The significance of this period in sociohistorical terms has been studied at length in the work of Georges Duby and will be summarized at the end of this Introduction.

23. Paul Zumthor, *Essai de Poétique Médiévale* (Paris: Seuil, 1972), pp. 104–6.

24. On the etymology and usage of *vilain* and *courtois*, see K. J. Hollyman, *Le développement du vocabulaire féodal en France pendant le haut moyen âge: Etude sémantique* (Geneva: Droz, 1957), pp. 23, 72–77, and Glyn Sheridan Burgess, *Contribution à l'étude du vocabulaire précourtois* (Geneva: Droz, 1970), pp. 35–43.

25. Stanley Leman Galpin, *Cortois and Vilain: A Study of the Distinctions Made between them by the French and Provençal Poets of the Twelfth, Thirteenth, and Fourteenth Centuries* (New Haven: Ryder's Printing House, 1905).

26. Jean de Condé, "Des vilains et des courtois," in *Dits et contes de Baudoin de Condé et de son fils Jean de Condé* (Brussels: Auguste Scheler, 1866–67), 3:189–95. See also *Le dit sur les vilains*, by Matazone de Calignano, ed. Paul Meyer, in *Romania* 12:20–24, vv. 8–18.

27. Marcabru, *Poésies complètes du troubadour Marcabru*, ed. J. M. L. Dejeanne (Toulouse: Edouard Privat, 1909), p. 141.

28. *Gaydon,* ed. François Guessard and S. Luce (Paris: A. Frank, 1862).

29. The present openness between the fields of history and literature is examined in Brian Stock's article "History, Literature, and Medieval Textuality," *Yale French Studies* 70 (1986): 7–17. It was sketched out as early as 1977 in R. Howard Bloch's *Medieval French Literature and Law* (Berkeley and Los Angeles: University of California Press, 1977), pp. 1–12.

30. Michel Foucault, *The Archeology of Knowledge,* trans. Alan Sheridan (New York: Pantheon, 1970).

31. Georges Duby, *The Early Growth of the European Economy: Warriors and Peasants from the Seventh to the Twelfth Century*, trans. Howard B. Clarke (Ithaca: Cornell University Press, 1974), pp. 257–58.

32. Ibid., p. 168.

33. Ibid., pt. III, "Peasant Conquests: Middle of the Eleventh to the End of the Twelfth Century," pp. 155–256. For an instructive account of earlier representations of peasants, see Jacques LeGoff, "Les paysans et le monde rural dans la littérature du Haut Moyen Age (Ve–Xe siècle)," in *Pour un autre Moyen Age: Temps, travail et culture en Occident* (Paris: Gallimard, 1977), pp. 131–45, and also the classic work by Marc Bloch, *Feudal Society*, trans. L. A. Manyon (Chicago: University of Chicago Press, 1961), esp. vol. 1, pt. 5, "The Ties of Dependence among the Lower Orders of Society," pp. 241–79.

34. Guy Fourquin, *Lordship and Feudalism in the Middle Ages*, trans. Iris Sells and A. L. Lytton Sells (London: Allen and Unwin, 1976), pp. 180–81.

35. M. Bloch, "Lords and Tenants," in *Feudal Society*, 1:248–54.

36. Fourquin, *Lordship*, pp. 171–72.

37. Marie-Thérèse Lorcin, *Les campagnes de la région lyonnaise aux XIVe et XVe siècles* (Lyon: Bosc Frères, 1974).

38. Theodore Evergates, *Feudal Society in the Bailliage of Troyes under the Counts of Champagne*, 1152–1284 (Baltimore: Johns Hopkins University Press, 1975), esp. "The Peasantry," pp. 16–30, and "The Aristocracy: Counts, Lords, and Knights," pp. 96–127.

39. Duby, *Early Growth*, and also his *Le temps des cathédrales: L'art et la société*, 980–1420 (Paris: Gallimard, 1976), esp. "L'âge de raison," pp. 163–93.

40. M. Bloch, *Feudal Society*, 2:288–89, 320–25, 339–421; Guy Bois, *The Crisis of Feudalism: Economy and Society in Eastern Normandy c.* 1300–1550 (Cambridge: Cambridge University Press, 1984).

41. One of the vilain heroes discussed below, Fergus (Chapter 1) is ignorant of chivalry but is the son of a noblewoman; he learns very quickly to ride, fight, joust, and kill. Another of the heroes in the texts to be studied, Audigier, is the son of a count; he knows perfectly well how to ride and bear arms, but is a poor fighter, a coward, and loser in every battle. Yet another hero, Trubert, of pure peasant birth, can scarcely hang on to a horse's back, let alone manage a lance and shield.

CHAPTER 1: FERGUS

1. Aristotle, *Poetics*, trans. Leon Golden (Englewood Cliffs, N.J.: Prentice-Hall, 1968), pp. 4–5; Northrop Frye, *Anatomy of Criticism*, (Princeton, N.J.: Princeton University Press, 1957), p. 33.

2. Guillaume le Clerc, *Fergus*, ed. Ernst Martin (Halle: Verlag der

Buchandlung des Waisenhauses, 1872). A first, inferior edition was published in 1841 by Francisque Michel, *Le Roman des Aventures de Fregus* (Edinburgh: Abbotsford Club). Two manuscripts of the *Fergus* exist: MS. A (Musée de Chantilly 472) was copied in the second half of the thirteenth century. The dialect is Picard. The codex includes Chrétien's *Erec* and *Yvain*, the vulgate *Lancelot*, several Arthurian romances (*Rigomer, L'Atre Perilleux, La Vengeance Raguidel, Perlesvaux*) and four branches of the *Roman de Renart*. A new edition of MS. A has just appeared: *The Romance of Fergus*, ed. Wilson L. Frescoln (Philadelphia: William H. Allen, 1983). MS. P (Bibliothèque Nationale fonds français 1553) was copied in the second half of the thirteenth century as well. The codex consists of an immense and varied grouping of religious poems, romances, and a few lais and prose pieces. The dialect is Picard. This is the manuscript that was edited by Michel, with many errors and faulty readings.

3. Ernst Martin's introduction and annotations document allusions to and quotations from Chrétien. Wilhelm Marquardt, *Der Einfluss Kristians von Troyes auf den Roman "Fergus" des Guillaume le Clerc* (Diss. Göttingen University, 1906), provides an extensive and detailed catalogue of verses, characters, and narrative sequences common to both authors. See also Alois Stefan, *Laut- und Formenbestand in Guillaume Li Clers' Roman "Fergus"* (Klagenfurt: Bertschinger, 1893), and Helen Newstead, "The Besieged Ladies in Arthurian Romance," *PMLA* 62 (1948): 803–30.

4. Bakhtin, *Rabelais*, pp. 135–36.

5. Chrétien de Troyes, *Le Chevalier au Lion*, ed. Mario Roques (Paris: Champion, 1975); *Le Chevalier de la Charrette*, ed. M. Roques (Paris: Champion, 1975); *Cligès*, ed. Alexandre Micha (Paris: Champion, 1975); *Erec et Enide*, ed. M. Roques (Paris: Champion, 1973); *Le Conte du Graal*, ed. Felix Lecoy (Paris: Champion, 1975).

6. Wilson L. Frescoln, "A Study on the Old French Romance of *Fergus*" (Diss. University of Pennsylvania, 1961). Frescoln's work deals with questions of manuscripts, critical history, composition, authorship, and dialect.

7. Erich Köhler's model, which compares literary patterns to ideological projection, remains pertinent and useful: *Ideal und Wirklichkeit in der Höfischen Epik: Studien zur Form der Frühen Artus- und Graldichtung* (Tübingen: Max Niemeyer, 1956).

8. Two of the finest recent examples are E. Jane Burns, *Arthurian Fictions: Rereading the Vulgate Cycle* (Columbus: Ohio State University Press, 1985), and Matilda Bruckner, *Narrative Invention in Twelfth-Century French Romance: The Convention of Hospitality* (1160–1200) (Lexington, Ky.: French Forum, 1980). For an earlier, structuralist study, see Marie-José Southworth, *Etude comparée de quatre romans médi-*

évaux: Jaufré, Fergus, Durmart, Blancandin (Paris: Nizet, 1973). The limitation of Southworth's analysis of medieval romance is the limitation of structuralism as we judge it today. The narrative skeleton of each text is revealed exactly, but poetic modes such as irony or humor escape the formalist grid.

9. M. Schlauch, "The Historical Background of Fergus and Galene," *PMLA* 44 (1929): pp. 360–76, summarizes the debate. See also M. D. Legge, "Some Notes on the *Roman de Fergus*," in *Transactions of the Dumfriesshire and Galloway National History and Antiquarian Society* 27 (1950), and "Sur la genèse du *Roman de Fergus*," in *Mélanges de Linguistique Romane et de Philologie Médiévale offerts à Maurice Delbouille* 2 (1964): 399–408. Frescoln has presented a thorough discussion of the scholarship asserting that Soumillet was Somarled, that Fergus refers to the historical Fergus, a prince of Galloway who died in 1161, and that Fergus's great-grandson, Alan of Galloway, commissioned the romance. Frescoln judiciously shows why such suppositions are fanciful and unsubstantiated. Frescoln, "A Study," pp. 125–29.

10. Frescoln outlines the theories as to Guillaume's identity, again concluding that they are highly improbable. "A Study," pp. 114–16. All that is certain is that Guillaume wrote in Picard dialect, and also used many Francian word forms. See Stefan, *Laut- und Formenbestand,* for a discussion that remains seminal.

11. Frédéric Godefroy, *Dictionnaire de l'ancienne langue française et de tous ses dialectes du IXe au XVe siècle,* 10 vols. (Paris, 1881–1902).

12. Ernst Brugger, "The Hebrides in the French Arthurian Romances," *Arthuriana* 2 (1929–30): 7–19, and "'Pellande,' 'Galvoie,' and 'Arragoce' in the Romance of *Fergus*," in *Miscellany of Studies in Romance Languages and Literature Presented to Leon E. Kastner,* ed. Mary Williams and James A. de Rothschild (Cambridge: Heffer and Sons, 1932).

13. Arthur's court is at Caradigan, Wales, the white stag in the forest of Gorriende (thought to be Geltsdale, just east of Carlisle) near Carduel. The troupe travels into the forest of Gedeorde. Perceval goes through Landemore, which is in the forest of Glascou, then rides on to Aroie, Ayreshire. The stag is killed at Ingegal. On the following day the entourage passes by Pelande (in the Hebrides), en route to Carduel.

14. Zumthor, *Essai,* p. 104.

15. Paule Le Rider compares Rainouart, Ipomédon, Aiol, Fergus, and Audigier to Chrétien's Perceval "Le type littéraire de l'ingénu," in *Le chevalier dans "Le Conte du Graal" de Chrétien de Troyes* (Paris: SEDES, 1978), pp. 111–41. Philippe Ménard, *Le rire,* pp. 52–54, touches on these stock scenes of "l'adoubement comique" and the "combat du nice."

16. Chrétien, *Cligès,* ed. Micha, vv. 865–1041.

17. Many other examples could be cited: e.g., "Fergus s'en va par une lande, /Grande aleure chevauchant / Et aventures demandant./ Mais il n'en puet nule trover" (2537–40; Fergus sets off across the wooded land, riding at full gallop and looking for knightly adventure, but he can find none).

18. Grégoire Lozinski, *La Bataille de Caresme et de Charnage* (Paris: Champion, 1933), pp. 64, 69–70. Exclusion of food and eating is true of twelfth- and thirteenth-century romance, but by the fourteenth century, elaborate description of meals and eating is part of chivalric romance.

19. Fergus repeatedly gauges his hunger while seeking the wronged Galiene: "Tot le jor a erre ensi / C'ome ne feme ne trova / Ne qu'il ne but ne ne manga, / N'il ne s'esmaie de noient. / Ce li ert avenu sovent / Puis qu'il enprist ice voiage" (4377–82; Thus did he ride the whole day, without seeing either man or woman or drinking or eating. Nor does he become alarmed by any of this, for it had happened to him frequently since undertaking this trip).

20. The three-day tournament is a well-known Arthurian convention; see Jessie Weston, *The Three Days' Tournament: A Study in Romance and Folklore* (London: D. Nutt, 1902). *Fergus* comically undercuts each of the three days by punctuating the hero's return with food: "Apres ce commande a souper, / Que jehune ot langement. / Celes salent plus tost que vent, / Se li ont tantost aporte: / Car il estoit bien apreste" (5011–15; After which [Fergus] ordered food to be brought in, for he had fasted a long time. [The maidens] leapt to their feet and ran like the wind to bring it to him, for he was more than ready).

21. Ernst Curtius, *European Literature and the Latin Middle Ages*, trans. W. Trask (Princeton: Princeton University Press, 1953). Curtius's excursus, "Jest and Earnest in Medieval Literature," pp. 417–35, is especially relevant. See also "Kitchen Humor and Other 'Ridicula,'" pp. 431–35.

22. Curtius, *European Literature*, pp. 432–33.

23. Chrétien, *Le Conte du Graal*, ed. Lecoy, vv. 633–778.

24. On the variation in spelling Ferragus and Fernaguz, see Gaston Paris's review of Paul Gehrt, *Zwei Altfranzoesische Bruchstücke des Floovent*, in *Romania* 26 (1897): 116.

25. Ernest Langlois, *Table des noms propres dans les chansons de geste* (New York: Burt Franklin, 1904), p. 215.

26. To the extent that Guillaume le Clerc is thoroughly familiar with all Chrétien's texts, he could not have been unaware of this tradition; in *Erec,* Ferraguz, or Fernaguz, is named as the pagan giant killed by Roland.

27. In *Mainet* (twelfth century), *Renaut de Montauban* (late twelfth century), and *Doon de Maience* (thirteenth century), Galiene is a Saracen

who converts to Christianity when she marries Charlemagne. See Langlois, *Table des noms*, p. 250.

28. "Guillaume's mention of olive trees in a Scottish setting . . . is an astonishing incongruity. This caused Francisque Michel to remark that 'il est douteux que cet arbre ait jamais pu venir en Ecosse,' and Bruce parenthetically calls attention to such a geographical absurdity in his analysis: 'On approaching the Black Mountain, he ties his horse to an olive-tree (in Scotland!).'" Frescoln, "A Study," p. 170.

29. Another example: "Lur chevals laisent dedesuz un' olive" (2705; They leave their horses underneath an olive tree). *La Chanson de Roland: Edition bilingue* (Paris: 10/18, 1968), pp. 196 and 204.

30. Indeed, MS. P of *Fergus* actually mentions "Rollant." See the Michel ed., p. 33, v. 16.

31. "Gueule baee," Flohart leaps after the Christians in *Aliscans,* where she is fifteen feet tall, wears a buffalo skin, and swings her scythe (6514–61). In *La Chevalerie Vivien,* 326–37, and *Anseis de Carthage,* 5544–51, she is the unnamed "vieille à la faux." In *Fierabras,* ed. A. Kroeber and G. Servois (Paris: Anciens Poètes de la France, 1860), Amiete stands at the passage of the Mautrible bridge, "plus noire que pevree" (5039–65). See Ménard, "Portraits horrifiques," in *Le rire,* pp. 48–51.

32. Gerald Bertin, "The Burlesque Elements in Old French Epic Poetry" (Diss. Columbia University, 1953), pp. 129–81 (a chapter entitled "Heroes of Low Degree"). See also W. W. Comfort, "The Character Types in the Old French Chansons de Geste," *PMLA* 21 (1906): 279–334. Arthur Dickson refers to this character as an avatar of the wild man, in *Valentine and Orson: A Study in Late Medieval Romance* (New York: Columbia University Press, 1929), pp. 179–80. Many German dissertations were written at the turn of the century on the vilain in Old French literature, including A. Hünherhoff, *Uber die Komischen "Vilain"-Figuren der Altfranzösischen Chansons de Geste* (Marburg: R. Friedrich, 1894). Jean Rychner discusses the vilain in his *La chanson de geste* (Geneva: Droz, 1955). See again Ménard, *Le rire,* pp. 39–46, 69–78, and 168–73.

33. Curtius, "Comic Elements in the Epic," in *European Literature,* pp. 429–30; Ménard, "Le rire dans les chansons de geste," pp. 19–144.

34. Bertin, "Burlesque Elements," pp. 129–63; Ménard, *Le rire,* pp. 39–85; Johannes Runeberg, *Etudes sur la geste Rainouart* (Helsingfors: Aktiebolaget Handelstryckeriet, 1905); Friederike Wiesmann-Wiedemann, *Le roman du "Willehalm" de Wolfram d'Eschenbach et l'épopée d' "Aliscans": Etude de la transformation de l'épopée en roman* (Göttingen: Alfred Kümmerle, 1976), pp. 188–226.

35. *La Chanson de Guillaume,* ed. Duncan McMillan (Paris: A. & J. Picard, 1949).

36. *Aliscans*, ed. F. Guessard and A. de Montaiglon (Paris: A. Franck, 1870).

37. For a critically well-informed rereading of the fabliaux, and the meaning of vilains in the fabliaux, see R. Howard Bloch, *The Scandal of the Fabliaux*.

38. Marie-Thérèse Lorcin comments: "Dans les 'fabliaux à triangle', le mari et l'amant appartiennent souvent à milieux différents, comme l'a montré P. Nykrog. Certains contes, avec ou sans triangle, poussent plus loin le contraste: mari et femme n'ont pas la même origine sociale. C'est le point de départ d'aventures et mésaventures variées. Les éléments essentiels sont cependant les mêmes, et permettent de définir la mésalliance vue par les auteurs de fabliaux. La mésalliance est le fait de la femme: un paysan ou un bourgeois épouse la fille d'un châtelain, d'un chevalier. Jamais n'est mis en scène un homme prenant pour épouse une fille placée plus bas que lui sur l'échelle de valeurs sociales." Marie-Thérèse Lorcin, "Quand les princes n'épousaient pas les bergères; ou, Mésalliance et classes d'âge dans les fabliaux," *Medioevo Romanzo* 3 (1976): 197.

39. *Berengier au Lonc Cul*, in *Recueil général et complet des fabliaux des XIIIe et XIVe siècles*, ed. A. Montaiglon and G. Raynaud (Paris: Librairie des Bibliophiles, 1872–90), 3:252.

40. Fergus's mother says: "Et si vous di de cest vallet,/ Se de prouece s'entremet,/ Ne vos en deves merviller. / Car il a maint bon chevalier / En son lignage de par moi. / Si i retrait, si con je croi" (*Fergus* 495–501; And as for this young man, I tell you that you ought not be surprised if he aspires to chivalric achievements, for many of his forefathers on my side of the family were good knights. He takes after them, as I see it).

41. The foolish husband mistakes "Berenger"'s female genitalia for one long crevice, whence the fabliau's title. The "baiser honteux" is a popular motif in medieval literature, well-known for its place in Chaucer's *Canterbury Tales* and in Rabelais's *Gargantua et Pantagruel*.

42. *Le Roman de Renart*, ed. Mario Roques (Paris: Champion), in 6 vols.: Branch I (1951), Branches II–VI (1951), Branches VII–IX (1951), Branches X–XI (1958), Branches XII–XVII (1960), Branches XVIII–XIX (1963). Hereafter cited by branch and verse numbers in Roques's edition.

43. A few examples of hunger used as narrative transition in the *Roman de Renart*: II, 3291–3312; III, 4021–28; IIIa, 4655–57, 4797–99; VIIa, 5566–92 (the theft of food); XII, 12943–45.

44. *Renart* IIIa, 4168–76; X, 10177–79; *Fergus* 910–17.

45. A father, mother, and three sons in a rustic castle: *Renart* I, 1593–1633; a lovesick female character: Ib, 2703–10; a hunt scene: Ia, 1803–30; the fear of an animal character who hides: X, 9900–10018; the theft of food: VIIa, 5566–92.

46. Frescoln, "A Study," pp. 74–76.

47. Louis-Fernand Flutre, *Table des noms propres des romans du moyen âge* (Poitiers: Publications du CESCM, 1962), pp. 75–76; G. D. West, *French Arthurian Prose Romances: An Index of Proper Names* (Toronto: University of Toronto Press, 1978), p. 113. West also includes references to the *Alixandre l'Orphelin: A Prose Tale of the Fifteenth Century,* ed. Cedric Pickford (Manchester: University of Manchester Press, 1951), p. 8, v. 29, and p. 9, vv. 2 and 6.

48. *Le Livre du Lancelot del Lac,* vols. 3–5 of *The Vulgate Version of the Arthurian Romances,* ed. H. Oskar Sommer (Washington, D.C.: Carnegie Institution, 1910–12); *Les Prophecies de Merlin de Maître Richard d'Irlande,* ed. Lucy A. Paton (New York and London: D. C. Heath and Oxford University Press, 1926–27); *Le Roman de Tristan en prose française,* ed. Joseph Bédier in an appendix to the fragment of Thomas (Paris: Société des anciens textes français, 1905); *Le Roman en Prose de Tristan: Analyse critique,* ed. Eilert Loseth (Paris: Champion, 1890); *Perceforest* (Paris: Printed by Nicolas Cousteau, 1528). In volume 3 of *Perceforest* another Fergus is the king of Norway. See L.-F. Flutre's articles, "Etudes sur le roman de Perceforest," *Romania* 70 (1948–49): 474–522; 71 (1950–51): 374–92; and 74 (1953): 44–102. Although in *Guiron le Courtois,* Fergus le Grant is an evil knight, he reaches the Renaissance in a preface to the 1501 printing of *Guiron, Les Devises des Armes de Tous les Chevaliers de la Table Ronde,* as Fergus du Blanc Lieu (a deformation of Guillaume le Clerc's "Blanc Ecu"), companion of the Round Table. See Roger Lathuillère's edition, *Guiron le Courtois: Etude de la tradition manuscrite et analyse critique* (Geneva: Droz, 1966).

49. M. Bloch, *Feudal Society,* Köhler, *Ideal und Wirklichkeit,* Duby, *Trois ordres,* and Bois, *Crisis of Feudalism.*

CHAPTER 2: AUDIGIER

1. Robert M. Adams, *Bad Mouth: Fugitive Papers on the Dark Side* (Berkeley and Los Angeles: University of California Press, 1977). The chapter epigraph is from p. 122.

2. The edition I use is that of Omer Jodogne, "*Audigier* et la chanson de geste, avec une édition nouvelle du poème," *Le Moyen Age* 66 (1960): 495–526. The text was first edited and published in Etienne Barbazan and Dominique Méon, *Fabliaux et contes des poètes français des XIe, XIIe, XIIIe et XIVe siècles* (Paris: Crapelet, 1808), 4:217–33, then by Edmond Faral, in *Le Manuscrit 19152 du Fonds Français de la Bibliothèque Nationale* (Paris: Droz, 1934). *Audigier* has been dated, with difficulty, as belonging to the late twelfth or early thirteenth century. The sole manuscript is written in Picardian dialect.

3. René Louis, *Girart, comte de Vienne, dans les chansons de geste*

(Auxerre: L'Imprimerie moderne, 1947), pp. 305–15; Paul Zumthor, *Histoire littéraire de la France médiévale (VIe–XIVe siècles)* (Paris: PUF, 1954), p. 190; Rychner, *La chanson de geste*, pp. 18, 128–30; Jodogne, *Audigier*, pp. 502–11. Charles Lenient, *La satire en France au Moyen Age* (Paris: Hachette, 1877), pp. 123–28, interpreted *Audigier* as both parody and satire.

4. This tendency is one manifestation of the increasing conflation of romance and epic themes in the late twelfth and thirteenth centuries. It also reveals of conflation of epic and hagiographic models, in its focus on *moniage* and miracles. The *Chanson de Roland* is continued in the *Enfances Roland*; the *Chanson de Guillaume* is followed by the cycle of Guillaume's great-grandfather, *Garin de Monglane*; *Aimeri de Narbonne* is followed by the invention of the hero's father, in the *Girard de Vienne*; *Aiol* gives rise to *Elie de Saint Gilles*; *La Chevalierie Vivien* precedes the *Enfances Vivien*. The ancestral romance, which appeared in the twelfth century, grows increasingly popular through the fourteenth century. See M. Dominica Legge, *Anglo-Norman Literature and Its Background* (Oxford: Clarendon Press, 1963), pp. 139–75. For a theoretical discussion of continuations as a form of second-degree literature and their relation to parody, see Genette, *Palimpsestes*, pp. 177–236.

5. Rychner, *Chanson de geste*, pp. 128–53.

6. Bertin, "Burlesque Elements," p. 332.

7. F. J. Lelievre, "The Basis of Ancient Parody," *Greece and Rome*, 2nd ser., 1 (1954): 66–81. Genette offers a thorough discussion of the etymology of *parody* in *Palimpsestes*, pp. 17–32.

8. Louis, *Girart*, pp. 303–5, 311–15. It should be noted that *Girart* comments directly on the opposition of vilain and courtois: "Oh God! how ill is recompensed the good warrior who knights the son of a vilain" (stanza LX). Paul Meyer, in his 1884 translation of the chanson de geste, points to the mistrust of vilains as one of the constants of medieval literature, in texts of all types, and quotes similar outcries in the *Couronnement de Louis*, the *Roman d'Alexandre*, and *Cléomades*. Paul Meyer, *Girart de Roussillon* (Paris: Champion, 1884), p. 28, n. 2.

9. Louis, *Girart*, p. 304. See M. Théodore Gérold, *La musique au Moyen Age* (Paris: Champion, 1932).

10. Jean Beck, "La musique des chansons de geste," in *Comptesrendus des Séances de l'Académie des Inscriptions et Belles-Lettres* (1911), p. 42, as quoted in Louis, *Girart*, p. 303.

11. Genette, *Palimpsestes*, p. 67.

12. Ibid., p. 35, and also the diagram on p. 157.

13. Since the nineteenth century, *Audigier* has been identified as a parody of *Girard de Vienne* (by Joseph Bédier, *Les fabliaux*, 2nd ed. [Paris: Emile Bouillon, 1895]), of *Girard de Roussillon* (by René Louis, *Girart*,

1947, and Paul Meyer, *Bibliothèque de l'Ecole des Chartes*, vol. 22 [1861], pp. 40–41, cited in René Louis, *Girart*), and of the *Chanson de Guillaume* (by Jodogne, *Audigier*, 1960). These varying identifications confirm the fact that the *Audigier* parodies a cohesive and fixed medieval tradition, with all its conventions and clichés.

14. Rychner, *Chanson de geste*, pp. 128–53.

15. The similarities of *Girart de Roussillon, Audigier,* and *Aiol* are discussed in useful detail by Louis, *Girart,* pp. 303–15, who gives vv. 3253–56 of this passage of *Girart* from the Paris manuscript.

16. Paul Zumthor, *Essai,* p. 105.

17. See, for a typical example, the indignation of Thomas D. Cooke, *The Old French and Chaucerian Fabliaux: A Study of Their Comic Climax* (Columbia: University of Missouri Press, 1978), p. 167.

18. "Turgibus" is a learned play on the Latin *turgere,* "to swell."

19. Rychner, *Chanson de geste*, p. 129.

20. Paul Zumthor uses the term "incompossibility" in Zumthor, E.-G. Hessing, and R. Vijlbrief, "Essai d'analyse des procédés fatrasiques," *Romania* 84 (1963): 145–70.

21. Hans-Robert Jauss, "Littérature médiévale," pp. 79–101. In addition to Zumthor et al., "Essai d'analyse," see an earlier Zumthor article which places the fatrasie in a historical perspective: Paul Zumthor, "Fatrasie et coq-à-l'âne (de Beaumanoir à Clement Marot)," in *Fin du Moyen Age et Renaissance: Mélanges de philologie française offerts à Robert Guiette* (Anvers: De Nederlandsche Bockhandel, 1961), pp. 5–18. All references to the fatrasies will be to the edition of Lambert Porter, *La fatrasie et le fatras: Essai sur la poésie irrationnelle en France au Moyen Age* (Geneva: Droz, 1960).

22. Zumthor et al., "Essai," p. 140.

23. Jauss, "Littérature médiévale," pp. 91–97.

24. Curtius, *European Literature*, pp. 94–95.

25. Both manuscripts are edited in Porter, *La fatrasie,* pp. 109–44. Translations are mine.

26. Zumthor, *Essai,* p. 141; Zumthor et al., "Essai d'analyse," pp. 145–70.

27. The "chanson de merde" epithet comes from Paul Brian, ed., *Bawdy Tales from the Courts of Medieval France* (New York: Harper and Row, 1973), p. 69. My reading of scatological parody owes a great deal to Michael Riffaterre's analysis of stercoraceous parody in Lautréamont, in "Sémiotique intertextuelle," pp. 128–50.

28. Norman O. Brown, "The Excremental Vision," in *Life against Death: A Psychoanalytic View of History* (New York: Vintage Books, 1959), pp. 179–201. Brown's work is discussed by Gustave Legman, *Ra-*

tionale of the Dirty Joke (New York: Breaking Point, 1975), with relation to scatological humor, in section 15, "Scatology," pp. 810–987.

29. Adam de la Halle, *Le Jeu de Robin et de Marion,* ed. Ernest Langlois (Paris: Champion, 1965).

30. Paul Meyer, "La chanson *Doon de Nanteuil* (Fragments inédits)," *Romania* 12 (1884): 1–18; Ernst Langlois, *Recueil d'arts de seconde rhétorique* (Paris: Champion, 1902), pp. 64–65; Bertin, "Burlesque Elements," pp. 327, 333; Jodogne, *Audigier,* p. 495; Cooke, *The Old French and Chaucerian Fabliaux,* p. 167. Jodogne prefaces his edition of *Audigier* with the following disclaimer: "Pour les contemporains d'*Audigier* la scatologie était l'attrait principal de l'oeuvre. Je n'en dirais pas plus, car notre français, dans ses mots, ne peut braver l'honnêteté" (p. 511). As we will see in the following discussion, it is the modern, not medieval, reader who sees nothing but scatology in this text.

31. In classes in medieval literature, it can sometimes be difficult to generate student interest in the canonical texts, but in my own experience no group of students has ever failed to be delighted by and interested in *Audigier.* Moreover, their interest is not of the sophomoric nature one might expect. The text consistently stimulates discussion among the noninitiated who are otherwise uninterested in the Middle Ages or in literary theory, and who subsequently raise many questions about medieval literature and culture.

32. See Ashley Montagu, *The Anatomy of Swearing* (New York: Macmillan, 1967), who views the pleasure involved in the use of such language as healthy and cathartic. My own views owe a great deal to a conference paper by Nancy Freeman Regalado, "The Poetic Functions of Body Talk," presented at the 1982 "Poetics Colloquium," Maison Française, Columbia University, November 1982.

33. Each critic manages to find a distancing vocabulary in working on scatological texts. Michael Riffaterre favors "stercoraceous," rather than the more familiar "scatological"; Jeffrey Henderson relies heavily on "crepitation," and avoids "flatulence"; R. Howard Bloch prefers "coprophagy" to the already distant "scatophagy." I am grateful to each of them for providing me with this reassuring terminology.

34. Jeffrey Henderson, *The Maculate Muse: Obscene Language in Attic Comedy* (New Haven: Yale University Press, 1975). See especially "Scatological Humor," pp. 187–99, and "The Dramatic Function of Obscenity in the Plays of Aristophanes," pp. 62–65.

35. Freud, "The Tendencies of Wit," in *The Basic Writings,* trans. A. A. Brill (New York: Random House, 1938), pp. 692–97. Legman also espouses the Freudian view of scatology as an expression of aggression and hostility: the teller of the scatological joke actually does to the lis-

tener what he recounts in the joke. It is interesting to note that Legman views the hostility of scatological language as directed against women in particular. For him, the "anti-gallantry" of scatological jokes constitutes a form of woman-hating. See "Cloacal Intercourse," *Rationale*, pp. 329–48, and sec. 15, "Scatology," ibid. Legman's theory cannot, however, account for the "joyous scatology" in *Audigier*.

36. On the question of social class and dirty words, see Edward Sagarin, *The Anatomy of Dirty Words* (New York: Lyle Stuart, 1962), esp. pp. 34–35. For a specific discussion of social class in the fabliaux, see R. Howard Bloch, *Scandal*, esp. his introduction.

37. I am grateful to R. Howard Bloch for making this point clear to me. This understanding of excrement has grown out of Marquis de Sade studies, whose locus classicus is Jane Gallop, *Intersections: A Reading of Sade with Bataille, Blanchot, and Klossowski* (Lincoln: University of Nebraska Press, 1981); see especially Ch. 2, "Friends / Corpses / Turds / Whores: Blanchot on Sade," pp. 35–65.

38. Omer Jodogne documents eleven important medieval references to the text between 1173 and 1432, in his edition of *Audigier* (pp. 495–511). Bertin also discusses the popularity of *Audigier* in "Burlesque Elements," p. 334.

39. *Oeuvres Complètes de Rutebeuf,* ed. Edmond Faral and Julia Bastin (Paris: A. & J. Picard, 1960), 2:308. In the text of *Audigier,* it is the father, Turgibus, who "a chié plaine s'aumuce" (verse 12).

40. Langlois, *Recueil*, p. 64.

41. *Aiol,* ed. Jacques Normand and Gaston Raynaud (Paris: Société des anciens textes français, 1877). See also Le Rider, *Le chevalier,* pp. 114–37.

42. *Florent et Octavian,* ed. K. Vollmoller (Heilbronn: n.p., 1883), vv. 2279–85.

43. Quoted in K. V. Sinclair, "Comic *Audigier* in England," *Romania* 100 (1979): 257–59.

44. Gunnar Tilander, *Remarques sur le "Roman de Renart"* (Göteborg: Boktryekeri Aktiebolag, 1923), p. 116. Tilander quotes one of the variants of the branch entitled "Pelerinage Renart": when the "archeprestres" tries to flee the wolves but cannot move his feet, the narrator quips, "C'est de la menie Audigier." In Gerbert de Montreuil's *Roman de la Violette,* ed. D. Labarée Buffum (Paris: Société des anciens textes français, 1928), the hero uses the name as an insult: "Audigier, estes le vous venus vengier?" (vv. 4503–4).

45. Meyer, "La chanson *Doon de Nanteuil*," pp. 1–18.

46. Langlois, *Recueil*, pp. 64–65.

47. Julia Kristeva, *Powers of Horror: An Essay On Abjection*, trans.

Léon Roudiez (New York: Columbia University Press, 1982), pp. 3, 21.

48. See Legman, "Cloacal Intercourse," in *Rationale*, pp. 329–48.

49. Bakhtin, *Rabelais*. The following discussion can be read as an imagined dialogical exchange between Bakhtin and *Audigier*, a medieval text not mentioned in his book.

50. Bakhtin, *Rabelais*, p. 224; François Rabelais, *Oeuvres Complètes*, ed. Jacques Boulenger (Paris: Gallimard, 1955), p. 15.

51. Bakhtin, *Rabelais*, p. 224.

52. Ibid., p. 152.

53. Such a comparison would be especially interesting if we were to place Legman's theory that scatological humor is essentially antigallant next to the gallantries of the courtly love tradition.

54. Bakhtin, *Rabelais*, pp. 177–78.

55. Ibid., p. 96.

56. The pronunciation of the two names is identical except for the initial *G*, and many critics as well as authors confused the two names throughout the Middle Ages. In the *Jeu de Robin et de Marion*, for example, Adam de la Halle makes this "mistake," giving the words "Audigier, bouse vos di" not to the enemy but to the mother. The modern critic René Louis made another telling error when he identified Grimberge as Audigier's bride, speaking of "les amours et les noces d'Audigier et de Grimberge." Louis, *Girart*, p. 315.

CHAPTER 3: LE ROMAN DE RENART

1. See Linda Hutcheon's discussion on the time-honored confusion in *A Theory of Parody*, pp. 43–49.

2. Lenient, *La satire en France*, p. 129.

3. In this chapter I will use the title *Roman* to refer to the late twelfth- and early thirteenth-century branches of the *Roman de Renart*, some of which are signed and others anonymous, to avoid confusion with other Renardian texts. The earliest branch of the *Roman* is dated between 1174 and 1177. The first twelve branches are dated between 1175 and 1205; the terminus ad quem for the others is fixed as 1250. In this chapter references are to Mario Roques's edition (6 vols.; Paris: Champion, 1951–63), except for those branches not edited by Roques, which are cited from a much earlier edition by Ernst Martin (Strasbourg: K. J. Trübner, 1882). Recently a fine new bilingual edition has appeared, translated by Micheline de Combarieu du Grès and Jean Subrenat, published in the Bibliothèque Médiévale series (Paris: 10/18, 1981).

4. Nivardus, *Ysengrimus*, ed. Ernst Voigt (Halle, 1884).

5. See John Flinn, *Le "Roman de Renart" dans la littérature française*

et dans la littérature étrangère au moyen âge (Paris: PUF, 1963), for a discussion of the political satires.

6. Philippe de Novare, *Mémoires*, 1218–1243, ed. Charles Kohler (Paris: Champion, 1913), p. 29.

7. Genette, *Palimpsestes*, pp. 14–39, 29–30, 30–32.

8. Hutcheon, *A Theory*, pp. 16, 43. Parody is, of course, not limited to literature, but is practiced in all arts, ranging from the plastic arts and cinema, to architecture, as Hutcheon shows.

9. Jean V. Alter, *Les origines de la satire anti-bourgeoise en France: Moyen âge–XVIe siècle* (Geneva: Droz, 1966).

10. Per Nykrog, *Les Fabliaux* (Geneva: Droz, 1973), ch. 3, "La parodie dans les fabliaux"; Zumthor, *Essai*, pp. 105–6, 134–37, 251, 408; R. Howard Bloch, *The Scandal of the Fabliaux*. See also Charles Muscatine's recent study, *The Old French Fabliaux* (New Haven: Yale University Press, 1986), which reads the components of the fabliaux as symptomatic of their sociocultural context in thirteenth-century France.

11. Sigmund Freud, "Jokes and Their Relation to the Unconscious," *Standard Edition*, 8:73–74.

12. Bakhtin, *Rabelais*, pp. 13–15, 83–88.

13. Hutcheon, *A Theory of Parody*, pp. 4, 20, 59–64.

14. For the following discussion of satire and its definition, I am indebted to Karen Klein's *The Partisan Voice: A Study of the Political Lyric in France and Germany*, 1180–1230 (The Hague: Mouton, 1971), esp. pp. 31–54.

15. See my "Kings and Kingship in the *Roman de Renart*," *Kings and Kingship*, ACTA (1986): 113–20.

16. This chapter owes a great deal to the invaluable editions and studies of the *Roman de Renart* published by Jean Dufournet, whose training and mentoring I gratefully acknowledge. See especially the following: "Littérature oralisante et subversion: La branche 18 du *Roman de Renart* ou le partage des proies," *Cahiers de Civilisation Médiévale* 22 (1979): 321–31; "L'originalité de la branche XVII du *Roman de Renart*; ou, Les trois morts du goupil," in *Mélanges Camproux*, 2 vols. (Montpellier, 1977–78), 1:345–63; "Rutebeuf et le *Roman de Renart*," *L'Information Littéraire* 30 (1978): 7–15; and the preface to his edition of the *Roman de Renart* (Paris: Garnier-Flammarion, 1970), p. 22.

17. As early as 1959, H. R. Jauss described the *Roman de Renart* as parody in his *Untersuchungen zur Mittelalterlichen Tierdichtung* (Tübingen: Max Niemeyer, 1959). Jauss used the term *parody* in its broadest (rather than its classical) sense, as "Komik der Gegenbildlichkeit." Curiously, his interpretation has been overshadowed by that of John Flinn's 1963 book, *Le "Roman de Renart,"* which establishes the common interpretation of the text as satire. In the 1970s, most studies

maintained Flinn's view: see *Aspects of the Medieval Animal Epic,* ed. Edward Rombauts and Andries Welkenhuysen (The Hague: Martinus Nihoff, 1975). More recently, however, an attempt to reinvestigate the nature of the comic in *Renart* has been made in a collection of papers, published by Danielle Buschinger and André Crépin, entitled *Comique, satire et parodie dans la tradition renardienne et les fabliaux* (Goppingen: Kummerle Verlag, 1983). In this volume Jauss's ideas on parody are explored in Fritz-Peter Knapp, "Quelques procédés du comique dans l'épopée animale du moyen âge," pp. 93–102; in Jean Scheidegger, "Renart dans les branches: Comique et reflexivité," pp. 113–24, and in Jean Subrenat, "Le *Roman de Renart* et la parodie littéraire," pp. 125–38.

18. Flinn, Le *"Roman de Renart,"* pp. 41–44.

19. *Ysengrimus* is dated ca. 1150; for the *Ysopet* fables see Marie de France, *Poésies,* ed. B. de Roquefort (Paris: Marescq, 1832). "Dou Lion, dou Bugle et de un Leu" is Fable 11 in Roquefort's edition. The name *Ysopet,* or *Isopet,* derives from *Aesop.* In the Middle Ages the terms *Ysopet* and *Romulus* designated collections of beast fables. The beast fable was a hardy literary genre throughout the early medieval period; it grew very successful by the tenth century and gave rise to many new compilations in the eleventh century. Marie's *Ysopet* is in fact the translation of an Anglo-Saxon *Romulus,* itself adapted from a Latin collection. See Robert Bossuat, *Le Roman de Renard* (Paris: Hatier, 1967), p. 65.

20. My reading of this passage owes much to Léonard Willems's *Etude sur l'Ysengrinus* (Ghent: E. Van Goethem, 1895), pp. 13–18.

21. The "aumuce," or "aumusse," was a type of cap worn by canons in the Middle Ages.

22. *Beuve de Hamtome, Doon de Maience, La Chevalerie Ogier,* and *Gaufrey* are the chansons de geste which use the joke. See Gerald Bertin's unpublished doctoral dissertation, "Burlesque Elements," pp. 307–8.

23. Olga Dobiache-Rojdestvensky, ed., *Les poésies des Goliards* (Paris: Rieder, 1931), pp. 81–90. Useful complements to Dobiache-Rojdestvensky's invaluable edition are Helen Waddell's *The Wandering Scholars* (London: Constable, 1927) and George F. Whicher's edition and English translations, *The Goliard Poets: Medieval Latin Songs and Satires* (Cambridge: Cambridge University Press, 1949). Karen W. Klein's *The Partisan Voice* suggests that medieval political satire generally takes one of two forms: either clear, with an obvious use of topical allusions, or arcane, with allusions so cryptic as to be almost unrecognizable in later periods. Obscurantist satire does exist in the thirteenth century; there is, for example, Rutebeuf's *Renart le Bestourné.* See Nancy Freeman Regalado, *Poetic Patterns in Rutebeuf: A Study in Noncourtly Poetic Modes of the Thirteenth Century* (New Haven: Yale University Press, 1970), pp. 133–34, 151–52.

24. The allusions to "Petrus," Pierre de Pavie, become progressively more explicit: "Nos peccata relaxamus / et laxatos collocamus / sedibus ethereis. / Nos habemus Petri leges / ad ligandos omnes reges / in manicis ferreis" (stanza 16: We place our sins in you, to establish you, absolved, in celestial abodes; we have the power of rock [Pierre], to chain together all the kings with iron manacles). "Petrus foris, intus Nero, / intus lupi, foris vero / sicut agni ovium" (stanza 18: "Peter" on the outside, "Nero" within, wolves inside, but from outside they look like lambs). "Tales regunt Petri navem, / tales habent eius clavem, / ligandi potentiam" (stanza 19: Such are the men who steer the ship of Peter. They are the ones who hold his keys, and his power to bind). Dobiache-Rojdestvensky, *Poésies*, pp. 86–87.

25. Gabriel Bianciotto, "Renart et son cheval," *Etudes de langue et de littérature du moyen âge offertes à Félix Lecoy* (Paris: Champion, 1973), pp. 27–42; Omer Jodogne, "L'anthropomorphisme croissant dans le *Roman de Renart*," in Rombauts and Welkenhuysen, *Aspects of the Medieval Animal Epic*, pp. 25–41; Roger Dragonetti, "Renart est mort, Renart est vis, Renart règne," *Critique* 34 (1978): 783–98.

26. Flinn, *Le "Roman de Renart,"* pp. 55–68. Jean-Charles Payen, "L'idéologie chevaleresque dans le *Roman de Renart*," *Marche Romane* 28 (1978), 38–40, provided a good example of the antipeasantry explanation: while Payen announces that *Renart* is parody, he eventually reverts to the hypothesis that vilains are portrayed negatively in the text because the authors of the *Roman de Renart* despised peasants in real life.

27. Legal historians have shown the extent to which the *Roman de Renart* obeys twelfth-century legal procedure: see Yvonne Bongert, *Recherches sur les cours laïques du Xe au XIIIe siècle* (Paris: A. & J. Picard, 1949); Jean Graven, *Le procès criminel du "Roman de Renart": Etude du droit criminel féodal au XIIe siècle* (Geneva: Librairie de l'Université, 1950); Guido Van Dievoet, "Le *Roman de Renart* et *Van Den Vos Reynaerde*, témoins fidèles de la procédure pénale aux XIIe et XIIIe siècles?" in Rombauts and Welkenhuysen, *Aspects of the Medieval Animal Epic*, pp. 43–52. But can this faithfulness to medieval law, in the *Roman*'s courtroom scenes, be taken as proof that the text is satirical? The courtroom judgment is also a popular variant in the medieval animal fable. In Marie de France's Fable 48, "Dou vilain qui norri une choe," the just cause loses when a judge is bribed with a sheepskin pelt. In Fable 71, "Dou vileinz qui aveit uns cheval," the wronged peasant loses his case because he is not sufficiently eloquent. Yet critics do not, because of this, read these fables as satires of medieval society. For an excellent discussion on ways of understanding the relation between literary and legal discourses, see R. Howard Bloch, *Medieval French Literature and Law*, pp.

1–12. Bloch comments specifically on the *Roman de Renart* on pp. 24, 33, 77, 85, and 226–27.

28. Nancy F. Regalado, "Tristan and Renart: Two Tricksters," *Esprit Créateur* 16 (1976): 30–38.

29. For years scholars have criticized the *Roman de Renart* authors for the inconsistent appearance and disappearance of the animals' horses. Jodogne, "L'anthropomorphisme croissant," writes: "Ce qui est insupportable, c'est l'emploi de cheval là où il n'en est point. . . . Le recours trop fréquent aux images hippiques a quelque chose d'exaspérant" (p. 28). We find the same note of exasperation in Lucien Foulet, *Le Roman de Renard* (Paris: Champion, 1914), pp. 166–68.

30. "Mais que dire d'un cheval qui n'existe que dans la fuite, et dont le coeur bat à l'unisson de celui de son cavalier ou plutôt se substitue au sien? . . . L'image reste donc au niveau de la création verbale consciente, qui se juge avec humour et prend immédiatement ses distances par rapport au sens littéral des mots. . . . La surimpression des images confère ainsi aux mots une dimension parodique et poétique qu'ils ne possédaient pas à eux seuls." Bianciotto, "Renart et son cheval," pp. 41–42.

31. Galpin, *Cortois and Vilain,* pp. 5–6. For examples of complex texts dismissed as exceptions, see pp. 81–82, and p. 81, n. 1.

32. Although it is true that farm animals were tried, in the civil courts of fourteenth-century Paris, and even executed when found guilty. See L. Tanon, *Registre Criminel de Saint-Martin* in *Histoire des justices des anciennes églises et communautés monastiques de Paris des Champs* (Paris: Larose et Forcel, 1883), p. 554.

33. The morals that close the fables of Marie de France, like those found in Aesop's fables, are often morally ambiguous and cynical comments on the way of the world. The same may be said of the proverbs found throughout the *Roman de Renart;* like the famous medieval *Proverbes au Vilain* (ed. Adolf Tobler [Leipzig: S. Hirzel, 1895]), they are shrewd lessons in survival, rather than points of a moral code.

34. "Il semble bien, devant le caractère à la fois statique et incohérent de la structure, devant l'épuisement rapide de toute recherche idéologique, et eu égard au souci esthétique rigoureux et évident qui se manifeste à chaque page . . . que la signification du texte ne doive pas être recherchée au-delà du langage. Nous avons affaire à un jeu verbal parfaitement gratuit, à un récit qui se crée et se détruit au fur et à mesure qu'il avance, à une parole qui ne renvoie qu'à soi." Marie-Noëlle Lefay-Toury, "Ambiguité de l'idéologie et gratuité de l'écriture dans la branche I du *Roman de Renart,*" *Le Moyen Age* 80 (1974): 96.

35. I disagree with Robert Bossuat, who infers that the audience hopes to see Renart punished: "Ainsi Renard, traître à ses amis, cruel envers ses

ennemis, infidèle à son roi et suborneur d'honnêtes femmes, échappe encore au châtiment que le poète nous laissait espérer." Bossuat, *Le Roman de Renart*, p. 37. Although the narrators of *Renart* decry the perfidy of the fox, their denunciations were not necessarily to be received as sincere; such ironic disclaimers serve to underline the comedy of transgression and to authorize laughter.

36. Constant de Noes plays an important role in Branches IIa and VIIb (Roques), Frobert de la Fontaine throughout Branch VIIb (Roques) and XI (Martin), Liétart throughout Branch X (Roques), and Berthold throughout Branch XVIII (Roques). Curiously, one of the vilains in Branch XVII (Martin) is named Renart.

37. "Renart teinturier," "Renart jongleur," "Chantecler," "La femme du vilain," "L'escondit de Renart," "Le pélerinage Renart," "Liétart," "Les vêpres de Tibert," "Le bacon enlevé," "Le partage du Lion," "Berthold le Maire," and "La mort Renart."

38. I refer to the anthropological notion of the trickster, which will be discussed at length in the following chapter, on *Trubert*, by Douin de Lavesne. Trubert, the hero, is both vilain and trickster, yet another transgressive combination. The construct of the trickster presented in this book is essentially that presented by Paul Radin, *The Trickster: A Study in American Indian Mythology, with Commentaries by Karl Kerenyi and C. G. Jung* (New York: Schocken Books, 1972).

39. "The twelfth century reserves a special admiration for stories not about the everyday social world, not even about the hero's world, but stories that suggest a refusal of our imperfect and mortal world, whether they be stories of the asocial tricksters like the outlaw fox, of lovers who count the world well lost for love, or of the higher orders of monks and saints who lived, as the Rule of Saint Francis says, as pilgrims and strangers in this world." Regalado, "Tristan and Renart," p. 38.

CHAPTER 4: TRUBERT

1. Parts of this chapter were presented in a paper entitled "False Ladies, False Knights," at the Medieval and Renaissance Collegium Conference on "The Lady and the Knight," October 1984, at the University of Michigan–Ann Arbor.

2. The tale is found in E. Cosquin, *Contes populaires de Lorraine* (Paris: F. Vieweg, 1887), 2:338–41. See also R. Köhler's review of *Trubert* in *Zeitschrift für Romanische Philologie* 6 (1882): 483, in which Köhler recognizes the story of *Trubert* in "Le jeune homme au cochon." The typology referred to is that of A. Aarne and Stith Thompson, *The Types of the Folktale: A Classification and Bibliography* (Helsinki: Aktiebolaget Handelstryckeriet, 1928). The title of type number 1538 is "The Youth Cheated in Selling Oxen." In Thompson's motif index, *Trubert* is listed

under motif number K1825.1.3, "Trickster masks as doctor and punishes his cheaters." Stith Thompson, *Motif Index of Folk Literature*, 6 vols. (Bloomington: Indiana University Press, 1955). The two most important structuralist works on this subject are Vladimir Propp, *La morphologie du conte* (Paris: Seuil, 1965), and Claude Bremond, *Logique du récit* (Paris: Seuil, 1973).

3. The edition I use is *Trubert, fabliau du XIIIe siècle*, ed. Guy Raynaud de Lage (Geneva: Droz, 1974). See also Félix Lecoy's review of this edition in *Romania* 96 (1975): 278–81. Raynaud de Lage cites the various interpretations of *Trubert*, both in the introduction to his 1974 edition (pp. xix–xxii) and in his useful article "Trubert est-il un personnage de fabliau?" in *Mélanges d'histoire littéraire, de linguistique et de philologie romanes offerts à Charles Rostaing* (Liège, 1974), pp. 845–53.

The skeletal narrative of *Trubert* is as follows: A peasant boy sets out to sell the family cow. Trading the cow for a goat, the foolish lad spends his profit to have the goat painted in multicolored stripes. The duchess of Burgundy catches sight of the wondrous beast, and arranges to buy it from the boy; Trubert coaxes her into paying "un foutre et cinc sous." The duke of Burgundy then sees the goat, and decides he must have the animal at all costs. The boy tricks him into paying "quatre paus dou cul et cinc sous," humiliating and hurting the duke in front of his men.

On the following day, the peasant returns to the court, dressed as a carpenter, in order to obtain more money. The carpenter lures the duke into the forest, then beats and robs him.

On the third day, the boy returns disguised as a physician, and offers to heal the suffering duke. Left alone in the duke's chambers, the lad beats the duke, rubs his wounds with excrement, and makes off with money and a horse.

When war is declared between the duke and King Golias, the boy dresses as a knight and offers to help the Burgundian cause. The boy murders a woodcutter's wife and scalps "son cul et son con," which he uses to trick the duke into believing that he himself has killed the king, pretending the hair is the dead king's beard and moustache. When the boy's subterfuge is exposed, the duke sends soldiers to find the young peasant. The youth dresses as a girl, and befriends the soldiers. The enchanting girl is placed in the service of young Rosette, the daughter of the duke and duchess, at court. The two girls share a bed; Rosette soon becomes pregnant. When the king requests Rosette as his bride, the false girl must be sent in her place. The false girl marries the king, engineers a painful mock-castration that causes the king to faint with pain, then escapes the royal nuptial bed by deflowering a serving-girl and persuading her to go to the king's bed.

4. Regalado, "Tristan and Renart," p. 34; Ruth El-Saffar, "Tracking

the Trickster in the Works of Cervantes." *Symposium* (Summer 1983), pp. 106–24, esp. p. 110; Johannes Dietrich Schleyer, *Der Wortschatz von List und Betrug im Altfranzösischen und Altprovenzalischen* (Bonn: Romanistische Versuche und Vorarbeiten, 1961).

5. In medieval bestiaries, the goat is a signifier of lust. See Pierre de Beauvais, *Le Bestiaire de Pierre de Beauvais*, ed. Guy Mermier (Paris: A. G. Nizet, 1977), pp. 74–75.

6. This discussion of trickster texts is informed by the work of Claude Lévi-Strauss, *Le cru et le cuit* (Paris: Plon, 1964), and especially Lévi-Strauss, *Anthropologie structurale* (Paris: Plon, 1958).

7. Paul Radin, *The Trickster*. See also Norman O. Brown, *Hermes the Thief: The Evolution of a Myth* (Madison: University of Wisconsin Press, 1947).

8. El-Saffar, "Tracking the Trickster," pp. 106, 110.

9. Karl Kerényi, "The Trickster in Relation to Greek Mythology," in Radin, *The Trickster*, p. 185.

10. Regalado, "Tristan and Renart."

11. The name Trubert, or Estrubert, is that of Saint Trubert, believed to have lived in the Brisgau region of Germany in the seventh century. While that saint's name was never common in medieval France, *trubert* does become a noun and an adjective in Middle French, meaning "a debauched man," or "debauched." The transformation of the name was no doubt influenced by Eustache Deschamp's fourteenth-century farce, in which a lawyer named Trubert is a "deceiver deceived" in a dice game. Eustache Deschamps, *Oeuvres Complètes* (1859; rpt. New York: Johnson Reprint Corp. 1966), 7:155–74.

12. "En fabliaus doit fables avoir / s'i a il, ce sachiez de voir: / por ce est fabliaus apelez / que de faubles est aünez" (*Trubert* vv. 1–4: A fabliau must contain a fable, and this one has them, as you should know. That is why it's called fabliau, because it is composed of fables).

Per Nykrog and Joseph Bédier both conclude that *Trubert* cannot be classed as a fabliau. Guy Raynaud de Lage rejects their opinion but concedes that the role of parody is far greater in *Trubert* than in the fabliaux. Per Nykrog, *Les fabliaux* (Geneva: Droz, 1973), p. 15; Bédier, *Les fabliaux*, p. 32; Raynaud de Lage, *Trubert*, pp. xxi–xxii.

13. Robert W. Hanning, "*Engin* in Twelfth-Century Romance: An Examination of the *Roman d'Enéas* and Hue de Rotelande's *Ipomédon*," *Yale French Studies* 51 (1974): 82–101.

14. *Aucassin et Nicolette*, ed. Roques; *Gautier d'Aupais, Poème courtois du XIIIe siècle*, ed. Edmond Faral (Paris: Champion, 1919).

15. See Zumthor, *Histoire littéraire de la France médiévale*, pp. 122 and 150, for a discussion of the Byzantine genre.

16. *Guillaume de Palerme*, ed. H. Michelant (Paris: Société des anciens

textes français, 1876); Raoul de Houdenc, *Méraugis de Portlesguez,* ed. Martin Friedwagner (Halle: Waisenhaus, 1897). Two excellent papers on *Méraugis* were presented at the 1985 International Congress on Medieval Studies at Kalamazoo, Michigan, May 9–12, 1985: Renate Blumenfeld-Kosinski, "Méraugis de Portlesguez: A Reluctant Arthurian Hero," and Roberta L. Krueger, "Invention and Intervention in *Méraugis de Portlesguez* and *Durmart le Galois.*"

For a different type of romance tranvestitism, this time female, see *Le Roman de Silence,* ed. L. Thorpe (Cambridge: Heffer, 1974), and analyses by R. Howard Bloch, "Silence and Holes: The *Roman de Silence* and the Art of the Trouvère," *Yale French Studies* 70 (1986): 81–99, Kate Mason Cooper, "Elle and *L*: Sexualized Textuality in *Le Roman de Silence,*" and Michèle Perret, "Travesties and transexuelles: Yde, silence, Grisandole, Blanchandine," both in *Romance Notes* 25 (Spring 1985): 341–60 and 328–40, respectively.

17. Hue de Rotelande, *Ipomédon: Poème de Hue de Rotelande, fin du XIIe siècle,* ed. A. J. Holden (Paris: Klincksieck, 1979). William Calin's paper "The Exaltation and Undermining of Romance: *Ipomédon,*" also presented at Kalamazoo in May 1985 (see note 16), draws many of the same conclusions as this chapter does.

18. The relation between *Trubert* and Guillaume de Blois's *Alda* is discussed later in this chapter. Raynaud de Lage, "Trubert," p. 83, cites *Alda* as the source for the Couillebaude-Rosette scene. Pierre-Yves Badel, author of the only full-length study of *Trubert*—*Le sauvage et le sot: Le fabliau de "Trubert" et la tradition orale* (Paris: Champion, 1979)—presents Trubert as an avatar of the medieval wild man. Badel concentrates on those traits of the character that confirm his relation to the wildman stereotype: hunger, unbridled sexuality, forest dwelling, violent strength. But in looking at those traits in light of the wild man archetype, Badel obscures the fact that Trubert is a trickster and that the text is organized by the logic of the trick.

19. Ronald M. Spensley, "The Structure of Hue de Rotelande's *Ipomédon,*" *Romania* 95 (1974): 341–51. Paule Le Rider provides a useful discussion of the masks of fool and of knight in their relation to other medieval romances, including Chrétien's *Perceval, Fergus,* and *Aiol* in his *Le chevalier dans "Le Conte du Graal,"* pp. 137–41. M. D. Legge discusses *Ipomédon* as burlesque in her *Anglo-Norman Literature and Its Background,* pp. 85–96. For a summary of the debate on how to read the travestied knight, see Michel Stanesco, "Le secret de *l'estrange* chevalier: Notes sur la motivation contradictoire dans le roman médiéval" in Glyn S. Burgess and Robert A. Taylor, eds., *The Spirit of the Court: Selected Proceedings of the Fourth Congress of the International Courtly Literature Society* (Cambridge: D. S. Brewer, 1985), pp. 340–45.

20. Henderson views humor as a form of psychic exposure, and argues that in Attic comedy nudity satisfies the hostility of the audience, who identifies with the comic hero.

21. Galpin, *Vilain and Cortois,* pp. 82–84.

22. Kerényi, "The Trickster in Relation to Greek Mythology," p. 188.

23. "Les fabliaux peuvent se dérouler sous les yeux des personnages augustes, mais ne peuvent pas les engager activement. . . . La haute noblesse n'entre jamais dans le triangle érotique des fabliaux. Dans les contes sublimes d'amour courtois, par contre, les protagonistes sont volontiers des comtes, des ducs ou des rois. C'est une question de style." Nykrog, *Les fabliaux,* p. 122.

24. Alice Colby, *The Portrait in Twelfth-Century French Literature* (Geneva: Droz, 1965).

25. Legge, Le Rider, Spensley, and in general most critics said little if anything concerning the obscenity in *Ipomédon.*

26. Roberta L. Krueger offers a perceptive and extremely useful analysis of this romance in "Misogyny, Manipulation, and the Female Reader in Hue de Rotelande's *Ipomédon*" (forthcoming). Susan Crane focusses on social and political concerns implied in *Ipomédon* in *Insular Romance: Politics, Faith, and Culture in Anglo-Norman and Middle English Literature* (Berkeley and Los Angeles: University of California Press, 1986), esp. "*Ipomédon*: Love and Pleasure," pp. 158–74.

27. Holden was the first actually to draw attention to the role of obscenity in *Ipomédon*; see pp. 52–53 of his edition.

28. Renaut de Beaujeu, *Le Bel Inconnu,* ed. G. Perrie Williams (Paris: Champion, 1929). Renaut de Beaujeu stops the hero's love story on an unhappy note and informs his own cruel mistress that unless she acknowledges her love, the text's hero will never be reunited with his true love.

29. Hanning, "*Engin,*" p. 92, n. 12, and Holden, ed., *Ipomédon,* p. 56.

30. The case for the poem's parodic stance has been made by Holden, *Ipomédon,* pp. 52–57. "L'anti-féminisme de Hue est toujours présent, tantôt à l'état soujacent, tantôt éclatant en propos désabusés qui dépassent en aigreur tout ce qu'on trouve habituellement dans les romans qui se donnent pour courtois"(p. 55). "On ne saurait méconnaître le contraste entre les déclarations solennelles du prologue et la boutade indécente de la fin: contraste hautement instructif si l'on veut bien saisir les véritables intentions de l'auteur" (p. 56).

31. Gustave Cohen, *La comédie latine en France au XIIe siècle* (Paris: Belles Lettres, 1931), pp. 109–51.

32. For an analysis of Trubert's transvestite disguise and its relation to linguistic gender, see Bernard Cerquiglini, "Un phénomène d'énonciation: Ancien français *mar,*" *Romania* 97 (1976): 23–62.

33. *Trubert* actualizes many of the stereotypical jokes cited by Gustave Legman in his sections "Castration," and "Dysphemism and Insults," in *Rationale,* and specifically the subsections "Vagina Dentata," pp. 420–73, "Castration of Authority-Figures," pp. 490–93, "The Doctor as Castrator," pp. 508–19, "Symbolic Castrations," pp. 567–97, "Anti-Gallantry and Anti-Woman," pp. 704–27, "Mocking Authority-Figures," pp. 744–60, and "Mocking God," pp. 760–79. Legman's cataloguing of these jokes is truly exhaustive, and a quick perusal shows that the jokes in *Trubert* are universal and time-honored. In light of our study of medieval parody, it is ironic that Legman ascribes the number and popularity of castration jokes to a modern and highly generalized male anxiety about the loss of virility. See also Sagarin, *The Anatomy of Dirty Words,* esp. "The Policy of the Big Stick," pp. 79–104, and "Euphemist, What's the Good Word?" pp. 113–20.

34. *Trubert* has been termed an unfinished text because it has no epilogue and the manuscript appears to be incomplete; it stops at verse 2984. Yet its end obeys a clear logic, as F. Manoine has argued in "Ist der Trubertroman ein Fragment?" *Zeitschrift für Romanische Philologie* 50 (1930): 740–44.

35. Patricia A. Parker, *Inescapable Romance: Studies in the Poetics of a Mode* (Princeton: Princeton University Press, 1979), esp. "Fictional Deviance and the Problem of Closure," pp. 31–38.

36. "Toute autorité est tutélaire et bonne. On se garde bien de la tourner en ridicule; il semble même tout naturel de solliciter son intervention." Lorcin, "Quand les princes n'épousaient pas les bergères," pp. 196–97. "Chaque fois, l'autorité, quel que soit celui qui l'incarne, arrange tout, en donnant raison au personnage à qui l'auteur a donné le rôle sympathique, en donnant par conséquent satisfaction à l'auditeur" (p. 197). How very different from the "satisfaction" of the audience in *Trubert.*

37. Badel, *Le sauvage et le sot.*

38. Kerényi, "The Trickster in Classical Greek Mythology," p. 180.

39. The two common denominators of the transgressive medieval texts we have seen are the ridiculous failure of the comic knight and culinary humor. *Trubert* does not present a transgressive combat between the hero and a female enemy, as do *Fergus* and *Audigier,* nor does it use the humor of animal characters, as does the *Roman de Renart.*

40. Those who read the conclusion of *Trubert* as an indication of the hero's conversion to goodness, or to concern for society, may be thinking in a slightly anachronistic fashion. Amaury Duval, in his article "Trubert," in *Histoire littéraire de la France* 19 (1838): 734–47, sees *Trubert* as revolutionary satire "avant la lettre." Sending the serving-girl to the king's bed is not a "good" act in terms of medieval morality, but rather a

medieval actualization of the false bride motif. Douin de Lavesne presents no redeeming conversion in the hero's behavior. On the contrary, Trubert has just boasted of all the wicked tricks he has committed, in a mock-epic list of his feats (vv. 2902–12). While the poet is perfectly capable of depicting remorse and contrition (the duchess is repeatedly filled with guilty sorrow), there is no remorse in the heart of Trubert. If the reader seeks a repentance that cannot be found in the text, it is perhaps because unredeemed and unredeeming devilry is less easy to accept in a human character than in an animal character, such as a fox.

41. See Judson Boyce Allen, *The Ethical Poetic of the Later Middle Ages: A Decorum of Convenient Distinction* (Toronto: University of Toronto Press, 1982).

42. Hutcheon, *A Theory of Parody*, p. 72.

43. Bakhtin, *Rabelais*, p. 68.

44. Julia Kristeva, *Desire in Language*, trans. Thomas Gora, Alice Jardine, and Leon Roudiez (New York: Columbia University Press, 1980), p. 71.

45. Hutcheon, *A Theory of Parody*, p. 75.

46. For a valuable model of this type of study, see Larry D. Benson and John Leyerle, eds., *Chivalric Literature: Essays on Relations between Literature and Life in the Later Middle Ages*, Studies in Medieval Culture 14 (Kalamazoo: Western Michigan University, 1980).

47. Deschamps, "La Farce de Maître Trubert et d'Antrongnart." Here, Trubert is a lawyer who tries to cheat at dice and is himself tricked.

48. See note 11 above, and Godefroy, *Dictionnaire de l'ancienne langue française*, 8:96a; Adolf Tobler and Erhard Lommatzsch, *Altfranzösisches Worterbuch* (Weisbaden: F. Steiner Verlag, 1927–76), 10:702; and Walther von Wartburg, *Französisches Etymologisches Worterbuch* (Leipzig and Berlin: B. G. Teubner, 1940–65), 13(2):324b.

BIBLIOGRAPHY

MEDIEVAL WORKS

Adam de la Halle. *Le Jeu de la Feuillée*. Ed. Ernest Langlois. Paris: Champion, 1964.

———. *Le Jeu de la Feuillée*. Trans. Jean Dufournet. Gand: Editions scientifiques E. Story-Scientia S.P.R.L., 1977.

———. *Le Jeu de Robin et de Marion*. Ed. Ernest Langlois. Paris: Champion, 1965.

Aiol. Ed. Jacques Normand and Gaston Raynaud. Paris: Société des anciens textes français (SATF), 1877.

Aliscans. Ed. F. Guessard and A. de Montaiglon. Paris: Librairie A. Franck, 1870.

Alixandre l'Orphelin, A Prose Tale of the Fifteenth Century. Ed. Cedric Pickford. Manchester: University of Manchester, 1951.

Andreas Capellanus. *The Art of Courtly Love*. Trans. John Jay Parry. New York: W. W. Norton, 1969.

Aubailly, Jean-Claude, ed. *Deux jeux de carnaval de la fin du moyen âge: La bataille de Sainct Pensart à l'encontre de Caresme, et le Testament de Carmentrant*. Paris: Droz, 1978.

Aucassin et Nicolette. Ed. Mario Roques. Paris: Champion, 1975.

Audigier. In "*Audigier* et la chanson de geste, avec une édition nouvelle du poème." Ed. Omer Jodogne. *Le Moyen Age* 66 (1960): 495–526.

———. In *Fabliaux et contes des poètes français des XIe, XIIe, XIIIe et XIVe siècles*, Ed. Etienne Barbazan and Dominique Méon. 4:217–33. Paris: Crapelet, 1808.

———. In *Le manuscrit* 19152 du fonds français de la Bibliothèque nationale. Ed. Edmond Faral. Paris: Droz, 1934.

Augustine of Hippo. *Confessions*. Trans. R. S. Pine-Coffin. New York: Viking, Penguin Books, 1961.

———. *On Christian Doctrine*. Trans. D.W. Robertson, Jr. New York: Bobbs-Merrill, 1958.

Berengier au Lonc Cul. In *Recueil général et complet des fabliaux des XIIIe et XIVe siècles*. 6 vols. Ed. Anatole de Montaiglon and Gaston Raynaud. Paris: Librairie des Bibliophiles, 1890.

Bibliography

Béroul. *Le Roman de Tristan.* Ed. Ernest Muret. Paris: Champion, 1974.

Brian, Paul, ed. *Bawdy Tales from the Courts of Medieval France.* New York: Harper & Row, 1973.

La Chanson de Guillaume. Ed. Duncan McMillan. 2 vols. Paris: A. & J. Picard, 1949.

La Chanson de Roland. Ed. Pierre Jonin. Paris: Gallimard, 1979.

Chrétien de Troyes. *Les Romans de Chrétien de Troyes édités d'après la copie de Guiot (Bibl. Nat. Fr. 794).* Paris: Champion, 1973–75. Volumes are *Erec et Enide,* ed. Mario Roques; *Cligès,* ed. Alexandre Micha; *Le Chevalier de la Charrette,* ed. Mario Roques; *Le Chevalier au Lion,* ed. Mario Roques; *Le Conte du Graal,* ed. Félix Lecoy.

Condé, Jean de. "Des vilains et des courtois." *Dits et contes de Baudouin de Condé et de son fils Jean de Condé.* 3 vols. Brussels: Auguste Scheler, 1866–67.

Deschamps, Eustache. "La Farce de Maître Trubert et d'Antrongnart." In *Oeuvres Complètes d'Eustache Deschamps,* 7:155–74. 1859; rpt. New York: Johnson Reprint Corp., 1966.

Dickson, Arthur, trans. *Valentine and Orson.* Oxford: Oxford University Press, 1937.

Dobiache-Rojdestvensky, Olga, ed. *Les poésies des Goliards.* Paris: Rider, 1931.

Ferguut. Ed. G. S. Overdiep. Leiden: Bibliotheek van Middelnederlandsche Letterkunde, 1925.

———. Ed. Eelco Verwijs and Jacob Verdam. Leiden: Bibliotheek van Middelnederlansche Letterkunde, 1908.

Ferguut: Ridderroman uit den Fabelkring van de Ronde Tafel. Ed. L. G. Visscher. Utrecht, 1838.

Gautier de Coincy. "Du vilain qui a grant poine savoit la moitié de son Ave Maria." In *Les Miracles de Nostre Dame.* Ed. V. F. Koenig. Geneva: Droz, 1966.

Gaydon. Ed. François Guessard and S. Luce. Paris: A. Franck, 1862.

Gennrich, Friedrich, ed. *Altfranzösische Lieder.* 2 vols. Tübingen: Max Niemeyer, 1955.

Gerbert de Montreuil. *Le Roman de Violette.* Ed. D. Labarée Buffum. Paris: SATF, 1928.

Girart de Roussillon. Ed. W. Mary Hackett. Paris: SATF, 1953.

———. Ed. Paul Meyer. Paris: Champion, 1884.

Girart de Vienne: Chanson de Geste. Ed. Frederic G. Yeandle. New York: Columbia University Press, 1930.

Guillaume de Lorris and Jean de Meun. *Le Roman de la Rose.* Ed. Félix Lecoy. 3 vols. Paris: Champion, 1970–79.

Guillaume le Clerc. *Fergus.* Ed. Ernst Martin. Halle: Waisenhaus, 1872.

————. *The Romance of Fergus*. Ed. Wilson L. Frescoln. Philadelphia: William H. Allen, 1983.

————. *Le Roman des Aventures de Fregus par Guillaume le Clerc, trouvère du XIIe siècle*. Ed. Francisque Michel. Edinburgh: Abbotsford Club, 1841.

Guiron le Courtois: Etude de la tradition manuscrite et analyse critique. Ed. Roger Lathuillère. Geneva: Droz, 1966.

Hue de Rotelande. *Ipomédon: Poème de Hue de Rotelande, fin du XIIe siècle*. Ed. A. J. Holden. Paris: Klincksieck, 1979.

Le lai de l'oiselet. Ed. Gaston Paris. Paris, 1884.

Langlois, Ernest, ed. *Recueil d'Arts de Seconde Rhétorique*. Paris: Champion, 1902.

Lozinski, Grégoire. *La Bataille de Caresme et Charnage: Edition critique*. Paris: Champion, 1933.

Marcabru. *Poésies complètes du troubadour Marcabru*. Ed. J.M.L. Dejeanne. Toulouse: E. Privat, 1909.

Marie de France. *Die Fablen der Marie de France*. Ed. Karl Warnke. Bibliotheca Normanica VI. Halle: Niemeyer, 1898.

————. *Fables*. Ed. Harriet Spiegel. Toronto: University of Toronto Press, 1987.

————. *Poésies*. Ed. B. de Roquefort. Paris: Marescq, 1832.

Matazone de Calignano. "Dit sur les Vilains par Matazone de Calignano." Ed. Paul Meyer. *Romania* 12 (1883): 14–28.

Nivardus, *Ysengrimus*. Ed. Ernst Voigt. Halle: Waisenhaus, 1884.

Les Prophécies de Merlin de Maître Richard d'Irlande. Ed. Lucy A. Paton. 2 vols. New York and London: D. C. Heath and Oxford University Press, 1926–27.

Perceforest. See *Trèsélégante . . . Hystoire du Très Noble Roy Perceforest*.

Porter, Lambert C. *La fatrasie et le fatras: Essai sur la poésie irrationnelle en France au moyen âge*. Geneva: Droz, 1960.

Proverbes au Vilain. Ed. Adolf Tobler. Leipzig: S. Hirzel, 1895.

Raoul de Houdenc. *Méraugis de Portlesguez*. Ed. Martin Friedwagner. Halle: Waisenhaus, 1897.

Renaut de Beaujeu. *Le Bel Inconnu*. Ed. G. Perrie Williams. Paris: Champion, 1929.

"Richeut." Ed. I. C. Lecompte. *Romanic Review* 4 (1913): 261–305.

Le Roman de Renart. Ed. and trans. Micheline de Combarieu du Grès and Jean Subrenat. 2 vols. Paris: Editions 10/18, 1981.

————. Ed. Jean Dufournet. Paris: Garnier-Flammarion, 1970.

————. Ed. Ernest Martin. 3 vols. Strasbourg: K. J. Trübner, 1882–87. Vol. 1, *L'ancienne collection des branches*; Vol. 2, *Les branches additionnelles*; Vol. 3, *Les variantes*.

Bibliography

————. Ed. Mario Roques. 6 vols. Paris: Champion, 1951–63.

Le Roman de Tristan en prose française. Ed. Joseph Bédier. Paris: SATF, 1905.

Le Roman en prose de Tristan: Analyse critique. Ed. Eilert Loseth. Paris: Champion, 1890.

La Trèsélégante, Délicieuse, Melliflue et Trèsplaisante Hystoire du Très Noble, Victorieux et Excellentissime Roy Perceforest, Roy de la Grant-Bretaigne. Paris: Nicolas Cousteau, 1528.

Trubert, fabliau du XIIIe siècle. Ed. Guy Raynaud de Lage. Geneva: Droz, 1974.

Waddell, Helen, ed. *The Wandering Scholars*. London: Constable, 1927.

Whicher, George F., ed. *The Goliard Poets: Medieval Latin Songs and Satires*. Cambridge: Cambridge University Press, 1949.

MODERN WORKS

Aarne, A., and Stith Thompson. *The Types of the Folktale: A Classification and Bibliography*. Helsinki: Aktiebolaget Handelstryckeriet, 1928.

Abastado, Claude. "Situation de la parodie." *Cahiers du XXe Siècle* 6 (1976): 9–37.

Adams, Robert M. *Bad Mouth: Fugitive Papers on the Dark Side*. Berkeley and Los Angeles: University of California Press, 1977.

Alter, Jean V. *Les origines de la satire anti-bourgeoise en France: Moyen âge–XVIe siècle*. Geneva: Droz, 1966.

Aristotle. *Poetics*. Trans. Leon Golden. Englewood Cliffs, N.J.: Prentice-Hall, 1968.

Auerbach, Erich. *Literary Language and Its Public in Late Latin Antiquity and in the Middle Ages*. Trans. Ralph Manheim. New York: Random House, 1965.

————. *Mimesis: The Representation of Reality in Western Literature*. Trans. Willard R. Trask. Princeton: Princeton University Press, 1953.

Badel, Pierre-Yves. *Le sauvage et le sot: Le fabliau de "Trubert" et la tradition orale*. Paris: Champion, 1979.

Bakhtin, Mikhail. *The Dialogic Imagination*. Trans. Caryl Emerson and Michael Holquist. Austin: University of Texas Press, 1981.

————. *Rabelais and His World*. Trans. Helene Iswolsky. Cambridge: MIT Press, 1968.

Barthes, Roland. "L'effet de réel." *Communications* 11 (1969): 84–89.

Beck, Jean. "La musique des chansons de geste." In *Comptes-rendus des Séances de l'Académie des Inscriptions et Belles-Lettres*. 1911.

Bédier, Joseph. *Les fabliaux: Etudes de littérature populaire et d'histoire littéraire du moyen âge*. 2nd ed. Paris: Librairie Emile Bouillon, 1895.

Ben-Porat, Ziva. "Method in Madness: Notes on the Structure of Parody." *Poetics Today* 1 (1979): 245–72.

Benson, Larry D., and John Leyerle, eds. *Chivalric Literature: Essays on Relations between Literature and Life in the Later Middle Ages.* Studies in Medieval Culture 14. Kalamazoo: Western Michigan University, 1980.

Berman, Harold J. *Law and Revolution: The Formation of the Western Legal Tradition.* Cambridge: Harvard University Press, 1983.

Bernheimer, Richard. *Wild Men in the Middle Ages.* Cambridge: Harvard University Press, 1952.

Bertin, Gerald André. "The Burlesque Elements in Old French Epic Poetry." Diss. Columbia University, 1953.

Beyer, Jürgen. *Schwank und Moral: Untersuchungen zum Altfranzösischen Fabliau und Verwandten Formen.* Heidelberg: Carl Winter, 1969.

Bianciotto, Gabriel. "Renart et son cheval." In *Etudes de langue et de littérature du moyen âge offertes à Félix Lecoy,* pp. 27–42. Paris: Champion, 1973.

Bloch, Marc. *Esquisse d'une histoire monétaire de l'Europe.* Paris: Armand Colin, 1954.

———. *Feudal Society.* Trans. L. A. Manyon. 2 vols. Chicago: University of Chicago Press, 1961.

———. *French Rural History: An Essay on Its Basic Characteristics.* Trans. J. Sondheimer. Berkeley and Los Angeles: University of California Press, 1966.

Bloch, R. Howard. *Etymologies and Genealogies: A Literary Anthropology of the French Middle Ages.* Chicago: University of Chicago Press, 1983.

———. *Medieval French Literature and Law.* Berkeley and Los Angeles: University of California Press, 1977.

———. "Money, Metaphor, and the Mediation of Social Difference in Old French Romance." *Symposium* 35 (1981): 18–33.

———. *The Scandal of the Fabliaux.* Chicago: University of Chicago Press, 1986.

Bois, Guy. *The Crisis of Feudalism: Economy and Society in Eastern Normandy c. 1300–1550.* Cambridge: Cambridge University Press, 1984.

Bongert, Yvonne. *Recherches sur les cours laïques du Xe au XIIIe siècle.* Paris: A. & J. Picard, 1949.

Bossuat, Robert. *Le Roman de Renard.* Paris: Hatier, 1967.

Boswell, John. *Christianity, Social Tolerance, and Homosexuality: Gay People in Western Europe from the Beginning of the Christian Era to the Fourteenth Century.* Chicago: University of Chicago Press, 1980.

Bibliography

Bremond, Claude. *Logique du récit*. Paris: Seuil, 1973.

Brown, Norman O. *Life against Death: A Psychoanalytic View of History*. New York: Vintage, 1959.

Bruckner, Matilda T. *Narrative Invention in Twelfth-Century French Romance; The Convention of Hospitality (1160–1200)*. Lexington, Kentucky: French Forum, 1980.

Burgess, Glyn Sheridan. *Contribution à l'étude du vocabulaire précourtois*. Geneva: Droz, 1970.

Burns, E. Jane. *Arthurian Fictions: Rereading the Vulgate Cycle*. Columbus: Ohio State University Press, 1985.

Buschinger, Danielle and André Crépin, eds. *Comique, Satire et Parodie Dans La Tradition Renardienne et les Fabliaux*. Goppinger Arbeiten zur Germanistik, no. 391. Goppingen: Kummerle Verlag, 1983.

Carrière, Jean-Claude. "Le Carnaval et la politique: Une introduction à la comédie grecque." *Annales Littéraires de l'Université de Besançon* 212. Paris, 1979.

Cerquiglini, Bernard. *La parole médiévale*. Paris: Minuit, 1981.

———. "Un phénomène d'énonciation: Ancien français *mar*." *Romania* 97 (1976): 23–62.

Colby, Alice. *The Portrait in Twelfth-Century French Literature*. Geneva: Droz, 1965.

Colish, Marcia. *The Mirror of Language: A Study in the Medieval Theory of Knowledge*. Rev. ed. Lincoln: University of Nebraska Press, 1983.

Combarieu, Micheline de. "Image et représentation du vilain dans les chansons de geste (et dans quelques autres textes médiévaux)." *Exclus et Systèmes d'Exclusion dans la Littérature et la Civilisation Médiévales: Sénéfiance* 5 (1978): 7–26.

Comfort, W. W. "The Character Types in the Old French Chansons de Geste." *PMLA* 21 (1906): 279–334.

Cooke, Thomas D. *The Old French and Chaucerian Fabliaux: A Study of Their Comic Climax*. Columbia: University of Missouri Press, 1978.

———. "Pornography, the Comic Spirit, and the Fabliaux." In *The Humor of the Fabliaux*, pp. 137–62. Columbia: University of Missouri Press, 1974.

Cosquin, Emmanuel. *Contes populaires de Lorraine*. Paris: F. Vieweg, 1887.

Crane, Susan. *Insular Romance: Politics, Faith, and Culture in Anglo-Norman and Middle English Literature*. Berkeley: University of California Press, 1986.

Curtius, Ernst Robert. *European Literature and the Latin Middle Ages*. Trans. Willard Trask. Princeton: Princeton University, 1973.

Dane, Joseph A. "Mythic Parody in Jean Bodel's *Jeu de Saint Nicolas*." *Romance Notes* 22 (1981): 119–23.

———. "Parody and Satire: A Theoretical Model." *Genre* 13 (1980): 145–59.

Daniélou, Jean. *From Shadows to Reality: Studies in the Biblical Typology of the Fathers.* Trans. Wulston Hibberd. London: Burns & Oates, 1960.

Davis, Natalie Zemon. *Society and Culture in Early Modern France.* Stanford: Stanford University Press, 1975.

Derrida, Jacques. *Writing and Difference.* Chicago: University of Chicago Press, 1978.

Dickson, Arthur. *Valentine and Orson: A Study in Late Medieval Romance.* New York: Columbia University Press, 1929.

Dragonetti, Roger. "Renart est mort, Renart est vif, Renart règne." *Critique* 34 (1978): 783–98.

Duby, Georges. *The Early Growth of the European Economy: Warriors and Peasants from the Seventh to the Twelfth Century.* Trans. Howard B. Clarke. Ithaca: Cornell University Press, 1974.

———. *L'économie rurale et la vie des campagnes de l'occident médiéval (France, Angleterre, Empire, IXe–XVe s.).* 2 vols. Paris: Gallimard, 1962.

———. *Hommes et structures du moyen âge.* Paris: Mouton, 1973.

———. *Le temps des cathédrales: L'art et la société, 980–1420.* Paris: Gallimard, 1976.

———. *Les trois ordres; ou, L'imaginaire du féodalisme.* Paris: Gallimard, 1978.

Dufournet, Jean. "Littérature oralisante et subversion: La branche 18 du *Roman de Renart* ou le partage des proies." *Cahiers de Civilisation Médiévale* 22 (1979): 321–31.

———. "Rutebeuf et le *Roman de Renart*." *L'Information Littéraire* 30 (1978): 7–15.

———. "L'originalité de la branche XVII du *Roman de Renart*; ou, Les trois morts du goupil." In *Mélanges Camproux*, 1:345–63. 2 vols. Montpellier: Centre d'Etudes Occitanes, 1977–78.

Dupriez, Bernard. *Gradus: Dictionnaire des procédés littéraires.* Paris: Editions 10/18, 1980.

Duval, Amaury. "Trubert." *Histoire Littéraire de la France* 19 (1838): 734–47.

Eco, Umberto. "Peirce and Contemporary Semantics." *Versus* 15, no. 4 (1976): 49–72.

———. *Semiotics and the Philosophy of Language.* London: Macmillan, 1984.

Bibliography

————. *A Theory of Semiotics*. Bloomington: Indiana University Press, 1976.

Eagleton, Terry. *Literary Theory*. Minneapolis: University of Minnesota Press, 1983.

El Saffar, Ruth. "Tracking the Trickster in the Works of Cervantes." *Symposium* (Summer 1983), pp. 106–24.

Evergates, Theodore. *Feudal Society in the Bailliage of Troyes under the Counts of Champagne, 1152–1284*. Baltimore: Johns Hopkins University Press, 1975.

Faral, Edmond. *Les arts poétiques du XIIe et du XIIIe siècle*. Paris: Champion, 1971.

Ferrante, Joan M. *Woman as Image in Medieval Literature: From the Twelfth Century to Dante*. New York: Columbia University Press, 1975.

Flinn, John. *Le "Roman de Renart" dans la littérature française et dans la littérature étrangère au moyen âge*. Paris: Presses Universitaires Françaises (PUF), 1963.

Flutre, Louis-Fernand. *Table des noms propres des romans du moyen âge*. Poitiers: Publications du CESCM, 1962.

Foucault, Michel. *The Archaeology of Knowledge*. Trans. Alan Sheridan. London: Tavistock, and New York: Pantheon, 1970.

————. *The History of Sexuality*. Trans. Robert Hurley. Vol. 1. New York: Pantheon Books, 1978.

————. *Language, Counter-Memory, Practice*. Trans. Donald F. Bouchard and Sherry Smith. Ithaca: Cornell University Press, 1977.

————. *Madness and Civilization*. Trans. Richard Howard. New York: Random House, 1965.

————. *The Order of Things*. New York: Random House, 1970.

Foulet, Lucien. *Le Roman de Renard*. Paris: Champion, 1914.

Fourquet, J. "Le rapport entre l'oeuvre et la source chez Chrétien de Troyes et le problème des sources bretonnes." *Romance Philology* 9 (1956): 298–312.

Fourquin, Guy. *Lordship and Feudalism in the Middle Ages*. Trans. Iris Sells and A. L. Lytton Sells. London: George Allen and Unwin, 1976.

Frescoln, Wilson L. "A Study on the Old French Romance of *Fergus*." Diss. University of Pennsylvania, 1961.

Freud, Sigmund. *The Basic Writings*. Trans. A. A. Brill. New York: Random House, 1938.

————. *The Standard Edition of the Complete Psychological Works of Sigmund Freud*. 24 vols. London: Hogarth Press and the Institute of Psychoanalysis, 1953–74.

Frye, Northrop. *Anatomy of Criticism*. Princeton: Princeton University Press, 1957.

Gaignebet, Claude. *Le carnaval: Essais de mythologie populaire.* Paris: Payot, 1974.

Gallop, Jane. *Intersections: A Reading of Sade with Bataille, Blanchot, and Klossowski.* Lincoln: University of Nebraska Press, 1981.

Galpin, Stanley Leman. *Cortois and Vilain: A Study of the Distinctions Made between Them by the French and Provençal Poets of the Twelfth, Thirteenth, and Fourteenth Centuries.* New Haven: Ryder's Printing House, 1905.

Genette, Gérard. *Palimpsestes: La littérature au second degré.* Paris: Seuil, 1982.

Génicot, Léopold. *Le XIIIe siècle européen.* Paris: PUF, 1968.

Gérold, M. Théodore. *La musique au moyen âge.* Paris: Champion, 1932.

Godefroy, Frédéric. *Dictionnaire de l'ancienne langue française et de tous ses dialectes du IXe au XVe siècle.* 10 vols. Paris, 1881–1902; rpt. New York: Krauss Reprint, 1961.

Goosens, Jan, and Timothy Sodmann, eds. *Proceedings of the Third International Beast Epic, Fable, and Fabliau Colloquium.* Munster, 1979; Cologne and Vienna: Böhlau Verlag, 1981.

Goumarre, Pierre. "La sexualité infantile: Rabelais, Freud, et Jung." *Renaissance and Reformation* 16 (1980): 33–46.

Gravdal, Kathryn. "Kingship and Kingdoms in the *Roman de Renart.*" *Kings and Kingship, ACTA* 11 (1984): 113–20.

———. "Nouvelles approches du *Bel Inconnu* de Renart de Beaujeu, du *Méraugis de Portlesguez* de Raoul de Houdenc, du *Fergus* de Guillaume le Clerc." Diss. Université de Paris III, 1981.

Greenlee, Douglas. *Peirce's Concept of Sign.* The Hague: Mouton, 1973.

Hanning, Robert W. "*Engin*" in Twelfth-Century Romance: An Examination of the *Roman d'Enéas* and Hue de Rotelande's *Ipomédon.*" *Yale French Studies* 51 (1974): 82–101.

Hardison, O. B., Jr. *Christian Rite and Christian Drama in the Middle Ages: Essays in the Origin and Early History of Modern Drama.* Baltimore: Johns Hopkins Press, 1965.

Hardwick, Charles S. *Semiotic and Significs. The Correspondence Between C. S. Peirce and Victoria Lady Welby.* Bloomington: Indiana University Press, 1977.

Henderson, Jeffrey. *The Maculate Muse: Obscene Language in Attic Comedy.* New Haven: Yale University Press, 1975.

Highet, Gilbert. *The Anatomy of Satire.* Princeton: Princeton University Press, 1962.

Hollyman, K. J. *Le développement du vocabulaire féodal en France pendant le haut moyen âge: Etude sémantique.* Geneva: Droz, 1957.

Bibliography

Householder, Fred W., Jr. "Parodia." *Classical Philology* 39 (1944): 1–9.

Huizinga, Johan. *Homo Ludens: A Study of the Play Element in Culture.* Boston, 1960.

———. *The Waning of the Middle Ages.* Garden City, N.Y.: Doubleday, 1954.

Hünerhoff, A. *Uber die Komischen "Vilain"-Figuren der Altfranzösischen Chansons de Geste.* Marburg: R. Friedrich, 1894.

Hunt, Tony. "La parodie médiévale: Le cas d'*Aucassin et Nicolette.*" *Romania* 100 (1979): 341–81.

———. "Precursors and Progenitors of *Aucassin et Nicolette.*" *Studies in Philology* 74 (January 1977): 1–19.

Husband, Timothy. *The Wild Man: Medieval Myth and Symbolism.* New York: Metropolitan Museum of Art, 1980.

Hutcheon, Linda. *A Theory of Parody: The Teachings of Twentieth-Century Art Forms.* New York: Methuen, 1985.

Jackson, W.T.H. "The Medieval Pastourelle as a Satirical Genre." *Philological Quarterly* 31 (1952): 156–70.

Jameson, Fredric. *The Political Unconscious: Narrative as a Socially Symbolic Act.* Ithaca: Cornell University Press, 1981.

Jankélévitch, Vladimir. *L'ironie.* Paris: Flammarion, 1964.

Jauss, Hans Robert. "Littérature médiévale et théorie des genres." *Poétique* 1 (1970): 79–101.

———. *Untersuchungen zur Mittelalterlichen Tierdichtung.* Tübingen: Max Niemeyer, 1959.

Jauss, Hans Robert; Erich Köhler; et al. *Grundriss der Romanischen Literaturen des Mittelalters.* 13 vols. Heidelberg: Carl Winter, 1968–70.

Jodogne, Omer. "L'anthropomorphisme croissant dans le *Roman de Renart.*" In *Aspects of the Medieval Animal Epic: Proceedings of the International Conference,* pp. 25–41. Ed. E. Rombauts and A. Welkenhuysen. Louvain: Leuven University Press, 1975.

———. "La parodie et le pastiche dans *Aucassin et Nicolette.*" *Cahiers de l'Association Internationale des Etudes Françaises* 12 (June 1960): 53–65.

Jolles, André. *Einfache Formen.* 2nd ed. Tübingen: Max Niemeyer, 1958.

Karrer, Wolfgang. *Parodie, Travestie, Pastiche.* Munich: Wilhelm Fink, 1977.

Kerényi, Karl. "The Trickster in Relation to Greek Mythology." In Paul Radin, *The Trickster,* pp. 173–91. New York: Schocken Books, 1972.

Klein, Karen W. *The Partisan Voice: A Study of the Political Lyric in France and Germany, 1180–1230.* The Hague: Mouton, 1971.

Köhler, Erich. *Ideal und Wirklichkeit in der Höfischen Epik: Studien zur Form der Frühen Artus- und Graldichtung.* Tübingen: Max Niemeyer, 1956.

Kristeva, Julia. *Desire in Language*. Trans. Thomas Gora, Alice Jardine, and Léon Roudiez. New York: Columbia University Press, 1980.

——. *Powers of Horror: An Essay on Abjection*. Trans. Léon Roudiez. New York: Columbia University Press, 1982.

——. *Le Texte du Roman*. The Hague: Mouton, 1970.

Krueger, Roberta L. "Misogyny, Manipulation, and the Female Reader in Hue de Rotelande's *Ipomédon*." Forthcoming.

Lacy, Gregg F. "Fabliau Stylistic Humor." *Kentucky Romance Quarterly* 26 (1979): 349–57.

Langlois, Ernest. *Table des noms propres dans les chansons de geste*. New York: Burt Franklin, 1904.

Lecoy, Félix. "Compte rendu: Douin de Lavesne, *Trubert*, fabliau du 13e siècle, edition par G. Raynaud de Lage." *Romania* 96 (1975): 278–81.

Lefay-Toury, Marie-Noëlle. "Ambiguité de l'idéologie et gratuité de l'écriture dans la branche I du *Roman de Renart*." *Le Moyen Age* 80 (1974): 89–100.

Legge, M. Dominica. *Anglo-Norman Literature and Its Background*. Oxford: Clarendon Press, 1963.

Legman, Gustave. *The Horn Book: Studies in Erotic Folklore and Bibliography*. New Hyde Park, N.Y.: University Books, 1964.

——. *Rationale of the Dirty Joke: An Analysis of Sexual Humor*. New York: Breaking Point, 1975.

LeGoff, Jacques. *Pour un autre moyen âge: Temps, travail et culture en occident*. Paris: Gallimard, 1977.

Lehmann, Paul. *Die Parodie im Mittelalter*. 2nd ed. Stuttgart: Hiersemann, 1963.

Lelièvre, F. J. "The Basis of Ancient Parody." *Greece and Rome*, 2nd ser., 1 (1954): 66–81.

Lenient, Charles. *La satire en France au moyen âge*. Paris: Hachette, 1877.

Le Rider, Paule. *Le chevalier dans "Le Conte du Graal" de Chrétien de Troyes*. Paris: SEDES, 1978.

Levine, Jacob. *Motivation in Humor*. New York: Atherton Press, 1969.

Lévi-Strauss, Claude. *Anthropologie structurale*. Paris: Plon, 1958.

——. *Le cru et le cuit*. Paris: Plon, 1964.

Leyerle, John, and Larry D. Benson, eds. *Chivalric Literature: Essays on Relations between Literature and Life in the Later Middle Ages*. Kalamazoo, Mich.: Medieval Institute Publications, 1980.

Livingston, Charles H. *Le jongleur Gautier le Leu: Etude sur les fabliaux*. Cambridge: Harvard University, 1951.

Lorcin, Marie-Thérèse. *Les campagnes de la région Lyonnaise au XVIe et XVe siècles*. Lyon: Bosc Frères, 1974.

——. "Quand les princes n'épousaient pas les bergères; ou, Mésalliance et classes d'âge dans les fabliaux." *Medioevo Romanzo* 3 (1976): 195–228.

Louis, René. *Girart, comte de Vienne, dans les chansons de geste: Girart de Vienne, Girart de Fraite, Girart de Roussillon.* 2 vols. Auxerre: Bureaux de l'Imprimerie moderne, 1947.

Maddox, Donald. *The Semiotics of Deceit: The Pathelin Era.* Lewisburg, Pa.: Bucknell University Press, 1984.

Manoine, F. "Ist der Trubertroman ein Fragment?" *Zeitschrift für Romanische Philologie* 50 (1930): 740–44.

Marquart, Wilhelm. *Der Einfluss Kristians von Troies auf den Roman "Fergus" des Guillaume le Clerc.* Diss. Göttingen, 1906.

Ménard, Philippe. *Le rire et le sourire dans le roman courtois en France au moyen âge.* Geneva: Droz, 1969.

Mollat, Michel. *The Poor in the Middle Ages: An Essay in Social History.* Trans. Arthur Goldhammer. New Haven: Yale University Press, 1986.

Montagu, Ashley. *The Anatomy of Swearing.* New York: Macmillan, 1967.

Muscatine, Charles. *The Old French Fabliaux.* New Haven: Yale University Press, 1986.

———. "The Social Background of the Old French Fabliaux." *Genre* 9 (1976): 1–19.

Nichols, Stephen G., Jr. "*Canso* to *Consa*: Structures of Parodic Humor in Three Songs of Guilhem IX." *Esprit Créateur* 16 (1976): 16–29.

———. "Ethical Criticism and Medieval Literature." In *Medieval Secular Literature.* Ed. William Matthews. Berkeley and Los Angeles: University of California, 1965.

———. "Fission and Fusion: Mediations of Power in Medieval History and Literature." *Yale French Studies* 70 (1986): 21–41.

———. *Romanesque Signs: Early Medieval Narrative and Iconography.* New Haven: Yale University Press, 1983.

Nykrog, Per. *Les fabliaux.* Geneva: Droz, 1973.

Ong, Walter J. *Interfaces of the Word: Studies in the Translation of Consciousness and Culture.* Ithaca: Cornell University Press, 1977.

Owen, D.D.R. "The Craft of Guillaume le Clerc's *Fergus*." In *The Craft of Fiction: Essays in Medieval Poetics.* Ed. Leigh Arrathoon. Rochester, Mich.: Solaris Press, 1984.

Parker, Patricia A. *Inescapable Romance: Studies in the Poetics of a Mode.* Princeton: Princeton University Press, 1979.

Payen, Jean-Charles. "L'idéologie chevaleresque dans le *Roman de Renart*." *Marche Romane* 28 (1978): 33–41.

———. "Trubert ou le triomphe de la marginalité." In *Exclus et Systèmes d'Exclusion dans la Littérature et la Civilisation Médiévales: Séné-fiance* 5 (1978): 1–21.

Pearcy, Roy J. "An Instance of Heroic Parody in the Fabliaux." *Romania* 98 (1977): 105–8.

———. "Modes of Signification and the Humor of Obscene Diction in the Fabliaux." In *The Humor of the Fabliaux*, pp. 163–96. Ed. Thomas D. Cooke. Columbia: University of Missouri Press, 1974.

———. "Realism and Religious Parody in the Fabliaux: Watriquet de Couvin's *Les Trois Dames de Paris*." *Revue Belge de Philologie et d'Histoire* 50 (1972): 744–54.

Peirce, Charles S. *Collected Papers*. 8 vols. Cambridge: Harvard University Press, 1931–58.

Propp, Vladimir. *La morphologie du conte*. Paris: Seuil, 1965.

Radin, Paul. *The Trickster: A Study in American Indian Mythology, with Commentaries by Karl Kerényi and C. G. Jung*. New York: Schocken Books, 1972.

Raynaud de Lage, Guy. "Trubert est-il un personnage de fabliau?" In *Mélanges d'histoire littéraire, de linguistique et de philologie romanes offerts à Charles Rostaing*, pp. 845–53. Liège, 1974.

Regalado, Nancy Freeman. "Des contraires choses." *Littérature* 41 (1981): 62–81.

———. *Poetic Patterns in Rutebeuf: A Study in the Noncourtly Poetic Modes of the Thirteenth Century*. New Haven: Yale University Press, 1970.

———. "Tristan and Renart: Two Tricksters." *Esprit Créateur* 16 (1976): 30–38.

Rickard, P. *Britain in French Medieval Literature*. Cambridge: Cambridge University Press, 1956.

Riffaterre, Michael. "L'intertexte inconnu." *Littérature* 41 (1981): 4–7.

———. "La parodie à la lumière de la théorie de l'intertextualité." Paper presented to the Colloquium on the History and Theory of Parody, Queen's University, Kingston, Ontario, 10 October 1981.

———. *Semiotics of Poetry*. Bloomington: Indiana University Press, 1978.

———. "Sémiotique intertextuelle: l'interprétant." *Revue d'Esthétique*, n.s., 32 (1979): 128–50.

———. "La trace de l'intertexte." *La Pensée* 215 (1980): 4–18.

Rombauts, Edward, and Andries Welkenhuysen, eds. *Aspects of the Medieval Animal Epic*. The Hague: Martinus Nihoff, 1975.

Rose, Margeret. *Parody/Metafiction*. London: Croon Helm, 1979.

Runeberg, Johannes. *Etudes sur la geste Rainouart*. Helsingfors: Aktiebolaget Handelstryckeriet, 1905.

Bibliography

Rychner, Jean. *La chanson de geste: Essai sur l'art épique des jongleurs.* Geneva: Droz, 1955.

———. *Contribution à l'étude des fabliaux: Variantes, remaniements, dégradations.* 2 vols. Geneva: Droz, 1960.

Sagarin, Edward. *The Anatomy of Dirty Words.* New York: Lyle Stuart, 1962.

Said, Edward W. *The World, the Text, and the Critic.* Cambridge: Harvard University Press, 1983.

Schenck, Mary Jane. "Functions and Roles in the Fabliau." *Comparative Literature* 30 (1978): 22–34.

Schleyer, Johannes Dietrich. *Der Wortschatz von List und Betrug im Altfranzösischen und Altprovenzalischen.* Bonn: Romanistische Versuche und Vorarbeiten, 1961.

Schmolke-Hasselmann, Beate. *Der Arthurische Versroman von Chrestien bis Froissart.* Tübingen: Max Niemeyer, 1980.

Sinclair, K. V. "Comic *Audigier* in England." *Romania* 100 (1979): 257–59.

Southworth, Marie-José. *Etude comparée de quatre romans médiévaux. Jaufré, Fergus, Durmart, Blancandin.* Paris: Nizet, 1973.

Spencer, Richard. "The Courtois-Vilain Nexus in *La Male Honte.*" *Medium Aevum* 37 (1968): 272–92.

Spensley, R. M. "The Structure of Hue de Rotelande's *Ipomédon.*" *Romania* 95 (1974): 341–51.

Stanesco, Michel. "Le secret de *l'estrange* chevalier: Notes sur la motivation contradictoire dans le roman médiéval." In *The Spirit of the Court: Selected Proceedings of the Fourth Congress of the International Courtly Literature Society (Toronto 1983),* pp. 340–45. Ed. Glyn S. Burgess and Robert A. Taylor, Dover. N.H.: D. S. Brewer, 1985.

Stefan, Alois. *Laut- und Formenbestand in Guillaume Li Clers' Roman "Fergus."* Klagenfurt: Bertschinger, 1893.

Stevenson, Joseph. *Documents Illustrative of the History of Scotland, 1286–1306.* Edinburgh: H. M. General Register House, 1870.

Stewart, Susan. *Nonsense: Aspects of Intertextuality in Folklore and Literature.* Baltimore: Johns Hopkins University Press, 1978.

Stock, Brian. "History, Literature, and Medieval Textuality." *Yale French Studies* 70 (1986): 7–17.

———. *The Implications of Literacy: Written Languages and Models of Interpretation in the Eleventh and Twelfth Centuries.* Princeton: Princeton University Press, 1983.

Strubel, Armand. "Le rire au moyen âge." In *Précis de la littérature française du moyen âge.* Ed. Daniel Poirion et al. Paris: PUF, 1983.

Sudre, Léopold. *Les sources du Roman de Renart.* Paris: Bouillon, 1893.

Susskind, Norman. "Love and Laughter in the *Romans Courtois*." *French Review* 37 (1964): 651–57.

Tanon, L. *Histoire des justices des anciennes églises et communautés monastiques de Paris*. Paris: L. Larose et Forcel, 1883.

Thompson, Stith. *The Folktale*. New York: Dryden Press, 1951.

————. *Motif Index of Folk Literature: A Classification of Narrative Elements in Folktales, Ballads, Myths, Fables, Medieval Romances, Exempla, Fabliaux, Jest Books, and Local Legends*. 6 vols. Bloomington: Indiana University Press, 1955.

Tilander, Gunnar. *Remarques sur le "Roman de Renart."* Göteberg: Elanders Boktryekeri Aktiebolag, 1923.

Tobler, Adolph, and Erhard Lommatzsch. *Altfranzösisches Worterbuch*. 10 vols. Wiesbaden: F. Steiner Verlag, 1927–76.

Todorov, Tzvetan. *Les genres du discours*. Paris: Seuil, 1978.

————. *Mikhail Bakhtin: The Dialogical Principle*. Trans. Wlad Godzich. Minneapolis: University of Minnesota Press, 1985.

Vance, Eugene. *From Topic to Tale: Logic and Narrative in the Middle Ages*. Minneapolis: University of Minnesota Press, 1986.

————. "Greimas, Freud, and the Story of *Trouvère* Lyric." In *Lyric Poetry: Beyond New Criticism*, pp. 93–105. Ed. Chaviva Hošek and Patricia Parker. Ithaca: Cornell University Press, 1985.

————. "Love's Concordance: The Poetics of Desire and the Joy of the Text." *Diacritics* 5 (1975): 40–52.

————. *Mervelous Signals: Poetics and Sign Theory in the Middle Ages*. Lincoln: University of Nebraska Press, 1986.

von Wartburg, Walther. *Französisches Etymologisches Worterbuch*. 21 vols. Leipzig and Berlin: B. G. Teubner, 1940–65.

West, G. D. *French Arthurian Prose Romances: An Index of Proper Names*. Toronto: University of Toronto Press, 1978.

White, Hayden. "The Forms of Wildness: Archaeology of an Idea." In *The Wild Man Within: An Image in Western Thought from the Renaissance to Romanticism*, pp. 3–38. Ed. Edward Dudley and Maximilian E. Noble. Pittsburgh: University of Pittsburgh Press, 1972.

Wiesmann-Wiedemann, Friederike. *Le Roman du "Willehalm" de Wolfram d'Eschenbach et L'Epopée d' "Aliscans": Etude de la transformation de l'épopée en roman*. Göttingen: Verlag Alfred Kümmerle, 1976.

Willems, Léonard. *Etude sur l'Ysengrinus*. Ghent: E. Van Goethem, 1895.

Williams, Henry F. "French Fabliau Scholarship." *South Atlantic Review* 46 (1981): 76–82.

Zink, Michel. *La pastourelle: Poésie et folklore au moyen âge*. Paris and Montréal: Bordas, 1972.

Bibliography

———. *La subjectivité médiévale*. Paris: Minuit, 1986.

Zumthor, Paul. *Essai de poétique médiévale*. Paris: Seuil, 1972.

———. "Fatrasie et coq-à-l'âne (de Beaumanoir à Clement Marot)." In *Fin du moyen âge et Renaissance: Mélanges de philologie française offerts à Robert Guiette*. Anvers: De Nederlandsche Bockhandel, 1961.

———. *Histoire littéraire de la France médiévale (VIe-XIVe siècles)*. Paris: PUF, 1954.

———. "Intertextualité et mouvance." *Littérature* 41 (1981): 8–16.

———. *Le masque et la lumière*. Paris: Seuil, 1978.

———. *Speaking of the Middle Ages*. Trans. Sarah White. Lincoln: University of Nebraska Press, 1986.

Zumthor, Paul; E.-G. Hessing; and R. Vijlbrief. "Essai d'analyse des procédés fatrasiques." *Romania* 84 (1963): 145–70.

INDEX

Index

Index

Other volumes in the Regents Studies
in Medieval Culture include:

Speaking of the Middle Ages
By Paul Zumthor
Translated by Sarah White

Mervelous Signals
*Poetics and Sign Theory
in the Middle Ages*
By Eugene Vance

Giants in Those Days
*Folklore, Ancient History,
and Nationalism*
By Walter E. Stephens